THE NEW COUNTRYSIDE?

Ethnicity, nation and exclusion in contemporary rural Britain

Edited by Sarah Neal and Julian Agyeman

First published in Great Britain in March 2006 by

The Policy Press
University of Bristol
Fourth Floor
Beacon House
Queen's Road
Bristol BS8 1QU
UK

Tel +44 (0)117 331 4054
Fax +44 (0)117 331 4093
e-mail tpp-info@bristol.ac.uk
www.policypress.org.uk

All photographs in Chapter Six © of Mosaic: BEN/CNP

British Library Cataloguing in Publication Data
A catalogue record for this book is available from the British Library.

Library of Congress Cataloging-in-Publication Data
A catalog record for this book has been requested.

ISBN-10 1 86134 795 2 paperback
ISBN-13 978 1 86134 795 4 paperback
ISBN-10 1 86134 796 0 hardcover
ISBN-13 978 1 86134 795 4 hardcover

Sarah Neal is Senior Lecturer at The Open University, UK and
Julian Agyeman is Associate Professor at Tufts University, US.

Cover design by Qube Design Associates, Bristol.
Front cover: 'Pastoral Interlude', photograph supplied by kind permission of
Ingrid Pollard.
Printed and bound in Great Britain by Hobbs the Printers Ltd, Southampton.

For Brock, with love

Contents

List of illustrations and tables

Illustrations

Tables

Foreword

John Solomos

The study of race and ethnicity has been transformed beyond recognition over the past three decades. We have seen the emergence of new conceptual and empirical research by new generations of scholars that has opened up new arenas for research and has given voice to new critical perspectives in a field that was dominated by a limited range of analytical paradigms. Yet what also remains clear is that there are still a number of major absences in the research literature. Among the most important of these absences we can include the study of race and ethnicity within rural settings and communities. This is an issue that has received regular attention in media coverage in recent years, but the academic discourses of race and ethnicity have remained silent and largely ignorant of this important social and political phenomenon.

Such an absence is to some extent the result of the origins of the study of race and ethnicity in societies such as our own. From its earliest stages as a sub-discipline, the sociology of race and ethnicity has been constructed through an urban frame of reference, and researchers and policy makers have shared the view that the focus of research should be on urban environments that have been shaped by the impact of race and ethnicity. In the period since the 1960s this is pretty much the direction in which the study of British race relations has gone, and this is evident in the main books in this field as well as in the journals.

This important new collection of original research on contemporary facets of ethnicity, nation and forms of exclusion in rural Britain is therefore to be welcomed both by scholars and by policy makers working in this broad field. In putting together this masterful edited collection Sarah Neal and Julian Agyeman have sought above all to raise questions and issues for further research and analysis. Apart from the editors' opening and closing overviews, the collection provides us with important contributions from leading scholars and researchers in this area of research. It includes chapters on such topical issues as the experiences of minority ethnic communities in rural environments, the position of Gypsy Travellers and New Age Travellers, the role of ideologies of race and place in a range of different environments and the experiences of refugees in rural environments. The various chapters are the product of up-to-date research and have been carefully edited to produce a volume that allows for diverse views as well as emphasising a number of common themes throughout. This makes for a volume that moves easily from the specific experiences of Gypsy Traveller communities to wider debates about the construction of racialised spaces and identities. In doing so the book as a whole seeks to question both assumptions that race and ethnicity are not relevant issues in the countryside and assumptions that the countryside can be viewed as a monolithic and unchanging social and cultural environment.

Given the complex range of questions raised by all the contributors to this refreshing collection, it is somewhat invidious to focus on individual chapters as such. There are, however, a number of themes that run through the volume as a whole that need to be mentioned in the context of how we may move on from the current situation. First, and perhaps least controversially, there is the key refrain of the volume as a whole that we cannot ignore the impact of questions of race, racism and ethnicity in the rural landscapes of Britain. This is in some ways a simple point to make, but it is one that has been largely ignored by researchers in this field, with a few notable exceptions. What is important to note, however, is that the editors go beyond simply making this critical point and address in a serious and helpful way how researchers can move beyond the limits of existing research agendas.

Second, and perhaps most importantly in the context of current political debates, there is the important question of what it means to talk about living in a 'multicultural society' when little or no attention has been given to the realities of living with difference in the context of changing rural communities. Researchers in diverse arenas, such as education and social services, have highlighted the ways in which multicultural policies are seen as being relevant only in urban environments and as a result there are important lacunae in the implementation of policies at a national level. This is a concern that has been voiced recently by the Commission for Racial Equality, which has argued for the need to develop policy agendas around multiculturalism that are of relevance in largely rural environments. What this volume shows more clearly, however, are the consequences of a narrow vision of multiculturalism for specific communities.

Third, the various chapters in this volume point to the need for a better sociological understanding of the social makeup of rural communities and environments. The realities of what the editors call 'belonging and becoming' are complex and difficult to make sense of in any social situation, but they are surely right to argue that we need to develop a more nuanced and location-specific understanding of the meanings attached to race and ethnicity in rural environments. This implies both more research on these issues in the future, but perhaps more importantly the need for more dialogue about the parameters and focus of such research.

It is to be hoped that *The new countryside?* will act as a timely reminder to all those of us working on questions of race and ethnicity that we have to broaden our fields of vision beyond the urban and be more attentive to what is happening in rural environments. It is a fascinating book that evokes an amazing range of social, political, cultural and everyday issues about the role of race and ethnicity in rural environments. My main hope is that the challenge it makes to dominant research agendas in this field will be taken up in a positive manner and that the communities and issues to which it seeks to give voice become part of the evolving research and policy agendas in this field. The chapters that follow should be an important, if overdue, push in this direction.

John Solomos
City University, London

Acknowledgements

An edited collection always represents a piece of work in which many people have been involved. This collection is no exception and there are a number of people that we, as editors, would want to extend our thanks to. We have been extremely fortunate in being able to attract (or coerce!) the contributors who make up this volume. We want to thank each of them for their commitment to the project and for producing innovative, exciting and challenging material. We would also like to thank those that enabled the project along the way – the Leverhulme Trust, the ESRC and other funding bodies; the respondents and organisations in the various research projects who provided the authors with time and rich and important information; the Open and Tufts Universities; John Solomos for always being generous and for writing the Foreword; Ingrid Pollard for letting us use her beautiful and important pictures; and our patient and ever helpful editorial team – Dawn Rushen, Laura Greaves, Julia Mortimer, Emily Watt and Dave Worth at The Policy Press. We want to extend our thanks to those friends and colleagues who not only supported and encouraged us but at the same time pushed us along on the intellectual journey and did not tire of discussing the issues and themes – Sarah Bradshaw, John Clarke, Karen Duke, Lynn Hancock, Gail Lewis, Eugene McLaughlin, Janet Newman, Steve Pile, John Solomos, Carol Vincent, Sue Walters and Joanne Winning. Needless to say they are in no way responsible for any weaknesses or limitations within the collection.

A few final words of love and thanks are of course owed to our families for their love and constancy and for being such an important part of our own relation to rural spaces. Sarah thanks Su, Brock, Mum, Dad, Tom and Joe. Julian thanks his mother, Margaret, for developing his interest in the countryside and he thanks those members of black and minority ethnic communities who continually push the boundaries.

Notes on contributors

Julian Agyeman is Associate Professor of Urban and Environmental Policy and Planning, Tufts University, Boston/Medford, US. His publications on sustainable development and environmental justice, which number over 115, include books, peer reviewed articles, book chapters, published conference presentations, reports, book reviews, newspaper articles and articles in professional magazines and journals. His most recent books are *Just sustainabilities: Development in an unequal world* (Cambridge, MA: MIT Press, 2003), which was voted one of the most important new books in environmental sociology in 2005, and *Sustainable communities and the challenge of environmental justice* (New York, NY: NYU Press, 2005). Both books call for coalition building between environmental justice and sustainable development advocates and activists.

Kye Askins is a Lecturer in Human Geography at the University of Northumbria. Her chapter is drawn from her doctoral research, recently completed at the University of Durham, from which a policy guidance document was also written for the National Park Authorities of England. This report is available online at www.moors.uk.net/learning/index.php?mid=115. Pre-academia, Kye held a range of 'social work' positions, including working within the homelessness and mental health fields She is obsessive about composting, and strongly believes in a holistic approach to environmental and social agendas for transformative action on either: that is, the 'just sustainability' approach. She would like to teach the world to sing in perfect harmony, but – being a touch tone deaf – instead lobbies for smiling to be given tax relief.

Kalwant Bhopal is a Senior Lecturer in Education at the University of Greenwich. Her research interests include gender, 'race' and minority ethnic groups. She has been researching the Gypsy diaspora since she published *Working towards inclusive education: Aspects of good practice for Gypsy Traveller pupils*, with J. Gundara, C. Jones and C. Owen (London: Department for Education and Employment, 2000). She is currently working on issues of social exclusion and marginalisation in relation to the social status of Gypsies in an inner London borough. Her other publications include, *Gender, 'race' and patriarchy* (Aldershot: Ashgate, 1997) and *Connecting children: Care and family life in later childhood*, with J. Brannen and E. Heptinstall (London: RoutledgeFalmer, 2000).

Paul Connolly is Professor of Education and Head of Research at the School of Education, Queen's University Belfast. He is also Director of the NFER at Queen's Centre for Educational Research. He has researched and published widely on issues of racism and ethnic relations both in England and in relation to Northern Ireland. His books include: *Racism, gender identities and young children* (London: Routledge, 1998) and *Researching racism in education*, with Barry Troyna (Buckingham: Open University Press, 1998). In recent years, Professor Connolly has led a major government-funded research study into the nature and extent of racism in Northern Ireland. Further details on this and his other publications can be found at: www.paulconnolly.net.

Philomena de Lima works as a Development Officer and Researcher with UHI Policy Web – UHI Millennium Institute. She has more than 15 years of research and consultancy experience with a wide range of clients. She authored the first publication in 2001 on rural minority ethnic groups in Scotland, *Needs not numbers* (London: CRE and Community Development Foundation) and completed a mapping exercise on rural 'race' issues in the British context for the Commission for Racial Equality in 2002/03. She contributed to an audit of research on ethnic minorities in Scotland in 2001 and has recently completed a study on access to further and higher education among minority ethnic groups in the Highlands and Islands. Recent publications include book chapters (in *Rural racism* edited by Chakraborti and Garland, Cullompton: Willan Publishing, 2004) and journal articles (in *Policy Futures in Education*). She is actively involved regionally and nationally on policy issues, including the Scottish Further Education Council (2000–05) and is a member of the Scottish Advisory Group for the Equal Opportunities Commission.

Perminder Dhillon BSc, MA was a senior lecturer at the Centre for Ethnicity and Health, University of Central Lancashire where for the past six years, she researched and lectured on drug issues and diverse communities and equality and diversity issues. She managed a number of drug education projects and produced video resources in a range of languages. She also set up and managed the centre's equality training function. Currently, Perminder manages a drug education charity and is a freelance trainer and Master NLP Practitioner with Third Vision Consultancy. Perminder has worked in a variety of equality settings and her research interests are racial equality, personal and community empowerment. Perminder has authored a number of publications on equality, media, Black women's issues, drug education and mental health.

She has also worked on a number of broadcast documentaries, many dealing with racial equality issues.

Hannah Gardner is a Senior Research Assistant within the School of Geography at the University of Wales Swansea. Her research interests centre upon issues of rurality and ethnicity, and she is currently investigating the experiences and attitudes of black and minority ethnic people and the criminal justice system in parts of rural Wales. Before that, Hannah researched the lived experiences of black and minority ethnic individuals in rural Wales for her doctoral thesis at the same institution. She has co-authored a research paper and book chapter on some of her initial findings from her doctoral research with Vaughan Robinson.

Kevin Hetherington is Professor of Geography at The Open University, UK. Previously, he held a Chair in Cultural Sociology at Lancaster University. He has published widely on issues of consumption, spatiality, identity and material culture. His books include *Badlands of modernity* (New York, NY: Routledge, 1997), *Expressions of identity* (London: Sage, 1998), *New Age travellers* (London: Cassell, 2000) and *Capitalism's eye* (New York, NY: Routledge, forthcoming). He has also published many journal articles and book chapters. He is co-editor of the journal *Museum and Society.*

Sarah Neal is Senior Lecturer in the Faculty of Social Sciences at The Open University, UK. Her research interests cover the areas of race and ethnicity and the relationship of these with equality policy processes, media and representation and rural landscapes and formations of belonging. Her publications include *The making of equal opportunities policies in universities* (Buckingham: Open University Press, 1998) and a number of journal articles and chapters in books. She is currently co-authoring with John Solomos *Race, multi-culturalism and social policy in Britain* (Houndmills: Palgrave, forthcoming) and writing up her recent research project on rurality and identity.

Vaughan Robinson is Professor of Human Geography and Director of the Migration Unit at the University of Wales Swansea. His research interests are in human migration broadly, and in the social demography of minority populations, and geographies of asylum- and refuge-seeking in particular. He has written or edited eight books on these themes, the three most recent being *Spreading the 'burden'? European policies to disperse asylum seekers*, with Roger Andersson and Sako

Musterd (Bristol: The Policy Press, 2003); *Understanding the decision making of asylum seekers*, with Jeremy Segrott (London: Home Office, 2002), and *Migration and public policy* (Cheltenham: Edward Elgar, 1999).

Katharine Tyler is a Lecturer in the Department of Sociology, University of Surrey. She was previously a post-doctoral Research Fellow on an EU-funded project exploring public understandings of 'race', genealogy and genetics based at the Department of Social Anthropology, University of Manchester, where she studied for her PhD. Her doctoral thesis examined ethnographically the ways in which Englishness/Britishness is portrayed as essentially white, suburban/ rural and middle class. Recent publications based on this research include: 'Racism, tradition and reflexivity in a former mining town', *Ethnic and Racial Studies*, vol 27, no 2, 2004, pp 290-309; and 'The racialised and classed constitution of English village life', *Ethnos*, vol 68, no 3, 2003, pp 391-412.

Introduction

Sarah Neal and Julian Agyeman

Beginnings

In Kazuo Ishiguro's wonderful *The remains of the day*, a 1950s-set novel about class, love and social change, the central character, Stevens, an ageing butler to a country house, embarks on tour of England's West Country. Stopping outside Salisbury Stevens is advised by a local man to climb a hill for the view. Rather crossly (the hill is steep) he does so and encounters 'the most marvellous view over miles of surrounding countryside ... field after field rolling off into the far distance. The land rose and fell gently and the fields were bordered by hedges and trees ... To my right, almost on the horizon, I thought I could see the square tower of a church' (Ishiguro, 1989, p 26). Later that night in his hotel room in Salisbury it is this view that Stevens recalls:

> the English landscape at its finest − such as I saw this morning − possesses a quality that the landscapes of other nations, however more superficially dramatic, inevitably fail to possess. It is I believe, a quality that will mark out the English landscape to any objective observer as the most deeply satisfying in the world, and this is probably best summed up by the term greatness. (Ishiguro, 1989, p 28)

We begin by quoting from Ishiguro because he describes, through Stevens, the sensuous appeal of the English countryside and its core place in an imagining of not only nation but the superiority of a nation. What is apparent in the figure of Stevens is Rodaway's (1994, p 5) distinction between sense and senses. Stevens' gaze from the hill across the pastoral English landscape incorporates a process of making sense, 'sense as meaning' (seen in his connection between the view and the 'greatness' of England) *and* a process in which the senses, particularly sight, shape his emotional experience of 'feeling' the view (its 'pleasures', 'fineness', 'marvellousness'). This is an important and perhaps overlooked point in discussions of the race–ethnicity–rural relation. The rural landscape itself gets a little lost in research and arguments about the extent and experiences of racism and marginalisation and exclusion. The loveliness of the rural sweeps of Britain tends to vanish in critiques of its constructedness and its potency as a signifier of a very particular version of national belonging and culture. Of course, in part it is the loveliness of rural landscapes, the ways in which they are seen and made sense of that underpin discourses and practices of inclusion and exclusion. Relph (1976, p 122) argues that 'landscape is not merely an aesthetic background to life, rather it is a setting that both expresses and conditions cultural attitudes and activities ... landscapes are therefore always imbued with meanings that come from how and why we know them'. This observation is particularly pertinent to rural landscapes that are able to act as persuasive settings for ideas of what the nation 'is'. This is echoed in Cosgrove's suggestion that 'landscape is a social and cultural product, a way of seeing projected onto the land' (1984, p 269). A 'way of seeing' Englishness in particular has been to project it onto a rural landscape although, as Connolly, de Lima, and Robinson and Gardner (this volume) all show, this projection is not confined to England but extends to Northern Ireland, Scotland and Wales. The powerfulness of a dominant way of seeing can be reflected in hiddenness and invisibility, subordination and marginalisation, absences and problematic/dangerous presences. As Kinsman (1993, p 2) notes, 'if a group is excluded from the [rural] landscape, then it is excluded to a large degree from the nation'.

This introduction seeks to explore this exclusionary way of seeing nation through notions of the rural and examines the outcomes of this and the nature of the challenges to it. We argue that this way of seeing is inherently unstable and is constantly open to contestation and change. This is increasingly so in a contemporary context in which perceptions of expanding geopolitical borders (for example, the European Union) and globalisation processes (transnational movements of people, goods, services, capital) have unsettled and destabilised the 'national spaces' within, and boundaries of, nation-states (Clarke, 2005, p 81). The anxieties that these unsettlements produce – what Clarke defines as 'internalised globalisation' (2005, p 80) – can mean that particular spaces become (re)valorised as essences of nation. At the same time these spaces are themselves part of the unsettlement and re-formation processes. Such spaces are subject to diverse claiming processes by those identified as included *and* those identified as excluded.

The first part of the introduction looks at the connections between rural spaces, identity and nation formation. The second part scrutinises the discourses and practices of exclusion. The final section of the introduction outlines the organisation of this book and introduces the concerns of the chapters within it.

Ways of seeing: rural spaces, whiteness[1] and senses of nation

We have cited Stevens' view out across the hills of Wiltshire and his reflection on the greatness of England as a fictional example of the sensuousness of landscape and its meaning. Stevens' gaze works as an example of how a particular space is seen and understood and experienced as *the* nation. That there is an alchemic process by which the countryside is converted into the essence of the country is not a new argument and has been made cogently by a number of commentators. Raymond Williams begins *The country and the city* by noting the power of the term 'country' and reminding how 'in English the "country" is both a nation and a part of a "land"; the country can be the whole society or its rural area' (1979, p 9). Splitting country/side with the oblique stresses the duality that Williams identifies, the way in which countryside can simultaneously flag and stand in for nation, even a highly urbanised nation. For us, what is of pertinence is the alchemic process itself; countryside becoming country/side. In what ways and why does Stevens' gaze from the hill not simply see other hills but rather 'see' England?

Sarah was reminded of this passage from *The remains of the day* during a particular encounter in a recent research project. This project involved a series of focus group interviews with members of local Women's Institutes and Young Farmers' Clubs in three areas of rural England[2]. In one Young Farmers' Club interview in Northumberland the group discuss their attachments to Northumberland and the pleasures of a return to it after being away. Chris explains this seeing/feeling/belonging to the country/side moment: 'If you stand again and look at the view that we've got and you see the trees and the moors and the land, the free land, you think that's it you're in England.' For us, understanding the alchemic process of the country/side has taken us to the work of social theorists and cultural geographers such as Henri Lefebvre (1991) and Edward Soja (1996). While it is not our intention to review this body of work we want to suggest that the arguments put forward by them on the ways in which spaces and social relations each shape and embed the other – that is, they are mutually constitutive – is one that is highly appropriate to the analysis of the relationship between rural spaces, constructions of nation and racialisation. As space moves increasingly to the centre of social science analysis (Morgan, 2000), it becomes evident that a concern with the rural is a concern with the social production and interpretation of a particular form of space and spatial practice. While much of Lefebvre's work and that of those influenced by him has tended to focus on the urban and metropolitan environment (Soja, 1996; Pile, 1996), there is a very evident applicability of the core tenets of these arguments to rural spaces. What we want to take from this Lefebvreian work is the concept that spaces are socially produced and 'made'; that this production and making of space incorporates gendered, raced, ethnicised, sexualised, classed social power and political relationships; that spaces are never inert and immobile but are constantly subject to social and economic change and processes of reproduction and reinvention and that within those processes contestations, claims and counter claims will be key drivers and shapers. How do we map this onto rurality? What the contributors to this volume and other scholars have been able to show is that the countryside is not a blank or neutral space. It is politically charged space and one that has been adept at signifying nation. While English rural spaces may be repositories of nation *par excellence*, as Connolly, de Lima and Robinson and Gardner (this volume) show, rural space exists at the heart of other narratives of nation. However, the particular place that the rural takes up in the English narrative of nation is significant. It reflects the country-house base of the traditionalist political system of England and, perhaps above all, it appears to speak of a system of social order (Scruton, 2000; Neal, 2002). The production of the orderly English rural space requires a certain imagining that vigorously attempts to delineate between those groups who are included – the rural presences – and those that are excluded – the rural absences. It is the accounts and analysis of these processes that concern all of the contributors in this volume.

Rural spaces, trialectics of space and ethnicity

Lefebvre argued that space could be understood as operating through three fields or moments – perceived space, conceived space and lived space – *simultaneously*. These are not discrete, bounded spaces but domains that melt, and spill over, into each other. Lefebvre stressed the social production of all the three spaces. The cultural geographer, Edward Soja, has detailed this triad and developed a trialectics of space – firstspace, secondspace and thirdspace – based on the Lefebvre's delineations. Perceived space, firstspace, also referred to by Lefebvre as spatial practice, is the domain in which the reality of space and its material form is apparent. It is, according to Soja, 'directly sensible and open, within limits, to accurate measurement and description' (1996, p 66). Conceived space, secondspace, also described as representations of space, is the domain in which the meanings or ways of imagining space are identified and discursively set 'via control over knowledge, signs and codes' (1996, p 67). Lived space, thirdspace, also described as spaces of representation is Lefebvre's 'disrupter' of the real–imagined binary. It is the moment and location of 'thirdings', of insertions, of the choice of another. Lived space incorporates both the real and the imagined and unsettles these. Soja (1996, p 2) defines thirdspace as, 'a purposefully tentative and flexible term that attempts to capture what is actually a constantly shifting and changing milieu of ideas, events, appearances, and meanings'. The combination of real and imagined and the (emotional, intellectual, physical) experience of space render 'lived space [thirdspace] as a strategic location from which to encompass, understand and potentially transform all spaces simultaneously ... [it is] the space of perils and possibilities, the space of radical openness, the space of social struggle' (Soja, 1996, p 68).

In thinking the countryside into Soja's trialectics of spatiality it is possible to understand the countryside in firstspace or perceived space terms. It has a materiality and 'realness' that is, while evolving and shifting, nevertheless concrete and mappable (Soja, 1996, p 75). The particular, dominant imaginings of the countryside or ways of 'knowing' the countryside 'fit' with the conceived or secondspace domain. This is where our inclusion of the oblique in country/side can be fully appreciated. It relates to the populist and political constructions of the rural as problem-free, aesthetically and socially idyllic, culturally homogeneous zones signifying essentialist and familiar notions of nation – what Michael Billig has referred to as the very 'unimaginative imagining' of nation (1995, p 102). This secondspace meaning of the rural is, of course, metonymic and obscures, excludes and marginalises those that do not reinforce and reproduce a specifically imagined version of rural spaces. The secondspace is the moment in which meanings of space are institutionalised and compounded by the activities and discourses of the powerful and various actors and agencies within political and policy arenas within countryside areas. The findings of the early research into racism in the countryside (for example Jay, 1992; Derbyshire, 1994) are illustrative of this. Both studies found resistance on the part of actors and agencies active in the South-West of England and in Norfolk to conceive of the category race as having any relevancy to the countryside. Ironically, the assertion of the whiteness of rural spaces provided the basis from which respondents to Jay and Derbyshire claimed that there was 'no problem here'. As late as the late 1980s this conception of the rural as a white space in which race was not a relevant consideration was not confined to rural agencies and service deliverers. Urban-based racial equality and justice organisations such as the Commission for Racial Equality and Institute for Race Relations had, at that time, no perspectives on the issues of racism and racialised exclusions in the countryside (Neal and Agyeman, this volume).

The whitening of rural spaces has not been about whiteness per se. The whiteness that has been imagined in rural areas is particularly grained and hierarchically constructed as to its social and political desirability. Whiteness has never simply equated to belonging in racialised narratives. In rural spaces Gypsies and Travellers have been systematically undesired in both historical and contemporary countryside environments (see Bhopal and Connolly, this volume). In the 1980s and 1990s New Age Travellers and ravers who left urban and suburban places either temporarily or permanently met with local and national hostility culminating in restrictive legislation (Cresswell, 1996; Sibley, 1995; Hetherington, this volume). Alongside a privileging of cultural sameness the secondspace of the rural, particularly the English rural, has been about social order, regulation and stability. It is this orderly space that is called on in times of political crisis and anxiety: during the Second World War posters with views across the Sussex Downs rallied the population to defend the nation; in the 1980s former Conservative Home Secretary William Whitelaw, infamously looked to the rural view from his garden for reassurance of a stable country as urban unrest spread across inner-city areas of Britain (Neal, 2002). Equally infamously, in the early 1990s, former Conservative Prime Minister John Major evoked the constancy of a nation through a rurally imbued spacing of identity when he told the Conservative Party Conference in 1993 that '50 years from now Britain will still be the country of long shadows on county grounds, warm beer, invincible green suburbs ...'. As Billig argues, Major's unironic use here of Orwell's ironic framing of national identity was a spatialised strategy of 'playing the patriot card' (1995, p 102).

This particular and necessarily narrow imagining of the rural has long held an appeal for the political right, both for those with conservative tendencies and those on the extreme right (Iganski and Levin, 2004). The rural imaginary and its connections with national-identity formation have had a much more elusive place in leftist political discourse. There had been no New Labour government equivalent of Major's long shadows speech. Indeed, New Labour have been closely connected to the urban. In the early days of the Blair administration, the embracing of 'Cool Britannia' was an attempt to rebrand Britain through an appeal to Britain's urbanness and multiculturalness. For example, writing in 1995 Jack Straw, former Home Secretary, argued that England needed 'a modern sense of shared identity, one that is based as much on place as on past and that elaborates the reality not the myth of modern England [and] that reality is urban, multicultural and multiethnic' (cited in Lee, 2000, p 10). There has been a marked retreat from this, made evident in Straw's cool, and the media's hostile, reception of the *Future of multi-ethnic Britain* report (2000) that, with the rural as a notable absence, called for post-nation national identity (McLaughlin and Neal, 2004). The valorisation of multiculturalism has, since the 2001 attack on the Twin Towers and the Pentagon, the unrest in the Northern Pennine towns, the war on Iraq, the 'war on terrorism' and the London bombings in 2005, rapidly vanished into an agenda of community cohesion and the need to assert core national values. However, the urban association of the New Labour government has not only remained but escalated in the face of the hunting debate and the formation of the Countryside Alliance.

We have stressed the ways in which a particular, English-dominated, regulatory rural imaginary has filled the secondspace of rural spaces. Through this framing it is possible to understand how such constructions of rural spaces demonstrate the broader ways in which space is an 'active component of hegemonic power' (Keith and Pile, 1993). However, that there are shifts, tensions, contestations, contradictions and limits of this particular way of seeing the countryside speaks to the multiplicities and complexities of spaces and their inhabitants and users. The collisions, combinations and intersections between the real and imagined spaces produce the moment of Lefebvre's lived space or Soja's thirdspace. The lived space is then the way is in which the real and imagined space is navigated, reinvented and experienced, the ways in which possibilities are opened up and closed down. Soja argues that this thirdspace offers a 'terrain of "counter spaces", spaces of resistance to the dominant order arising precisely from their subordinate, peripheral or marginalized positioning' (1996, p 68). We want to suggest that the contemporary British countrysides are terrains that exhibit some of these counter spaces. The work of the photographer Ingrid Pollard invites us in to view a moment of apparent disjuncture between the black body and the (English) rural setting. With her inclusion of written text in her pictures Pollard challenges the notion of a disjuncture *and* details the sense/experience of living the disjuncture.

... death is the bottom line. The owners of these fields; these trees and sheep want me off their GREEN AND PLEASANT LAND. No trespass, they want me DEAD. A slow death through eyes that slide away from me ... (Pastoral Interlude by Ingrid Pollard, original in colour)

The presence, activities and multivocality of those 'transgressive' groups excluded from the dominant rural imaginary within the rural landscape reflect newer, dynamic and shifting boundaries of rural social relations that stand apart from the whitened, small-scale, orderliness of the inert, sanitised countryside.

Rural studies scholars have, throughout the 1990s, argued that there had been a neglect of the 'transgressive' constituents of rural spaces and examined the diversity of those living in and belonging to the rural (Philo, 1992; Murdoch and Pratt, 1993; Cloke et al, 1994; Cloke and Little, 1997; Hetherington, this volume; Chakraborti and Garland, 2004). This edited collection similarly represents a contribution towards the telling of a more contemporary rural narrative. Each of the chapters in this collection documents the fluidity of the rural and in so doing stresses the heterogeneity of countrysides and the ways in which countrysides are always in processes of becoming'. This is by no means to underplay the tenacity of the idea of the fixity or completeness of rural spaces in populist, political and policy delivery imaginations. Nor is it an attempt to underestimate the extent of the resistance to the process of becoming and remaking. Clearly the chapters in this collection provide evidence and discussion of those forms and instances of such continuing racist hostility and contestation.

This tension is reflected/flagged in the title of the collection itself. We raise the possibilities of a reconstituted rural, a 'new countryside', framed through the lens of ethnicity, but at the same time our inclusion of the term 'exclusion' helps stress the limits and conditionality of the remaking. We have purposely selected the category *ethnicity* as opposed to *race* as the central conceptual driver of the book for a number of reasons. First, the highly problematic nature of the concept of 'race' with its absence of a scientific basis and its stress on phenotype has meant that increasingly ethnicity is the category mobilised in discussions of racism, exclusion and multiculturalism. Second, ethnicity allows us to step away from an assumption in which visible physical difference is the *only* marker of racialised exclusion and discrimination in rural spaces. Third, ethnicity opens up the gaze to majoritised ethnic formations, particularly Englishness. However, as Hall (2000) alerts us, ethnicity, with its stress on culture, similarly presents a series of problematics, not least the extent of the linkages between essentialised biologicalism of race and the essentialised culturalism of ethnicity:

> The biological referent is therefore never wholly absent from discourses of ethnicity, though it is more indirect. The more ethnicity matters the more its characteristics are represented as relatively fixed, inherent within a group, transmitted from generation to generation, not just by culture and education but by biological inheritance, stabilized above all by kinship and endogamous marriage rules that ensure that the ethnic group remains genetically and therefore culturally 'pure'. (Hall, 2000, p 223)

From this Hall argues that there is a need to recognise the ways in which this produces two converging 'logics or registers of racism' that are simultaneously 'in play'. We need then to be wary of simply inserting ethnicity in place of race. Ethnicity complexly interacts with ideas of race. What ethnicity does offer is a lens through which the social constructedness of culture and difference can be viewed. Identifying ethnicity in this way enables this collection to engage with a broader concept of exclusion on the basis of ethnicity. The chapters by Hetherington (New Age Travellers), Connolly (Irish Travellers) and Bhopal (Gypsy Travellers) all illustrate the complex intersections between undesirable forms of 'ethnic whiteness' within wider discourses of place, whiteness and identity. The chapters by de Lima, Connolly, and Robinson and Gardner all document the configurations of an ethnicised national identity in which claims on Scottishness, Irishness, Britishness and Welshness possibly unsettle and disrupt the visible ethnicity–rural relation. For example, how is it possible to understand rural racism in a context in which, as Robinson and Gardner record, respondents spoke of hating not black people or asylum seekers in Wales, but the English? This is not to argue that this is 'a truth' but it is a narrative that requires attention to ethnic claiming and recognition of relationality and historical context. In privileging ethnicity in the text this allows us to examine majoritised ethnicities and, in particular, how white Englishness has secured such a hegemonic position in discourses of rurality (see Tyler, and Neal and Agyeman, this volume). While there is then a focus on visible ethnicity and the rural running through many of the chapters (see for example Askins, Dhillon and de Lima) the 'stretch' in the category ethnicity creates a space in which the slipperiness and complexities of racialised exclusions and inclusions can be interrogated.

Rationale and organisation of the book

In 2002 the journal *Ethnic and Racial Studies* (*ERS*) published an article by Sarah that examined notions of a rural multiculturalism and policy making (Neal, 2002). Julian, now based in the Department of Urban and Environmental Policy and Planning at Tufts University in Boston, Massachusetts, saw this article on *ERS*'s electronic site and made contact with Sarah. From being one of the earliest contributors to this debate, Julian thought he had 'closed the door' on this area of research and had moved on to concepts such as environmental justice and sustainable development. In the discussions we had following on from our initial contact we kept returning to the levels of interest in the racism–ethnicity–rurality relation. This interest was apparent in the media, in tentative moves by welfare organisations and agencies and among academics. While the research and theorisation of racism, multiculturalism, nation and ethnicity has tended to reflect the urban associations of multi-ethnicity in Britain there had been a long-standing empirical concern with *place* in this literature (see Robinson and Gardner, this volume). These places and localities were, admittedly overwhelmingly urban, but the focus on these reflected an acknowledgement of the centrality of space in the efforts to analyse the concepts of race and racism in Britain (Pryce, 1978; Rex and Tomlinson, 1979, Solomos and Back, 1995; Back, 1996; Alexander, 1999).

If the importance of space was implicit rather than explicit in this work the explicit focus on space in geography was also shifting and refocusing as cultural and feminist geographers and social theorists increasingly looked to the social and cultural construction of spaces and their political content and associated meanings (Lefebvre, 1991;

Keith and Pile, 1993; Massey, 1993; Soja, 1996;Valentine, 1996; Crang and Thrift, 2000). Rural geographers, too, engaged with the cultural turn and the scrutiny of the meanings of 'the rural'. As Cloke et al (1994, p 3) argue, 'to accept the rural as a social and cultural construct allows the rural to be rescued as an important research category, as the way in which the meanings of rurality are constructed, negotiated and experienced will interconnect with the agencies and structures being played out in the space concerned'. What has occurred as a result of the spatial turn in sociology and the cultural turn in geography is a concern with the relation between the rural and formations of ethnicity and identity. Influenced by the need for more finely grained accounts of racism and exclusion and alive to the specificity of historical and geographical contexts, the research and commentary on the ethnicity–rural relation has expanded significantly since the early days of Julian's work (Agyeman, 1989).There now exists a sort of disciplinary 'mezze', an assortment, as this collection illustrates, mainly of geographers and sociologists but reaching out to those in anthropology, criminology and social policy, who are concerned with the ways in which the rural is being deconstructed and remade and with forms of resistance, challenge, exclusion and inclusion. Our awareness, and own part in these intersections, led our conversations to the possibilities of capturing this moment through some of the academic work that we knew was taking place and through the policy developments that were becoming evident, all of which were occurring at a time when the rural occupies an increasingly prominent place on public agendas (Neal and Agyeman, this volume).

The book is divided into two broad parts. At one level the first section looks to the devolved (or partially devolved) Britain of the late 1990s and 2000s but at another level this first section represents the ways in which we are cognisant of what we have earlier called the Englishness of the dominant rural imaginary (and the Home Counties/southern England ruralness that forms the heart of this imaginary). The importance of recognising the relationship between historical and geographic specificity and the ethnicity–rural relation shapes the first part of the book. Paul Connolly's chapter highlights this with his examination of the place of the rural in nationalist and unionist identity formations in Northern Ireland. Connolly shows how the nature and development of these two political projects have been based upon essentially racialised and exclusionary foundations in which whiteness has been a key element. Using quantitative and qualitative data from three separate studies, Connolly demonstrates the nature and extent of that exclusion. National stories, national-identity formations and the discourses of exclusion similarly occupy Vaughan Robinson and Hannah Gardner's excavation of contemporary Welshness and its coordinates of belonging. Like Connolly, Robinson and Gardner draw on a rich source of quantitative and qualitative data in order to examine the contradictions and tensions between a national imagining of radicalism, an abiding memory of English imperialism, extensive English settlement in Wales and a multi-ethnic population. Robinson and Gardner question the nature of the distinctiveness of Welsh rural racism and problematise the notion of a singular Welsh rural racism. They stress the importance of the recognition of different minority ethnic people having different experiences of living in Wales and racism in Wales. Philomena de Lima is similarly occupied by the complexities and contradictions involved in the examination of identity and racism in rural areas within a devolved national context. While de Lima details her research findings on the experiences of rural minority ethnic households/dwellers in the Scottish Highlands and Islands, she also draws attention to the declining Scottish population and the implications of this for the creation of multi-ethnic Scottish identity. The notion of a differently constituted rural identity within a broader national frame underpins the chapter by Neal and Agyeman. Drawing on the Marshallian concept of social citizenship Neal and Agyeman think this into a related concept of 'rural citizenship' to examine the changing contours of the English rural and to map a racialised landscape in which the questions of inclusion, exclusion, legitimacy and condtionality have been particularly struggled over. Neal and Agyeman argue that in the contemporary countryside these questions are being framed through a fractured narrative of 'rural idyll/rural crisis'. The ways in which the concept of rural citizenship and the discourse of rural idyll, rural crisis inflect and cut across each other is a key concern of the chapter. The chapter uses the story of the Black Environment Network (BEN) and empirical data from a recent research project as the lens through which to examine what happens when particular claims to rural citizenship are made in multicultural Britain.

The second part of the book deals with particular 'cuts' or ways into the idea of the contemporary rural and configurations of exclusion and claiming of a right to be in and to belong. While there is a focus on England in Part Two, each of the chapters make arguments that extend beyond the borders of the nation-state context. The second section begins with Katharine Tyler's account of Greenville, a semi-village on the outskirts of Leicester. Tyler shows us how Greenville has been, and is, actively constructed as 'a village' by its residents. Greenville, an affluent 'ruralised' settlement has increasingly appealed to affluent families of South Asian origin moving from Leicester. Based on her ethnographic study of the village Tyler identifies and analyses white middle-class discourses and practices that justify the marginalisation of wealthy and middle-class South Asian residents from participation in the social networks and activities that constitute the patterns of the imagined 'village' community.

The changing patterns of rural residential settlement and the appeal of the rural to middle-class minority ethnic populations forms the link to Kye Askins chapter on national parks and visible minority visitors to these particular spaces. Using quantitative and qualitative research concerning visible communities' perceptions and use of the English national parks Askins considers, through the concept of resistance, visible community challenges to what she describes as a 'mythologised absence in the countryside through both their *presence in* the rural and their *desire to be present*'. While Askins acknowledges she is revealing a particular account that should not obscure or marginalise experiences of exclusion from, and racism in, the rural Askins theorises particular purchases on the countryside that go beyond resistance, and focuses on the variety of ways in which rurality may be implicated in, and/or extricated from, national-identity formation.

The relationship between the production of social and cultural spaces that are inhabited by particular figures that confirm or challenge national identity formations is examined in Kevin Hetherington's chapter. This chapter focuses on the disruptions and unsettlements produced by the entry of Other figures within those social and cultural spaces. Like Askins', Hetherington's account of New Age Travellers examines the notion of a desire to be *in* the rural. Hetherington argues that New Age Travellers are able to construct an ethnicised identity that draws heavily on a different rural imaginary. This is a rural imaginary that challenges, resists and subverts the dominant rural imaginary detailed by Tyler. The final two chapters in this collection address the attempts by policy makers and service deliverers to engage with the issues of rural multiculturalism and rural racism. While Hetherington details the contested place of New Age Travellers within rural landscape Kalwant Bhopal examines the place of the rurally authentic but still highly contested Other group – Gypsy Travellers – in relation to educational policy making in South-West England. Within the context of examining aspects of good practice in a mixed comprehensive school in a rural village attended by a significant number of Gypsy Traveller children Bhopal highlights the need for educational policy-makers to consider a raft of issues from curriculum content to playground segregation and experiences of racism which are faced by many Gypsy Traveller pupils. Drawing on case-study data Bhopal urges the development of innovative practices in order to meet the needs of pupils with nomadic lifestyles that present significant challenges to educators and local education authorities. Policy development and the need for service delivery agencies and rural organisations to recognise rural multiculturalism and the specificity of rural racism and exclusion is the focus of Perminder Dhillon's chapter. Active in rural anti-racist campaigns since the late 1980s, Dhillon provides a reflexive account of the early struggles for recognition and interventions through her involvement in the Rural Anti-Racism Project. The chapter provides an examination of the issues that have subsequently reshaped the contours of rural anti-racism interventions – asylum seekers and refugees, the 2000 Race Relations (Amendment) Act, the new community cohesion/valuing diversity language in 'race' policy making and the current policy limitations of mainstream rural agencies and organisations.

What binds all of the chapters are the tensions between fluid and frozen countryside spaces. Ishiguro's story of Stevens' journey across the England's West Country is a narrative of England's social change. Similarly the narratives presented here are ones that document rural spaces and old and new contestations, desires and insertions and the wider linkages of these with national identity, multicultural citizenship and belonging. The different pulls on what rural spaces represent and the legitimacies and illegitimacies of presences within rural landscapes brings us back to the key notion of a socially produced space and Soja's 'perils and possibilities' of real-and-imaginary lived thirdspace.

Acknowledgements

We are very grateful to Gail Lewis for reminding us of the relevance of Ishiguro and to Steve Pile for discussing ideas of space.

Notes
[1] Regarding terminology: contributors in the collection vary in their choice of language and writing style in their scrutiny of ethnicity and particular populations and communities. In a reflection of the lack of consensus as to the language and terms used in the discussion and analysis of racialised social relations the different authors in this collection write with both lower and upper case spelling of categories – both white and White and black and Black appear. Race features with and without inverted commas. Some authors use the term 'minority ethnic' and others 'visible minority'. This lack of

'standardisation' reflects each contributor's intellectual and/or political preferences and the differing contexts in which the terms are being used as well as the broader and ongoing debate as to the inherent problematics of language, terminologies and categorisations. As editors we have not attempted to impose any 'one way' terminology in the collection. However, as a collection, there is an implicit, and, at times, explicit recognition of the limitations of current terminologies and categorisations and a constant emphasis on the unstable, incomplete, fluid, political, problematic, constructed and contested nature of these. It is not our, or any of the contributors', intention to homogenise and/or minimise the diversity of, and differences between, the various groups and populations that may be encompassed by racialised and ethnicised categorisations in terms of either identities or experiences.

² This 12-month qualitatively designed project was funded by Leverhulme Trust (2003-04). The data collection was based on series of focus group interviews with members of local Women's Institutes and Young Farmers' Groups in three different areas of rural England. All the views expressed are the respondents' own and not those of either the Women's Institute or Young Farmers' organisations.

References

Agyeman, J. (1989) 'Black-people, white landscape', *Town and Country Planning*, vol 58, no 12, pp 336-8.

Agyeman, J. and Spooner, R. (1997) 'Ethnicity and the rural environment', in P. Cloke and J. Little (eds) *Contested countryside cultures: Otherness, marginalization and rurality*, London: Routledge.

Alexander, C. (1999) *The Asian gang, ethnicity, identity, masculinity*, London: Berg.

Back, L. (1996) *New ethnicities and urban culture*, London: UCL Press.

Billig, M. (1995) *Banal nationalism*, London: Sage Publications.

Bunce, M. (1994) *The countryside ideal: Anglo-American images of landscape*, London: Routledge.

Chakraborti, N. and Garland, J. (2004) (eds) *Rural racism*, Devon: Willan.

Clarke, J. (2005) *Changing welfare, changing states: New directions in social policy*, London: Sage Publications.

Cloke, P., Doel, M., Matless, D., Phillips, M. and Thrift, N. (1994) *Writing the rural, five cultural geographies*, London: Chapman.

Cloke, P. and Little, J. (1997) (eds) *Contested countryside cultures: Otherness, marginalization and rurality*, London: Routledge.

Cosgrove, D. (1984) *Social formation and symbolic landscape*, London: Croom Helm.

Crang, M. and Thrift, N. (2000) (eds) *Thinking space*, London: Routledge.

Cresswell, T. (1996) *In place/out of place*, Minneapolis, MN: University of Minnesota Press.

Derbyshire, H. (1994) *Not in Norfolk: Tackling the invisibility of racism*, Norwich: Norwich and Norfolk Racial Equality Council.

Future of Multi-Ethnic Britain Commission Report, (2000) *Future of multi-ethnic Britain*, London: Profile Books.

Hall, S. (2000) 'The multicultural question', in B. Hesse (ed) *Un/settled multiculturalisms: Diasporas, entanglements, transruptions*, London: Zed Books, pp 209-41.

Iganski, P. and Levin, J. (2004) 'Cultures of hate in the urban and the rural: assessing the impact of extremist organisations', in N. Chakraborti and J.Garland (eds) *Rural racism*, Cullompton: Willan Publishing, pp 108-21.

Ishiguro, K. (1989) *The remains of the day*, London: Faber and Faber.

Jay, E. (1992) *Keep them in Birmingham*, London: Commission for Racial Equality.

Keith, M. and Pile, S. (1993) (eds) *Place and the politics of identity*, London: Routledge.

Kinsman, P. (1993) *Landscapes of national non-identity: The landscape photography of Ingrid Pollard. Working Paper 17*, Nottingham: University of Nottingham, Department of Geography.

Lee, S. (2000) 'The lion that never roared: the death of Britain and the awakening of England', unpublished paper presented to the Political Studies Association Conference.

Lefebvre, H. (1991) *The production of space*, Oxford: Blackwell.

McLaughlin, E. and Neal, S. (2004) 'Misrepresenting the multicultural nation: the policy process, news media management and the Parekh report', *Policy Studies*, vol 25, no 3, pp 155-73.

Massey, D. (1993) 'Politics and space/time', in M. Keith and S. Pile (eds) *Place and the politics of identity*, London: Routledge, pp 141-61.

Morgan, J. (2000) 'Critical pedagogy: the spaces that make the difference', *Pedagogy, Culture and Society*, vol 8, no 3, pp 273-88.

Murdoch, J. and Pratt, A. (1993) 'Rural studies: modernism, postmodernism and the post-rural', *Journal of Rural Studies*, vol 9, no 4, pp 411-28.

Neal, S. (2002) 'Rural landscapes, racism and representation: examining multicultural citizenship and policy-making in the English countryside', *Ethnic and Race Studies*, vol 25, no 3, pp 442-61.

Philo, C. (1992) 'Neglected rural geographies: a review', *Journal of Rural Studies*, vol 8, no 2, pp 193-207.

Pile, S. (1996) *The body and the city, psychoanalysis, space and subjectivity*, London, Routledge.

Pryce, K. (1979) *Endless pressure: A study of West Indian lifestyles in Bristol*, London: Penguin Education.

Relph, E. (1976) *Place and placelessness*, London: Pion.

Rex, J. and Tomlinson, S. (1979) *Colonial immigrants in a British city*, London: Routledge and Kegan Paul.

Rodaway, P. (1994) *Sensuous geographies, body, sense and place*, London: Routledge.

Scruton, R. (2000) *England, an elegy*, London: Chatto and Windus.

Sibley, D. (1995) *Geographies of exclusion*, London: Routledge.

Soja, E. (1996) *Thirdspace, journeys to Los Angeles and other real-and-imagined places*, Oxford: Blackwell.

Solomos, J. and Back, L. (1995) *Race, politics and social change*, London: Routledge.

Valentine, G. (1996) '(Re)negotiating the heterosexual street', in N. Duncan (ed) *Bodyspace: Destabilizing geographies of gender and sexuality*, London: Routledge, pp 146-55.

Williams, R. (1979) *The country and the city*, London: Chatto and Windus.

Part One:
Notions of nation and
national contexts

ONE

'It goes without saying (well, sometimes)'

Racism, Whiteness and identity in Northern Ireland

Paul Connolly

Introduction

Northern Ireland is a predominantly rural region with the majority of its population (60%) living in villages, open countryside and small towns outside the two principal urban areas of Greater Belfast and Derry/Londonderry (DRD, 2001: 86). Characteristic of other rural areas across the UK, Northern Ireland is also an overwhelmingly White population. Data from the 2001 census estimate that there are only around 14,300 minority ethnic people living in the region, representing just 0.8% of the total population. Within this, the largest minority ethnic groups are the Chinese (4,100), followed by South Asians (2,500), Irish Travellers (1,700) and African Caribbeans (1,100). In terms of settlement patterns, each of these main ethnic groups tends to be fairly evenly distributed across the five education and library board areas that comprise the region, with the majority tending to live in rural and semi-rural areas. Only around a third of the Chinese, South Asian and African Caribbean populations and a quarter of the Irish Traveller population reside in the two principal urban areas of Belfast and Derry/Londonderry.

Given these relatively small numbers, and also characteristic of many other rural areas, there has also tended to be a strong denial that racism is a problem or even a significant political issue in Northern Ireland (Mann-Kler, 1997; Hainsworth, 1998; Connolly, 2002). This is most clearly evident, for example, by the fact that the core provisions of the 1976 Race Relations Act were not even applied to the region until just a few years ago via the implementation of the 1997 Race Relations

(Northern Ireland) Order. Only since then have issues of 'race' and ethnicity begun to find their way onto the local political agenda.[1] Up until this point, racism was rarely mentioned or discussed among politicians or the media, being seen as a problem that happened elsewhere; one associated mainly with the large multi-ethnic conurbations of England (Connolly, 2002).

The aim of this chapter is to show that, far from it being a distant concern, 'race' is actually a fundamental aspect of life within Northern Ireland. The chapter begins with a brief discussion of the salience of the rural in relation to constructions of identity and senses of belonging in Northern Ireland. It will be shown how rural discourses have played very different roles in informing the two main political projects within Northern Ireland – nationalism (which tends to be associated with Catholics) and unionism (which tends to be associated with Protestants). In looking briefly at the nature and development of these two political projects it will be shown how both have been based upon essentially racialised and exclusionary foundations.

In drawing upon data from three separate studies led by the present author, the chapter will then demonstrate the nature and extent of that exclusion. More specifically, while the significance of 'race' is often denied, the chapter will show how 'Whiteness' has nevertheless been a key element of nationalism and unionism within the region and thus, by implication, tends to remain a key aspect of how the two main majority ethnic groups in Northern Ireland – Catholics and Protestants respectively – see themselves. However, while this sense of 'Whiteness' is so normalised that it often 'goes without saying', the presence of even relatively small numbers of minority ethnic people presents a fundamental challenge to these racialised senses of identity. As will be shown, there are thus times when it is 'stated' more explicitly – often through acts of racial discrimination and harassment – in an attempt to shore up this equation of being Catholic or Protestant with being White. With these arguments in mind, the chapter concludes with a brief discussion of their implications for understanding the nature and extent of racism in other rural areas across the UK.

Rural discourses and racialised identities in Northern Ireland

Notions of the rural idyll are certainly evident in relation to how Northern Ireland as a region has attempted to brand itself as a tourist destination.[2] While images and constructions of rurality at this level may be similar to many other regions within Britain, the way in which rural discourses feed into constructions of identity and belonging are inevitably complicated by the intense conflict that has beset the region for the last 30 years; a conflict that has resulted in over 3,600 deaths and well over 40,000 people being injured (Morrissey and Smyth, 2002). The evolution of this conflict can, itself, be traced back many centuries and related to Britain's attempts to colonise Ireland. It is this history that can help explain the very different ways in which rural discourses have come to shape the two main political projects of nationalism and unionism within the region.

For nationalists in Northern Ireland, their collective identity has tended to be associated with a sense of being Irish and a desire for Northern Ireland to be 're-united' with the south. Historically it is a sense of identity born out of the resistance to British colonial exploits in Ireland and this has tended to encourage the creation and maintenance of a strong sense of Irish national identity. This sense of national identity has, itself, often relied upon stirring images of a romantic, mystical and essentially rural Ireland (Coulter, 1999). Moreover, this elevation of the rural in depictions of Ireland and consequent constructions of Irishness is not coincidental but is arguably a central part of the project of establishing the Irish nation as a natural entity and thus, as Coulter (1999) has argued, seeking to confer onto it a moral authority that is natural and timeless and thus much greater than the current (imposed) political structures associated with Northern Ireland.

Not surprisingly, therefore, the active process of nation building that took place particularly following the partition of Ireland in the 1920s, both in relation to the newly independent Irish state in the south and among the now politically isolated minority Catholic population in the north, tended to be not only built upon a strong rural idyll but was also inevitably exclusionary, constructing Irishness as an homogeneous identity that was essentially Catholic and nationalistic as well as rural (MacLaughlin, 1999; McVeigh and Lentin, 2002). Moreover, the timeless depiction of Irishness and the continued evocation of an ancient and mystical past have ensured that such an identity remains essentially White.

For unionists in Northern Ireland, their collective sense of identity has tended to be much less influenced by such rural discourses. It is a collective identity that tends to continue to identify with Britain and to desire the maintenance of the political union between Northern Ireland and the 'mainland'. Many unionists are descended from earlier Scottish and English Protestant settlers loyal to the Crown who were encouraged by Britain from the 1600s onwards as part of its plantationist strategy to maintain and extend control over the island of Ireland (Darby, 1995). They settled largely in the north-eastern corner of Ireland that became the island's main industrial and trading centre, particularly in the production of linen, cotton and in ship building (Munck, 1993).

From the very beginning, therefore, the unionist collective identity tended to be informed by this sense of having to defend itself against the threat of the native Irish (Darby, 1995). Moreover, this sense of defensiveness and the need to protect their 'heritage' continued after the partition of Ireland and led the leaders of the newly created unionist majority within Northern Ireland to strive to create 'a Protestant Parliament for a Protestant State' as the then Northern Ireland Prime Minister James Craig stated in 1933 (cited in McVeigh and Lentin, 2002, p 20). Being unionist, therefore, has tended partly to be associated explicitly with Northern Ireland as a distinct political and geographical entity and partly with the defence of its Protestant heritage, the latter evident most clearly in relation to the importance of the annual Orange parades that tend to celebrate the ascendancy of Protestantism in the region.

Given this emphasis on the defence of land, it would be expected that such constructions of unionism would also be infused with rural discourses. However, there is very little attempt to associate unionism explicitly with any form of rural idyll (Coulter, 1999). This is not to suggest that the unionist collective identity is essentially urban. Indeed, sizeable numbers of unionists continue to live and work in rural areas. Rather, it is to suggest that unionist identity tends to be much more ambivalent about embracing rural discourses as part of their identity. Possibly one reason for this is simply that the rural has become associated with Irish nationalism. Moreover, and historically in relation to colonialism, there has tended to be a contrast made between the uncivilised Irish and the civilised and more industrially developed British. This in turn would then sometimes equate Catholics with the rural and Protestants with the urban. Whatever the reasons, the unionist collective identity was partly based upon exclusionary foundations, not just in relation to excluding Catholics but also, by default, other minority ethnic groups. Just as with the Catholic collective identity, therefore, the significance of the historical means that Protestantism tends also to remain infused with discourses of Whiteness.

The ultimate consequences of the conflict and the divisions between Protestants and Catholics are not just to be found in terms of the creation of two majority ethnic identities (each with very different associations with the rural but both nevertheless racialised and exclusionary) but also in terms of a heightened sense of locality and place. Clearly, the high levels of violence found in Northern Ireland over the last 30 years have led to huge population shifts as Catholics and Protestants have either been forced to move out of particular areas or have chosen to flee for their own safety (Smyth, 1998; Murtagh, 2002). The 2001 census gives some indication of the extent of these divisions suggesting that a quarter of wards (25%) in Northern Ireland consist of populations that are at least either 90% Protestant or Catholic and well over half of all wards (58%) have populations that are at least 75% Catholic or Protestant. Such spatial segregation is not just to be found in urban areas of Northern Ireland, however, but also in rural ones as well. As Murtagh (2003) has found, for example, neighbouring Catholic and Protestant villages can often be clearly demarcated with residents of each essentially living separate lives; not just living apart but also tending to work, shop and enjoy their leisure time in different areas.

Overall, therefore, it can be seen that the conflict in Northern Ireland has tended to produce two overarching majority ethnic identities – being Protestant and Catholic respectively – that are both informed by very different political projects that make use of rural discourses in differing ways but which are both, nevertheless, racialised and founded upon a sense of Whiteness. Moreover, and within this, both identities place a particular emphasis on land and territory; an emphasis that is not just found at a national level in terms of the tendency for Catholics to associate with Ireland and Protestants with Britain but also at the local level – in urban and rural areas where notions of locality and place take on special significance and tend to inform an individual's specific sense of identity and belonging. These are themes that will now be demonstrated empirically by considering the findings derived from three separate studies led by the present author. Before outlining the key findings it is necessary first to provide a brief overview of the methodology used for each study.

Methodology

The first study of the three to be considered below consisted of an attitudinal survey of a representative sample (n=380) of adults selected from across Northern Ireland undertaken in October 2002.[3] The main aim of this survey was to gain some appreciation of the nature of people's identities within the region and the significance of 'race' within this. As such, and inspired by a method previously used by Emmison and Western (1990) in a different context, the survey consisted of respondents completing a written questionnaire that included a module of questions headed: 'How you see yourself'. This module provided a list of 19 different characteristics that respondents were asked to individually rate on a five-point scale in relation to how important they felt each one was to how they saw themselves. A list of the characteristics provided and how they were worded is provided in Table 1.1. The characteristics were chosen to reflect as broad a range of items as possible that people may have found significant in terms of their sense of identity.

The second source of data consisted of the findings of a larger-scale survey (n=1,267) of a random sample of adults selected from across Northern Ireland conducted in November 1998.[4] The aim of this survey was to gain some appreciation of the nature and extent of racial prejudice among the general population in the region. Two sets of questions were asked of respondents in this regard. The first consisted of a slight adaptation of the classic Bogardus social distance scale

Table 1.1: Questions asked of respondents regarding how they see themselves

How you see yourself

When a person is asked to describe who they are, they are likely to answer in a number of different ways eg 'I am a woman', 'a Protestant', 'a father', and so on.

Now, how important are the following characteristics in describing how you see yourself?[a]

1. Your gender (ie being a man or a woman)
2. Your age (ie being young, middle-aged, retired etc)
3. The cultural tradition you are from (ie being Catholic or Protestant)
4. Your racial identity (ie being White, Chinese, African etc)
5. Your class background (ie being working class or middle class)
6. Your local neighbourhood (ie I'm from the Falls or the Shankill etc)
7. Your social activities (ie I go clubbing, I go to night classes etc)
8. Being a member of your family
9. Your political beliefs (ie I'm a Unionist, Nationalist, Socialist, Liberal, Loyalist, Republican etc)
10. Exercising and keeping fit (ie I go swimming, I go to aerobics, I play squash etc)
11. Your religious faith (ie being a Christian, Jew, Muslim etc)
12. Your occupation (ie being a secretary, plumber, social worker, teacher etc)
13. Being a football supporter (ie I'm a Liverpool fan, a Linfield supporter, a Celtic or Rangers fan)
14. Your nationality (ie being Irish or British)
15. The music you listen to
16. The county you come from (ie I'm from Tyrone, South Armagh etc)
17. The clothes you wear
18. Your star sign (ie I'm an Aries, Scorpion etc)
19. Your educational background (ie I studied psychology, history at college/ university)

[a] For each characteristic provided, respondents were asked to rate it either: 'Very important', 'Fairly important', 'Not very important' or 'Not at all important'. An additional option of 'Don't know' was also available.

(Bogardus, 1925) whereby respondents were asked how willing they would be to accept specific groups of people as:

- tourists visiting Northern Ireland;
- citizens of Northern Ireland who have come to live and work here;
- residents in my local area;
- a colleague at my work;
- a close friend of mine;
- a relative by way of marrying a close member of my family.

The specific groups that respondents were asked about were: African-Caribbean people; Chinese people; Asian people; Irish Travellers; and those from 'the other main religious tradition to themselves' (ie either Protestants or Catholics). Such questions give at least some idea of the general levels of prejudice found among the general population. In identifying where each respondent tends to 'draw the line' in terms of the contact they would ideally like to have with each group, it also provides some indication of the relative levels of prejudice held towards different minority ethnic groups.

The second set of questions consisted of a series of statements covering a range of issues relating to 'race' such as immigration, equal opportunities and multicultural education.[5] For each statement respondents were asked to indicate how much they agreed or disagreed with it on a five-point scale (that is, strongly agree, agree, undecided, disagree, strongly disagree). Rather than analysing the results of each of these statements individually, the main reason for asking these questions was to use the responses to construct an overall measure of racial prejudice for each respondent, a measure that consequently proved to be internally reliable and valid.[6] While it is not possible to interpret a respondent's individual score in isolation, such a measure does allow for comparison between groups of respondents in that higher scores can be interpreted as reflecting higher levels of racial prejudice. Moreover, and of particular concern for this chapter, it also provides the basis for further analyses to ascertain whether levels of prejudice are more likely to be found among some groups compared to others.

It is accepted that both these sources of data tend to provide rather crude and simplistic measures of people's racial attitudes and beliefs in Northern Ireland. As a wide range of qualitative, often ethnographic, studies have shown, racial attitudes and identities are not uniform and static but are inherently open and fluid and tend to develop and change over time and from one context to the next (see, for example, Keith, 1993; Back, 1996; Connolly, 1998). They are thus context-specific and tend to be much more complex and contradictory than such crude quantitative indicators can capture (Donald and Rattansi, 1992; Rattansi and Westwood, 1994; Cohen, 1999; Solomos, 2003). However, while far from perfect, such attitudinal surveys are the only means of developing some sense of the 'bigger picture' with regard to racism in Northern Ireland and thus to allow for broader generalisations to be made about the relative salience and importance of 'race' to the lives of the general population in the region. While it is important not to dwell too much on the detail of the findings, therefore, much can still be gained from the more general trends that such analyses do produce, as will be seen.

However, given these limitations, the final source of data that will be used here consisted of in-depth, qualitative interviews with minority ethnic people in Northern Ireland. A total of 101 people were interviewed with the aim of learning more about their experiences and perspectives and thus providing some insights into how the broader tendencies and processes identified through the survey data actually impact upon minority ethnic people's lives in the region. The respondents were contacted via local minority ethnic organisations and were drawn in equal numbers from the four largest groups in Northern Ireland: Chinese, Irish Travellers, Asians and African Caribbeans. Interviews were usually conducted in small groups (of typically two to four respondents) and, other than following a small number of key themes, were largely unstructured, with the emphasis on encouraging respondents to raise and discuss what issues concerned them. Further details on the methodology used and key findings to arise from the research can be found elsewhere (see Connolly and Keenan, 2001).

What 'goes without saying'

It has been argued above that being White is an essential factor in the political projects of both nationalism and unionism and thus, by implication, in the collective identities of both Catholics and Protestants in Northern Ireland. It is interesting to note, however, that the racialised nature of these respective identities is rarely stated explicitly in the region. Because of the general denial that racism is an issue (Hainsworth, 1998; Connolly, 2002), the significance of 'race' therefore tends to 'go without saying'. However, the fact that Whiteness is an integral element of both Protestant and Catholic identities can be demonstrated through an analysis of the findings gained from the first survey of people's attitudes in Northern Ireland that focused on their identities. As has been explained, the respondents were presented with 19 different items and asked to indicate how important each was to their sense of identity. One useful way of analysing the responses provided is to see whether there is any underlying pattern to the answers given. Is there a tendency, for example, for those who rate particular items as important to also rate certain others in the same way? Such a question is, in effect, asking whether the 19 items can be reduced to a much smaller number of underlying factors that tend to structure people's responses and thus which, ultimately, form the main dimensions of people's identities in the sample. These questions can be answered through a technique known as factor analysis and the method will hopefully become clearer to the reader by actually considering the results of such an analysis of the present data.

The results of the factor analysis on these 19 items are presented in Table 1.2. As can be seen, in examining the patterns of responses provided by those within the sample, the analysis has identified five main underlying factors. From the bottom of the table it can be seen that the first factor can account for just under a quarter (24.6%) of all variation in the responses given. Factor 2 can account for 14.2%,

Table 1.2: Factor analysis of the items that respondents in Northern Ireland felt were important to them in relation to their identity[a]

Item	Factor				
	1	2	3	4	5
Neighbourhood	**0.772**	0.060	0.105	0.253	−0.064
Social class background	**0.748**	0.147	0.162	0.246	−0.200
Racial identity	**0.743**	0.156	0.250	0.341	0.069
Being Protestant/Catholic	**0.678**	0.049	0.372	0.394	0.249
Nationality	**0.618**	0.098	0.437	0.173	0.221
Political beliefs	**0.720**	0.067	**0.571**	0.226	0.167
Religious faith	0.407	0.014	**0.647**	0.143	0.008
Exercise	−0.022	0.379	**0.506**	0.106	−0.307
Family	0.124	0.199	**0.553**	0.129	−0.100
Clothes	0.081	**0.720**	0.172	0.212	−0.371
Star sign	−0.007	**0.573**	0.100	0.136	−0.260
Music	−0.017	**0.552**	0.116	0.195	−0.173
Social activities	0.136	**0.489**	0.088	0.440	−0.225
Age	0.279	0.230	0.022	**0.779**	−0.091
Gender	0.154	0.226	0.211	**0.640**	−0.105
Educational background	0.148	0.361	0.160	0.224	**−0.592**
Occupation	0.092	0.246	0.216	0.161	**−0.563**
County	0.385	0.394	0.272	0.135	−0.076
Football	0.194	0.346	0.167	0.236	0.069
Eigenvalues	4.677	2.694	1.538	1.249	1.202
% of variance explained	24.6	14.2	8.1	6.6	6.3

[a] Principal axis factoring with oblique rotation.

Factor 3 for 8.1% and so on. To put it simply, it can be seen therefore that these five factors, taken together, explain just under 60% (59.8%) of the variations in people's identities within Northern Ireland.[7]

In terms of making sense of what these five factors actually represent, it is necessary to examine which individual items relate most strongly to them (that is, those whose figures are in bold in each of the five columns).[8] If we look at Factor 1, for example, it would appear to represent that dimension of identity specifically associated with Northern Ireland. As can be seen, it would tend to represent the two majority ethnic identities within Northern Ireland given the stress placed on being either Protestant or Catholic and the emphasis on political beliefs and a sense of nationality (in this sense being British or Irish) as well as a strong sense of territoriality.

In a similar vein, Factor 2 would seem to represent that dimension of identity relating to style and consumerism with its emphasis on clothes, social activities, music and star signs, whereas Factor 3 would appear to reflect a more conservative and traditionalist identity given its emphasis on religious faith, family and political beliefs. In contrast, Factor 4 seems to reflect a dimension of identity that simply reflects physical appearance with its emphasis on age and gender and Factor 5 would seem to represent some measure of professionalism given that it relates most strongly to a person's occupation and educational achievements.[9]

Overall, it is clear from the analysis here that there appear to be five main dimensions to identity that, between them, can account for about 60% of the variation in responses between individuals. Each dimension is not mutually exclusive, however, and for each individual their specific sense of identity is likely, in part, to be made up of the influence of a combination of these five factors, with some being relatively more important for that individual than others.

In the context of this present chapter, the most important point to note from this analysis relates to Factor 1, which, it will be remembered, tends to reflect the underlying dimension to the ethnic identities of Protestants and Catholics in Northern Ireland. As can be seen, these identities are built upon such elements as the importance of being Catholic/Protestant, their political beliefs, feelings of nationality and sense of territory – very much what would be expected of such identities given the discussion earlier. However, the key point to note is the fact that a person's racial identity (or 'being White, Chinese, African etc' as explained to respondents in the questionnaire) is one of the items most strongly related to these identities. This is extremely significant and provides some empirical evidence to support the arguments made earlier regarding the continued importance of being White to both Protestant and Catholic identities.

What you find when you 'scratch beneath the surface'

The previous analysis tends to confirm therefore that 'race' is a central aspect of the Protestant and Catholic identities within Northern Ireland, even if its significance is often denied. This argument gains further empirical support from the findings of the second larger-scale survey aimed at eliciting respondents' attitudes towards issues of 'race' and ethnicity more directly. Their attitudes towards members of other ethnic groups, as measured by a slightly adapted Bogardus social distance scale described earlier, are summarised in Table 1.3. As also mentioned earlier, such findings do represent rather crude measures of people's attitudes towards others. For example, while the findings suggest that a quarter of respondents (25%) would not willingly accept a Chinese person as a resident in their local area or that a third (34%) would not accept them as a colleague at work, it is not possible to assess what these figures mean in practice. There is a huge difference, for example, between how a person responds to an abstract question asked in an anonymous survey and then how they would react, in practice, should they meet a resident in their local area or a colleague at work who is Chinese.

The most informative approach to take with the findings presented in Table 1.3 therefore is to compare the overall levels of the responses for the different ethnic groups listed. In doing this, three key findings emerge. First, the findings from this survey suggest that the most negative attitudes that people within Northern Ireland tend to hold are those directed towards Irish Travellers. As can be seen, twice as many respondents stated that they were unwilling to accept Irish Travellers in comparison with any other ethnic group. This requires some explanation because, while there is now a growing body of research detailing the generally high levels of prejudice directed at Travellers in general across Britain (Acton, 1997; Kenrick and Clark, 1999), it would have been reasonable to assume that it may have been less in Northern Ireland, and particularly among Catholics, given the indigenous nature of Irish Travellers and their associations with rural Ireland. However, MacLaughlin (1999) suggests one explanation for this apparent paradox in relation to the project of nation building within Ireland with its emphasis on modernisation, social progress and importantly the acquisition of land. Within such a context the

Table 1.3: Percentage of respondents in Northern Ireland stating that they would be unwilling to accept members of other ethnic groups

'I would not willingly accept the following person as ...'	Percentage of respondents agreeing with the statements in relation to the following ethnic groups				
	African Caribbean	Chinese	Asian	Irish Traveller	Protestant/ Catholic[a]
... a citizen of Northern Ireland who has come to live and work here'	18	16	20	45	10
... a resident in my local area'	26	25	27	57	15
... a colleague at my work'	35	34	36	66	19
... a close friend of mine'	42	41	43	70	26
... a relative by way of marrying a close member of my family'	54	53	54	77	39

[a] 'Protestant' if the respondent identified themselves as Catholic, and 'Catholic' if the respondent identified themselves as Protestant.

traditional and nomadic ways of life of Irish Travellers came to be distinctly at odds with such a project (see also Fanning, 2002).

Interestingly, this argument has been developed further by some who have claimed that this attempt to build a modern Irish nation has not included a direct challenge to the colonial 'othering' of the Irish in general as uncivilised and backward but rather has been characterised by a simple transference of that discourse onto Irish Travellers. As ní Shuinéar (2002, p 187) has argued, for example, it is in this sense that Travellers are seen as 'the descendants of those victims of colonial policy – famine, evictions, land clearances – who (unlike "us") stayed down when they were pushed down, and ceased to experience history. Travellers are [therefore] essentially Irish peasants in a timewarp.'

Alongside the much higher levels of prejudice expressed towards Irish Travellers, and thus the construction of Irish Travellers as an undesirable form of Whiteness, the second point to note from Table 1.3 is that there seems to be little difference in the attitudes expressed towards the other three minority ethnic groups, namely: African Caribbeans, Chinese and Asians. The third and final point worth drawing attention to is the fact that attitudes towards members of minority ethnic groups tend to be notably more negative than those held by respondents towards members of the other majority ethnic group (that is, Catholics' attitudes towards Protestants and vice versa).

This last point is perhaps the most salient with regard to the present chapter and provides further evidence of the significance of 'race' to the attitudes and identities of the majority White (and settled) ethnic groups within Northern Ireland. As explained earlier, the conflict and ongoing divisions that exist within the region between the majority ethnic Protestant and Catholic groups have tended to dominate the political agenda here (Hainsworth, 1998; Connolly, 2002). This, in turn, has had the consequence of further marginalising, and thus denying the importance of, racial divisions in Northern Ireland. And yet, as the findings presented here clearly show, even against the background of the conflict, Catholics and Protestants are more willing to mix with one another than with those from minority ethnic groups. Again, it is important not to read too much into this finding. Sectarianism and racism are very different processes that manifest themselves in very different ways. It would therefore be wrong, for example, to claim from these findings that racism 'is worse than', or 'is more of a problem than' sectarianism in Northern Ireland. Rather, the findings are important simply for the fact that they demonstrate that, far from being eclipsed by the sectarian conflict, 'race' is still a significant element of White and settled people's attitudes and identities in the region.

A final element to examine briefly here is the distribution of racial prejudice among the population in Northern Ireland. Using the measure of racial prejudice discussed earlier, it is possible to assess how well a person's levels of prejudice could be predicted from characteristics such as their gender, age, religion, area they live in (that is, rural or urban area) and social class. This has been done with the data from this large-scale survey by means of a linear multiple regression analysis and the findings are shown in Table 1.4. Perhaps the key point to draw from this analysis is that, even when all these variables are taken together, they provide a fairly poor predictor of an individual's levels of racial prejudice. More specifically, and as can be seen, when all of these factors are combined, they can only account for 11.3% of the variation in racial prejudice scores within the sample. This tends to confirm the point made earlier: that racism is complex and context-specific and is thus certainly not reducible to some simple predictive formula. Moreover, what this also shows is that racism and racial prejudice are not confined to certain sub-groups within the population but tend to be found within every group. As will be seen shortly, for minority ethnic people living in Northern Ireland this means that there are no guaranteed 'safe havens' or communities or places where they can live free from racial prejudice.

The fact that all of these variables taken together can only account for a small proportion of the variation in levels of racial prejudice also

Table 1.4: Results of linear multiple regression with racial prejudice as the dependent variable[a]

Independent variable	B	s.e.	t	Sig.
Constant	13.922	0.613	22.715	<0.001
Gender[b]	0.483	0.265	1.826	0.068
Age	0.310	0.007	4.389	<0.001
Religion[c]	1.948	0.264	7.377	<0.001
Area (rural/urban)[d]	0.757	0.270	2.801	0.005
Social class[e]				
Professional/managerial	−1.682	0.547	−3.077	0.002
Intermediate/non-manual	−1.460	0.596	−2.451	0.014
Junior non-manual	−0.333	0.548	−0.608	0.543
Skilled manual	0.603	0.533	1.131	0.259
Semi-skilled manual	−0.308	0.533	−0.578	0.563

[a] Adjusted R^2=11.3%; Model fit: $F_{(9,943)}$=14.427, p<0.001

[b] Dummy coded: females=0, males=1

[c] Dummy coded: Catholics=0, Protestants=1

[d] Dummy coded: urban=0, rural=1

[e] Dummy coded with unskilled manual=0

means that we need to be very careful in making any generalisations about differences in levels of prejudice between discrete groups within the population (that is, average differences between men and women or between Protestants and Catholics). However, one point is worth drawing out from the results contained in Table 1.4 relating to average levels of racial prejudice found in rural and urban areas within Northern Ireland. As can be seen, those living in rural areas tend to have marginally higher levels of prejudice than their urban counterparts. This point is not meant to encourage a crude generalisation that the rural population is more prejudiced than the urban one. There is actually so much overlap between the two groups that it is practically impossible to distinguish between them.[10] Rather, the key point to note from this is simply that it provides further evidence to suggest that racial prejudice in Northern Ireland is not something that is restricted mainly to urban areas but is equally likely to be found in rural areas as well.

As for reasons why there is little difference between levels of racial prejudice in urban and rural areas, the empirical evidence available here unfortunately provides few clues. Given the relatively small size of Northern Ireland, both geographically and demographically, it could be argued that the boundaries between rural and urban areas are less distinct. The principal urban areas of Belfast and Derry/Londonderry are actually relatively small and for those living in them it will usually be a matter of a 10-minute car journey at the most to be able to 'escape to the countryside'. Moreover, this blurring of the urban/ rural distinction is likely to be enhanced by the predominance of the wider political projects of unionism and nationalism as described earlier that continue to encourage a sense of identity that is essentially White and exclusionary in both rural and urban areas. Whatever the reason, it would be unwise simply to generalise this finding concerning the lack of difference in levels of racial prejudice between urban and rural areas beyond Northern Ireland.

Racist harassment, or those times when it no longer 'goes without saying'

So far the chapter has been dealing with quantitative data and, as such, the discussion has remained at a rather abstract level. It is therefore worth reporting, in this final section, some of the actual accounts of minority ethnic people living in Northern Ireland not only to corroborate the findings reported earlier but also to provide some sense of the consequences of these racial attitudes and identities for those at the receiving end of them. Given the limits of space, only a few indicative comments can be reported here. However, these are taken from a much more detailed qualitative study of racist harassment in Northern Ireland and, for those interested, a full report on the findings of this study is available elsewhere (Connolly and Keenan, 2001). Moreover, it needs to be stressed that the accounts provided here focus only on racist harassment and that this is not meant to imply that racism is restricted to this. While it is not possible to discuss it here, institutional racism is also a significant issue in the region (Mann-Kler, 1997; Hainsworth, 1998; Connolly and Keenan, 2000a, 2002; Connolly, 2002).

As regards racist harassment in Northern Ireland, the nature and extent of the problem was first established in 1997 with the publication of a report presenting the findings of a large-scale survey of 1,176 minority ethnic people living in the region (Irwin and Dunn, 1997). It was found that just under a half (44%) of all those surveyed had experienced verbal abuse and a little under a third (29%) had experienced criminal damage to their property because of their racial identity. Moreover, one in ten reported that they had actually been physically assaulted (Irwin and Dunn, 1997, p 101).

This level of direct racist harassment was certainly corroborated by the accounts of many of those interviewed. Moreover, and given the fact that racism is not simply restricted to certain areas or sub-groups within the population as argued earlier, such incidents of harassment were found to occur almost randomly, in a wide range of different situations and contexts in rural and urban areas. As Carol (aged 37, African-Caribbean female) explained, for example, she was harassed while sitting on a bus:

> 'This guy just on the bus [aged] 25, between 25 to 30. [He said to me] "You fucking black bastard! Why don't you go back to your country!" Instead, I laughed because it happened so suddenly and unexpectedly you know, like, everybody gets on the bus and then all of a sudden this one particular person just comes straight to where I was sitting. "Oh you black bastard! Why don't you go back to your country!" So how do you respond to that?'

Such incidents were also commonly found to occur when just walking along the street while, for others, harassment was found to take place when waiting in a queue at the local shop as Michael (aged 23, Irish Traveller male) recounted: 'I was getting fags and this young fella behind me [in the queue] said "why don't you go back to where you came from you dirty bastard ya!"' Such incidents are not restricted to verbal abuse, however, but can involve physical violence as well. For example, Cyril (aged 43, African–Caribbean male) was attacked while sitting in his car waiting for a friend to arrive at a train station. As he explained:

> 'I was at a train station and really I wanted to find my friend who was coming from the South. The train came late. As I was running these guys came and say "Negro! Negro! Negro!" I say, I just say ignore, ignore it. I just rushed to the car and this guy, they came up to the car, tried to push the car, kick the car and, ah, I drove quickly. I went to the security at the train station and I, I told them that I need your help. And then the security were very nice. Quickly they say come sit here, phone the police.'

Such forms of direct harassment were found not just to occur in public spaces, however, but also took place in and around the home. As Kim (aged 25, Chinese female) recounted for example:

> '[We] used to have NF [National Front] signs painted all over our driveway wall and every time we, me and my brother and my younger sister, went out to paint over it again they would paint it back on. And, … ahm, my auntie had "Chinks move out" painted in her driveway in big white letters.'

The significance of all of these incidents cannot be understated. Given the general prevalence of racist harassment as found in Irwin and Dunn's (1997) earlier survey, it is likely that most minority ethnic people in Northern Ireland have either experienced racist harassment directly or, if they have not, they are certainly likely to be aware of a family member or close friend who has. The consequence of this is to create a general climate of exclusion and a sense of being different and of 'not belonging'. This feeling was also something that some of the interviewees talked about. Even in the absence of direct incidents of harassment, there was sometimes a sense, nevertheless, of not being welcome – evident in the silences, stares and subtle gestures of others. As Carol (aged 37, African–Caribbean female) explained:

> 'Even if they don't say something, they don't say anything to you but it's the looks. Sometimes the way they can just look at you. You know, like drop dead […] The elderly

people, yes. Or they would just bump into you, you know what I mean? They don't say anything it's the way they look at you or push you.'

Overall, therefore, it can be seen that while 'race' is seldom acknowledged within Northern Ireland it is ever-present. The centrality of Whiteness to the popular constructions of Protestant and Catholic identities in the region tend to ensure that those who are not White tend to be hyper-visible. Even in the absence of racist harassment, the types of looks and stares and (at best) the sense of inquisitiveness that are routinely directed towards minority ethnic people are testament to the continued normalisation of Whiteness among the majority population and the exclusion of minority ethnic people from their sense of belonging.

Conclusion

The main point of this chapter has not been to imply that Northern Ireland is more racist than other regions within the UK. Nor is it to suggest that all, or even the majority, of people living in the region are racially prejudiced and/or engage in racial discrimination and harassment. While, for example, one in three people were found to state that they would not willingly accept a Chinese or Asian or African-Caribbean person as a work colleague this can also be read more positively as suggesting that two-thirds of people would be willing to do so. Moreover, the measure of racial prejudice used showed up significant numbers within the majority White population who held very positive views on issues of 'race' and ethnicity.

Rather, the key point to be made here is simply that far from racism being a problem confined to multi-ethnic, inner-city areas in England, it is a problem that can also be found in rural areas with predominantly White populations. In this sense the chapter is being offered as a case study that is likely to have wider applicability to other rural areas across the UK. One potential problem in stating this, however, is the fact that the political conflict and ongoing sectarian divisions within Northern Ireland make it fairly distinctive as a rural area. It could be claimed, therefore, that the conflict in the region has created a more general climate characterised by violence and divisions. As such, this has tended to increase the exclusivity of collective identities and thus levels of racial prejudice and harassment well above those likely to exist in other rural areas. There certainly might be some truth in this. However, in the absence of detailed comparative analyses, it is not possible to determine how much the levels of racism reported earlier arise from Northern Ireland simply being a predominantly rural and White region and how much they arise from the particular ethnic divisions and conflict that exist here.

Having said this, it would be wrong simply to dismiss Northern Ireland as a wholly exceptional case with no wider applicability. While the sense of territory and belonging within Northern Ireland may have acquired a very specific form given the nature of the conflict, they are certainly not peculiar to Northern Ireland. A number of studies now exist showing just how significant senses of territory and belonging are to other rural communities across Britain (see this volume). Many of these are also informed by strong associations with history and local traditions. While there is a need to be cautious about simply applying the findings outlined previously wholesale to other rural areas, there are still some important general themes and issues arising from the earlier discussion that are likely to have some relevance to other rural contexts and situations.

With this in mind, one of the key themes to emerge from this chapter is that racism can be a problem in mainly-White rural areas. As has been shown, the lack of a significant number of minority ethnic people does not preclude the members of the majority White population living in rural areas either holding racial prejudices or engaging in the racist harassment of others. Moreover, it also does not reduce the tendency for 'race' to remain a significant aspect of the ethnic identities of the majority White population. As has been demonstrated, for example, it would appear that being Protestant or Catholic in Northern Ireland continues to be strongly associated with being White. However, and as seen earlier, while Whiteness is a key marker around which lines of inclusion and exclusion are drawn, it remains a taken-for-granted and normalised aspect of identity – one which is rarely stated or critically interrogated (Dyer, 1997; Fine et al, 1997; Frankenberg, 1997). Rather, and as also shown, it only tends to become visible when it is challenged, usually by the presence of minority ethnic people living in the region. As has been illustrated previously, it is here where the exclusionary processes of Whiteness are so clearly evident as minority ethnic people are reminded, through acts of discrimination and harassment, of their outsider status.

Finally, it is worth stressing that none of the earlier analysis is meant to imply that nationalism and unionism, and thus by default Catholic and Protestant collective identities, are fundamentally and irrevocably racialised and exclusionary. As shown, all political projects and ethnic identities are socially constructed. The current tendency for Protestant and Catholic identities to be so strongly associated with Whiteness is a reflection of particular socio-economic and political historical developments. The task now within Northern Ireland is to take seriously the need to understand and challenge racism in the region and also to begin to undermine these associations of being Catholic or Protestant with being White and to construct more open and inclusive forms of identity.

Notes

[1] It should be noted that issues of 'race' have become much more prominent over recent years within Northern Ireland, at least in government and policy circles (Connolly, 2002). The introduction of the 1997 Race Relations (Northern Ireland) Order, following a number of years of campaigning on the part of minority ethnic communities and organisations, certainly provided an impetus for change. Alongside this, perhaps the other most important single development has been the equality provisions introduced through the 1998 Northern Ireland Act. These provisions formed part of the 'Good Friday Agreement' aimed at addressing the causes of the conflict in Northern Ireland and establishing a political settlement. Part of the Agreement involved the introduction of new legislation that placed a statutory duty on all public authorities to ensure equality of opportunity and promote good relations. This was supported by the requirement that each public authority produce an equality scheme detailing how, precisely, they intend to meet these statutory duties and to submit this to the newly established Equality Commission for Northern Ireland for approval. While the primary impetus for these developments was undoubtedly in relation to addressing relations between Protestants and Catholics, it also covered many other aspects of inequality, including – most notably for this present chapter – 'race' and ethnicity. At the public level, at least, such developments have therefore certainly played a significant role in increasing the prominence of the issues of 'race' and racism in the region and the receptivity of policy makers to the findings of a growing number of research studies on racism in the region (for a review see Connolly, 2002).

[2] See, for example, the official website of the Northern Ireland Tourist Board: http://www.discovernorthernireland.com.

[3] The survey consisted of a questionnaire that included a number of modules of questions designed by undergraduate students as part of a quantitative research methods course taught by the present author.

The topics ranged from experiences of education and attitudes towards music to reasons for drinking alcohol and experiences of street crime. The questions that provide the focus for this present chapter were added by the author as a discrete module. Each student took ten questionnaires that they were asked to give to family and friends to complete on a quota basis to ensure a spread of respondents in terms of age and gender. Given the diverse social backgrounds of the students, such an approach also ensured that the final sample included respondents from a range of social class backgrounds, locations within Northern Ireland and from both the Protestant and Catholic ethnic traditions.

A total of 380 questionnaires was completed and returned in October 2002. The key characteristics of the final sample are detailed in the Appendix. It can be seen that the sample contains a diverse range of respondents in relation to gender, community background, age, area of residence and socio-economic status. However, in comparing the characteristics of the sample with data from the 2001 census, it is clear that it was not sufficiently representative of the Northern Ireland population. With this in mind, the sample was weighted prior to analysis to render it more representative. The characteristics of the weighted sample, as used in the analysis to follow, are also shown in the Appendix. As can be seen, while some minor discrepancies remain, the weighted sample is largely representative of the broader population.

[4] Full details on the methodology used for this survey are provided in Connolly and Keenan (2000b).

[5] See Connolly and Keenan (2000b) for details on the seven statements used.

[6] The overall measure was derived by calculating the mean response to the seven Likert-style statements. The resultant scale was found to be sufficiently reliable (Cronbach's Alpha = 0.739) and valid (with a factor analysis of the seven items extracting just one factor with an eigenvalue greater than one). Further details on the reliability and validity of the scale used can be found in Connolly and Keenan (2000b).

[7] It is recognised that it is strictly incorrect to sum the percentage of variation explained together like this when using an oblique rotation. However, when an orthogonal rotation was used instead, very similar

figures emerged indicating that we can have some confidence in this estimate of the total variation explained.

[8] These figures in each column represent the relationship between each item and the factor concerned. These figures are actually the correlation coefficients between each item and the underlying factor. Values for coefficients can range from 0 (indicating that no relationship exists at all) to 1 (or –1) indicating that a perfect relationship exists. The interpretation of each factor is achieved by identifying those items that relate most strongly to it. In Table 1.2 this has been done by highlighting those coefficients that are 0.450 or higher. This choice of 'cut-off point' is essentially arbitrary. 0.450 is used here as it indicates that an item shares at least one-fifth (20.25%) of its variation with the factor concerned.

[9] The detailed interpretation of each of these five factors is not actually the main concern here. The comments made here are provided mainly for illustrative purposes and it is recognised that there may well be alternative interpretations for some of these.

[10] In fact the findings suggest that being in a rural area tends to increase a person's racial prejudice score on average only by less than one point (that is, 0.757) on a scale, it should be remembered, running from 0 to 28.

References

Acton, T. (ed) (1997) *Gypsy politics and traveller identity*, Hatfield: University of Hertfordshire.

Back, L. (1996) *New ethnicities and urban cultures*, London: UCL Press.

Bogardus, E. (1925) 'Measuring social distance', *Sociology and Social Research*, vol 9 (March), pp 299-308.

Cohen, P. (ed) (1999) *New ethnicities, old racisms*, London: Zed Books.

Connolly, P. (1998) *Racism, gender identities and young children*, London: Routledge.

Connolly, P. (2002) *'Race' and racism in Northern Ireland: A review of the research evidence*, Belfast: Office of the First Minister and Deputy First Minister, www.research.ofmdfmni.gov.uk/raceandracism/index.htm.

Connolly, P. and Keenan, M. (2000a) *Opportunities for all: Minority ethnic people's experiences of education, training and employment in Northern Ireland*, Belfast: Northern Ireland Statistics and Research Agency.

Connolly, P. and Keenan, M. (2000b) *Racial attitudes and prejudice in Northern Ireland*, Belfast: Northern Ireland Statistics and Research Agency.

Connolly, P. and Keenan, M. (2001) *The hidden truth: Racist harassment in Northern Ireland*, Belfast: Northern Ireland Statistics and Research Agency, http://www.research.ofmdfmni.gov.uk/thehiddentruth.doc.

Connolly, P. and Keenan, M. (2002) *Tackling racial inequalities in Northern Ireland: Structures and strategies*, Belfast: Northern Ireland Statistics and Research Agency, http://www.research.ofmdfmni.gov.uk/racereport4/index.htm.

Coulter, C. (1999) *Contemporary Northern Irish society*, London: Pluto Press.

Darby, J. (1995) 'Conflict in Northern Ireland: a background essay', in S. Dunn (ed) *Facets of the conflict in Northern Ireland*, London: Macmillan, pp 18-37.

Department for Regional Development (DRD) (2001) *Regional development strategy for Northern Ireland 2025*, Belfast: DRD.

Donald, J. and Rattansi, A. (eds) (1992) *'Race', culture and difference*, London: Sage.

Dyer, R. (1997) *White*, London: Routledge.

Emmison, M. and Western, M. (1990) 'Social class and social identity: a comment on Marshall et al', *Sociology*, vol 24, no 2, pp 241-53.

Fanning, B. (2002) *Racism and social change in the Republic of Ireland*, Manchester: Manchester University Press.

Fine, M., Weis, L., Powell, L. and Wong, L. (eds) (1997) *Off White: Readings on race, power and society*, New York: Routledge.

Frankenberg, R. (ed) (1997) *Displacing Whiteness: Essays in social and cultural criticism*, Durham, NC: Duke University Press.

Hainsworth, P. (ed) (1998) *Divided society: Ethnic minorities and racism in Northern Ireland*, London: Pluto Press.

Irwin, G. and Dunn, S. (1997) *Ethnic minorities in Northern Ireland*, Coleraine: Centre for the Study of Conflict, University of Ulster.

Keith, M. (1993) *Race, riots and policing*, London: UCL Press.

Kenrick, D. and Clark, C. (1999) *Moving on: The Gypsies and Travellers of Britain*, Hatfield: University of Hertfordshire Press.

MacLaughlin, J. (1999) 'Nation-building, social closure and anti-Traveller racism in Ireland, *Sociology*, vol 22, no 1, pp 129-51.

McVeigh, R. and Lentin, R. (2002) 'Situated racisms: a theoretical introduction', in R. Lentin and R. McVeigh (eds) *Racism and anti-racism in Ireland*, Belfast: Beyond the Pale Publications, pp 1-19.

Mann-Kler, D. (1997) *Out of the shadows: An action research report into families, racism and exclusions in Northern Ireland*, Belfast: Barnardo's.

Morrissey, M. and Smyth, M. (2002) *Northern Ireland after the Good Friday Agreement*, London: Pluto Press.

Munck, R. (1993) *The Irish economy: Results and prospects*, London: Pluto Press.

Murtagh, B. (2002) *The politics of territory: Policy and segregation in Northern Ireland*, Basingstoke: Palgrave.

Murtagh, B. (2003) 'Territoriality, research and policy making in Northern Ireland', in O. Hargie and D. Dickson (eds) *Researching the troubles*, Edinburgh: Mainstream Publishing.

ní Shuinéar, S. (2002) 'Othering the Irish (Travellers)', in R. Lentin and R. McVeigh (eds) *Racism and anti-racism in Ireland*, Belfast: Beyond the Pale Publications, pp 112-34.

Rattansi, A. and Westwood, S. (eds) (1994) *Racism, modernity and identity on the Western Front*, Cambridge: Polity Press.

Smyth, M. (1998) *Half the battle: Understanding the impact of the Troubles on children and young people*, Derry/Londonderry: INCORE.

Solomos, J. (2003) *Race and racism in Britain* (3rd edn), Basingstoke: Palgrave.

Appendix: Main characteristics of the sample used to survey people's identities in Northern Ireland

Table 1.5: Characteristics of the sample

	Original sample		Weighted sample (%)	Census 2001 (%)
	n[a]	%		
Gender				
Male	165	43.5	49.4	48.7
Female	214	56.5	50.6	51.3
Community background				
Catholic	235	62.3	41.7	43.8
Protestant	138	36.6	56.0	53.1
Other	4	1.1	2.3	3.1
Age				
18-29	165	43.8	21.2	22.1
30-44	63	16.7	30.8	30.4
45-59	88	23.3	24.6	23.5
60 and over	61	16.2	23.4	24.1
Education and library board area				
North-Eastern	102	27.6	25.8	23.4
South-Eastern	60	16.2	17.1	23.1
Belfast	76	20.5	21.6	16.5
Western	56	15.1	14.8	16.7
Southern	76	20.5	20.6	20.4
Economically active[b]				
Middle class[c]	52	14.0	16.9	16.4
Intermediate	62	16.7	16.5	12.9
Working class[d]	84	22.6	23.3	30.6
Economically inactive				
Retired	55	14.8	20.6	11.0
Permanently sick/disabled	10	2.7	3.5	9.3
Looking after home/family	24	6.5	7.7	7.4
Full-time student	85	22.8	11.5	8.1[e]
Other	–	–	–	4.3

[a] N=380. Due to some missing data, not all categories will sum to 380.

[b] Coded using UK NS-SEC Categories.

[c] Corresponding to NS-SEC 'Managerial and Professional Occupations' Category.

[d] Combination of NS-SEC Categories: 'Routine and Manual Occupations', 'Long-Term Unemployed' and 'Never Worked'.

[e] Comprising those classified as both economically active and inactive by the census 2001.

TWO

Place matters

Exploring the distinctiveness of racism in rural Wales

Vaughan Robinson and Hannah Gardner

Racism: place matters

Researchers have, for some time, argued that there is no single racism in the UK, and that different racisms manifest themselves in different ways in different places at different times. In line with the research paradigms of the day, early work tried to demonstrate this statistically, by mining large data-sets Schaefer (1975) and Robinson (1987) both used national data-sets to identify regional variations in the scale and form of expressed racism. Both found that the populations of different regions and cities had propensities to express racist sentiments that were significantly different. Robinson (1987, p 193) therefore concluded that the study of localities and places should be an 'active element within any explanatory framework' and that neglecting their importance would only serve to 'weaken our ability to understand real world situations'.

Later work then tried to explain such variations in racism by reference to the characteristics of specific places. Husbands (1983), for example, identified the East End of London as a place where anti-immigrant sentiment had been prevalent for many years. He accounted for this by reference to a local culture that had been forged by continuing immigration and the casual nature of employment in the docks.

More recently still, research and writing has tended to follow two divergent paths, neither of which has been centrally concerned with place and its significance. Those working within rural studies initially concentrated upon proving that racism does exist in rural areas, and is just as virulent there. Jay (1992) was the first to do this, with his study funded by the Commission for Racial Equality. But, while this was situated within the South-West of England, there was little effort to consider the distinctiveness of that place and how this might have shaped the racism on display there. The South-West was simply taken as an archetype of the 'rural'. Further work within rural studies has since concentrated on the generic processes that 'other' various minorities (such as Travellers or gays) within rural settings because they do not fit into a generic – rather than place-specific – rural idyll. Only recently have researchers realised that there is no such thing as *the* rural (see Murdoch and Pratt, 1993), and that there are multiple variants of rural racism. This has led Neal (2002, p 442), for example, to criticise the representation of a 'single monolithic racism' within the rural literature that is 'unchanging' in operation. And it has led Williams (1999b, p 269) to argue that because

> 'race' will change within a given context and across time … the pursuit of universal examinations has given way to an exploration of the specificities of distinct locales. It has become important to understand the way in which key variables in social structural arrangements of society such as class, cultural and other social groupings produce particularized racialized relations.

In contrast, those working in fields other than rural studies have tended to focus upon a different agenda. They have been concerned increasingly either with the equal opportunities debate, with institutional racism or with the impacts of racism on (mainly urban) people, either through their exposure to, or fear of, racial attacks, or through how they have to modify their behaviour to avoid racism. Chahal and Julienne (1999), for example, have shown how individual families have had to change their everyday routines to avoid exposure to the racism of their neighbours. While some of this work has been overtly spatial (for example Chahal and Julienne's analysis of the use of different rooms in a house), much has not been concerned with variations between places, but with systems, policies and practices.

Devolution offers an opportunity to reinvigorate studies of how racism varies between places, not least given that this process may itself invigorate issues of national and regional identity. As policies have been tailored to the specific needs of the different nations of the UK, and resources applied in different ways, so there has been a need to provide evidence-bases and understandings that are unique to England, Wales, Scotland, Northern Ireland and even to regions within these nations. We are therefore seeing a rebirth in interest in the power of place.

In Wales, the present authors, and others, have started to sketch out the uniqueness, or lack of uniqueness, of racism there. A central consideration here has been the critical interrogation of the concept of *gwerin*, seen by many as a central aspect of Welsh (rural) culture (see Williams, Evans and O'Leary, 2003). *Gwerin* can be translated as an expression of Welsh traditional qualities: God-fearing, moral and tolerant towards others (also explored by Evans, 1991; Williams, 1999b). Thus, if the *gwerin* concept holds true, we would expect relatively little racism in the Welsh countryside. Complicating this, however, is the long legacy of English governance in Wales, where resentment of and resistance to the Westminster hegemony can easily spill over into more prejudicial anti-English feeling. Moreover, this may be intensified in the present day in rural Wales due to in-migration of English people, and the resulting locals vs newcomers conflicts (see Cloke, Goodwin and Milbourne, 1995). Thus may racism as conventionally understood overlap with more general prejudice against perceived 'others'.

Turning now to studies of racism in Wales, Robinson (1985) demonstrated how the levels of expressed racism in the city of Swansea were little different to those in multiracial England. Evans (1991) reviewed the long history of race relations in Wales and concluded that Wales had been no more tolerant of visible minorities than other parts of the UK. And, most pertinently, Williams (1995) contrasted this rather intolerant reality with the tolerant imaginings embedded within Welsh culture, particularly the notion of *gwerin*.

More recently these same authors have returned to some of these themes. Robinson (1999, p 78) has argued that attitudes towards asylum seekers in Wales are characterised by 'cultures of ignorance, disbelief and denial', and he and Gardner (Robinson and Gardner, 2004a, 2004b) have described the lived experience of black and ethnic minorities in rural Wales and the ways in which this is distinctive, and in many ways positive. In a substantial edited collection, Evans, O'Leary and Williams (2003) have developed their thesis that Wales is not the tolerant nation that it fondly imagines, with Robinson (2003) critiquing both English notions that Wales is a parochial and monoethnic society, and Welsh notions of *gwerin*. Nonetheless, while this work has been invaluable in charting the contours of Welsh racism, much of it has sought simply to establish that there is a distinctively Welsh form of racism that differs from its English and Scottish counterparts: that there is something unique to explain.

What we seek to do in this chapter is expose the distinctiveness of Welsh rural racism, and, in particular, two dimensions of this. First, we want to explore whether there is a single Welsh rural racism, or whether different minority ethnic people have different experiences, depending on who they are, where they live and who they come into contact with. Second, we will consider whether rural racism in Wales is distinctive by virtue of who perpetrates it. In the context of the long-scale migration of English people into rural Wales (as explored by Day, 1989), is it local Welsh residents or English incomers?

The distinctiveness of minority ethnic experiences in rural Wales: what the literature says

The following review of literature draws out in more detail ways in which the Welsh Black and Minority Ethnic (BME) experience is particularly distinctive. We will explore how the cultural, linguistic and social contexts in rural areas of Wales differ in six ways from the more generalised discussions of 'rural racism' that appear elsewhere in the UK literature.

The first theme is whether there is a common awareness of the 'race' issue throughout Wales. Williams (2003, p 227) explains how concern about race is restricted to a particular part of Wales, namely urban South Wales. As a result, 'white', predominantly rural, Wales is effectively distanced from the issue, creating a bicultural (as opposed to multicultural) Wales, that does not recognise diversity. She explains how this can impact directly on rural BME families who 'continue to live in rural areas but never become part of the life of the place and never achieve any sense of belonging'.

The second theme is that Wales has a unique history of ethnic diversity and conflict. The history of multiculturalism in Wales is long-standing, and pre-dates post-war mass migration to the UK. Fryer (1984) dates the earliest community of black people in Wales at 1874, but notes a longer history of individual settlement throughout Wales. Evans (1991) described how this had produced a diverse ethnic population within Wales, made up of significant numbers of Italians, Russians, Jews, Spaniards, Africans and West Indians. However, most of this long history has been characterised by racial conflicts that 'have been among the most vicious in Britain' (Evans, 2003, p 30), such as the well-documented and violent clashes between the Welsh and the Irish in the 1800s (Parry, 1983; O'Leary, 1991, 2000) and the anti-Jewish riots in 1911 (Alderman, 1972; Holmes, 1982). As a result, Evans (1991, p 21) noted 'there is little evidence of inherent tolerance in the Welsh psyche'. Later, in the post-war period, Wales ceased to be a major destination for international migrants (Evans, 2003), and as a result there has been a paucity of recent academic research on BME populations, with Robinson (2003, p 160) commenting that 'we have accumulated only limited knowledge to date about the nature of Wales' contemporary minority ethnic population or their experiences'. Much of the literature concerning ethnicity in Wales instead draws attention to the way 'race' has been missing from the political agenda (in comparison to England) causing complacency and 'a noticeable silence around the issue within the nation' (Williams, 1999b, p 270). Evans, O'Leary and Williams (2003, p 11) explain how this could be because racial issues in Wales are locally and popularly perceived as the conflict between the Welsh and the English, and as such, 'ethnic issues have forced race further down the agenda than in England'.

Related to this latter point, a third thematic concern is the three 'cultures' that underpin attitudes towards ethnic minorities in Wales (Robinson, 1998). Writing about refugees in Wales, Robinson described how a 'culture of disbelief' refused to acknowledge that Wales even had a minority ethnic population, a 'culture of ignorance' argued that because we know so little about the country's minority ethnic population we need not do anything about their special needs, and a 'culture of denial' simply claimed that Wales did not suffer the same blight of racism as England. This overall attitude of 'no problem here' has also been observed in relation to rural BME dwellers in Wales (Robinson, 2003), as it has elsewhere (Derbyshire, 1994; Nizhar, 1995; de Lima, 2001; Magne, 2003).

Fourth, is the idea that Wales as a country, and the Welsh as a people, are inherently more tolerant than their immediate neighbours. Williams (1995, 1999a) has carefully explained how this supposed tolerance is closely tied, as we have seen, to the Welsh belief that they live in a society and communities characterised by harmony, hospitality, open-mindedness and a tolerance of incomers. Robinson (2003) explored this imagined definition of the Welsh idyll through a 2001 questionnaire survey of local inhabitants of rural Powys. He found that residents regarded themselves as *more tolerant* than their counterparts in the rest of the UK, but were simultaneously prepared to express racist sentiments that were either as extreme or more extreme as those found in the rest of the UK. And he also found clear evidence of racism in the experiences of a number of BME residents in rural Wales. He concluded that 'contemporary Welsh imaginings of tolerance are just that' (Robinson, 2003, p 176). An associated facet of this claimed tolerance is the belief that the Welsh cannot but be tolerant, given their own history of oppression by the English. Williams (1995, p 120) writes 'The politics of Wales is the politics of English oppression: it therefore becomes easy to distance the Welsh from other elements of oppression, namely racism: the formula being, oppressed peoples cannot be oppressors'. Williams (1999b, p 279) goes on to claim that 'the common enemy of black people and of Welsh people is seen to be the English and in this common oppression there is potential for empathy, tolerance and solidarity'.

Another distinguishing factor in the minority ethnic experience in Wales is the Welsh language. Within Wales, different areas/spaces of language usage have been identified (see Osmond, 1985), which may in turn affect the way the politics of language is articulated and differentially experienced by minority ethnic residents. Williams (1995, p 124) expresses concern about how the Welsh language can serve to increase the visibility of minority ethnic inhabitants (an issue particularly important in rural areas, which tend to be more Welsh-speaking). She describes this situation as a 'double-edged sword' since non–Welsh-speaking incomers of all races will be regarded as threats to Welsh culture. However, Williams (1995, p 125) is not wholly pessimistic about the intersection of BME groups with Welsh-speaking Wales. In closing, she noted – 'it may well be that there is a higher level of social interaction between the dispersed individual from an ethnic minority group and Welsh-speakers in rural Wales'.

The last theme within the literature forms one of the dual foci of the remainder of this chapter. It is the view that racism in Wales is actually English racism, imported by the incomers who leave Birmingham and London and head for the rural idyll in Wales (see also Smith, 1993 on racism in Scotland). There have even been suggestions that these incomers are a self-selecting group who are moving specifically to escape English multiculturalism, that is, that they might be especially racist, even by English standards. Parker (2001, p 8) is the key proponent of this view, using his own experiences in Wales to produce a journalistic account of English racism in mid-Wales:

> it is a sad truth that many English immigrants into rural Wales are out-and-out racists ... the common defining feature is that their principal reason for leaving the English cities was to get away from multi-cultural society, from black and Asian people in particular, and they see rural Wales, with its largely white population, as a safe haven.

Such reasoning can then be used to absolve the Welsh of any responsibility for local racism as it is a problem unique to 'the English':

racism is generally perceived as a problem of the English. This level of detachment, distancing and denial is frequently articulated, the Welsh almost claiming a moral high ground as an oppressed people themselves. (Williams, 1995, p 120)

The research project

The research project utilised two main research methods and therefore datasets, and was completed as a joint venture between the authors and Victim Support Powys, with funding from Powys County Council. Powys was chosen as the initial case-study area as Victim Support Powys had identified a significant number of minority ethnic residents in the area with distinctive experiences and problems. They also found that many local people and service providers were in denial, refusing to acknowledge the local presence of a BME population. In order to explore the impact of this, in-depth qualitative interviews were undertaken in 2003 and 2004 with 40 BME residents in rural Powys. The research sample was derived over two years by snowballing, aiming to capture a wide range of experiences. Initial interviews were facilitated as a result of a Victim Support helpline set up in Powys for those wishing to report racial harassment (see Robinson, 2003). We also approached residents who had experienced racial harassment and chosen not to report their experiences, as well as those who had made no claims of victimisation whatsoever. Visiting schools, colleges and English-language classes, and working through 'community leaders' were also fundamental aspects of the snowballing process. We also sought variety in the ethnic identification of interviewees, with the final sample consisting of 24 females and 16 males, of whom nine were European, seven Black Caribbean, seven South-East Asian, six African, five Bangladeshi, three Indian, two Latin American, and one from the Middle East. The age of interviewees ranged from 15 to 54, and there was a variety of occupations. Interviews lasted an average of 120 minutes and were usually undertaken in the respondent's home.

For the second part of the project we organised a survey in Powys concerning attitudes to British and local dimensions of 'race' and immigration. This involved brief interviews with 300 people, with the sample matching the geographical distribution of the county's population, and its age structure and gender balance. The sample contained Welsh-born respondents and respondents who had moved into Wales from England. We employed on-street interviews to access village and town dwellers, and telephone interviews to access remote rural dwellers. Many of the questions we asked had been used in the

British Social Attitudes Survey (Jowell and Airey, 1984) and the EU's Eurobarometer (European Commission, 1998) survey of racism and xenophobia. They were therefore thoroughly pre-tested. Initial comparison of the socio-demographics of the Welsh and English samples indicated that they shared broadly similar social-class profiles, highest qualifications, age structures and gender balance. Differences in opinion between the Welsh and English cannot therefore be a byproduct of comparing dissimilar samples. However, the two groups did have rather different political outlooks, with the Welsh being more likely to vote Labour and Plaid Cymru, and the English being more likely to support the Conservatives.

Is there one racism in rural Wales or are there many?

This section focuses upon the findings derived from our qualitative interviews and argues that there is no single BME experience in rural Wales, as well as no single relationship between BME inhabitants and the communities in which they live. However, the interviewees did believe that their experience had been influenced by a series of dualisms – local/incomer, Welsh-speaking/non-Welsh-speaking, urban/rural – as well as by place. While, in keeping with the subject matter of this book, discussions of exclusion are central to this chapter, we are not suggesting that exclusion is the characteristic experience for every person (see Robinson and Gardner, 2004a).

Gaining entry to rural communities

A clear theme that came out of our interviews was the difficulty of penetrating what are seen to be cliquish rural communities and being accepted by them, regardless of skin colour. This was captured in the comments of three individuals:

> 'Even if you are white you can be an outsider.' (Female, children of dual heritage)

> 'Contacts with Welsh people aren't very, very easy in fact, because in Llandrindod Wells all peoples know each other, and they have, their views – I think they don't like the presence foreigners.' (Male, French)

'I find it in the Round Table. The ladies all compete and it's amazing to see them do it. You know, because they ... want to become president every year and vice president and secretary ... they'll all keep together and they try to out-do the other group. And they're all supposed to be one organisation but they're not, they're different groups, different cliques in their groups.' (Female, Jamaican)

Rural communities and minority ethnic residents

For other respondents, this general problem of exclusion was heightened for them personally because of their visible ethnicity:

'It was rural – there wasn't much black people, I just don't think I would fit in very easily.' (Female, Jamaican)

'Once people know you are from somewhere tropical, it didn't even matter where. Are you from abroad and that was it, you know, they didn't even class you as anything else.' (Female, Trinidadian)

'It doesn't matter how many generations you stay here you are never accepted 100 per cent because you're always going to be different. Unless you intermarry so much that you no longer look like. But as long as you are black it doesn't matter how long you're here, you're never ever going to be 100 per cent accepted. And I don't care what anybody else says. After 40 years, that's how I feel about it and I know that for a fact.' (Female, Jamaican)

Rural communities and a distinctive rural racism

Barriers to the entry of outsiders were also thought to be accentuated because of the limited prior contact rural communities had had with minority ethnic residents, and their consequent limited understanding of concepts of multiculturalism. For some, the attitudes they encountered were from an age gone by:

'A lot of these farmers, or whatever they are, they do tend to have that view that you know, you can't teach blacks anything, they're backward, you know, they're apes, you know, you just can't teach them anything. And it's that

> mentality that sort of drives a lot of the racists in this country. They also have that perception of black people as being ignorant and swinging from trees still.' (Female, Jamaican)

> 'Rural racism is more of an ignorance thing than it's racism, you know. The racism that you see in rural area, a lot of it is lack of knowledge and some of it racially motivated simply because you feel somebody else coming into your territory and both of it is quite naive really.' (Male, Bangladeshi)

As a result, rural racism is often not taken as seriously as it would be in an urban environment. The following people draw some interesting distinctions:

> 'Country people are not prejudiced, they are ... what they are, they are just country people. They are naive, but good-hearted people. The city life is different, they have the hatred.' (Female, Trinidadian)

> 'The problem a lot of ... racism here is ignorance rather than hatred. They don't know because they're not educated or experienced in other cultures. Whereas in London somebody might have a hatred, due to an experience, there's a difference. Because they are not used to see a lot of foreign people.' (Male, Bangladeshi)

Many interviewees identified a particular 'rural mindset' that almost excuses potentially racist behaviour as 'innocent' or unintended. For example, one girl commented, 'the Chinese takeaway had a few problems. But I don't think people mean it' (female, Mauritian). One boy recounted a similar experience: 'they are kind of blunt in what they say a lot of the time but they don't actually mean any harm I don't think' (male, Trinidadian). Another person explained how she also took no offence to potentially derogatory comments:

> 'I think we were treated more like children actually. We were ... not like mature people ... because I think they had no idea about the culture ... They had no idea about our people ... I remember a nurse saying to me, "do you come from the jungle?" ... It was said quite innocently.' (Female, Mauritian)

Certain interviewees even attribute attitudes towards them as cultural traits on the part of the Welsh. For example,

> 'Obviously you get the neighbours asking, that same question you mentioned … where's XXXXXX really from? But no, not with any malice, they were just curious … Just natural Welsh curiosity.' (Female, dual heritage)

The nature and practice of exclusion

How then is this exclusion manifested? Interviewees have drawn upon experiences of verbal and physical abuse, hate mail, public avoidance, stereotyping and gossip. Some had simply been made to feel different, and outsiders:

> 'They see me and I open my mouth and I have got a Nigerian accent, and that does shock a lot of people.' (Male, Nigerian)

> 'They [local inhabitants] just stare really and you can feel a sort of you know, a nudge, nudge, wink, wink, look at him.' (Male, Trinidadian)

Others had been excluded by overt collusion:

> 'There's a corner shop in town that's been taken over by Sri Lankans recently. And my brother's heard several people "oh we're not going in there anymore". He has a lot more to do with people in town and became aware of these things. And another friend of ours wanted to sell another corner shop to a person who wanted to change it to an Indian restaurant, takeaway Indian. Did that get planning permission? No way. All the residents objected. Not to it being a takeaway, but to it being an Indian takeaway.' (Female, dual heritage)

While yet others feel that racism is more covert:

> 'I have never seen that sort of prejudice you know and maybe because of the colour of my skin people know straight away – they either avoid me or they put up with

me. I think if there is any prejudice it's underground, it's not so blatant.' (Female, Jamaican)

'I don't look for things like that and I have never really you know been told to my face. I mean it's very, very underneath you know but you know it's there.' (Female, Mauritian)

Avoidance and exclusion are acts of rejection. However, there are also incidents that are exclusionary and are clearly racially motivated. As one lady, the recipient of hate mail, poignantly explained:

'One of the reasons I got the death threat is quite remarkable. I got the death threat because of what Robert Mugabe in Zimbabwe was doing to the white farmers. Not him personally, but when his war veterans were ransacking the white farms, raping women and killing some of the white farmers. And they said "we're going to do to you what had happened to them" ... And, you know, you think to yourself well I've got no connection with Robert Mugabe. Even going back generations I probably have no connection, even with Africa to Robert Mugabe's Zimbabwe. But you know it was just that whole business that prompted someone to send a death threat because they felt that it wasn't fair that I lived on a white farm. They didn't want me being on a white farm.' (Female, dual heritage)

Culture of denial

Many of our respondents commented on what Robinson (1999) has termed the Welsh 'culture of denial':

'The attitude and comments were [from service providers] "well there's not many black people here so racism is not a problem", if there's one black person or you know Asian or whatever then there's one who requires a service – you cannot deny them. That to say that there's not enough of us is just not acceptable.' (Mother of children with dual heritage)

Nor are service providers the only ones who practise a culture of denial:

Interviewer: 'What was the reaction of the local community when they heard about the death threats?'

Respondent: 'It's difficult. Because they don't believe that this is happening. Even now, even though the letters have been shown on telly for the world to see. Even now people say this hasn't happened and we're making this up effectively. You're doing it for publicity etc.' (Female, dual heritage)

A distinctive rural racism in Wales?

Overlaid on the more general processes of rural racism are those factors unique to Wales. One of these is the Welsh language, sensitivity to its future, and the way Welsh can be used to exclude or to gain inclusion. The way in which rural parts of Wales are culturally and linguistically sensitive to change was thought to be significant by many of our respondents:

Respondent 1: 'I understand their wish to preserve their culture and their language and they feel threatened. I just think it's such a shame. I mean we go up to London and it's so nice to see so many different people in different communities that are getting on with life.'

Respondent 2: 'It would be a total cultural shock for most of them round here if they actually took a day out and went to London or Birmingham for the day.'

Respondent 1: 'They don't see the benefits of it. They just don't.'

Respondent 2: 'They just don't see that, they don't see any of it.' (Male, English, and female of dual heritage)

The language could be used to exclude and include:

'[In work, staff talk] in Welsh if they want to talk about you.' (Male, Nigerian)

'I am Portuguese so I don't speak Welsh. You've got four people round the table and one starts speaking Welsh. And I can't speak Welsh. I think that's rude. They should speak

> English really, not Welsh. Welsh when they are by themselves
> but when they are altogether at a table.' (Female, Portuguese)

Having realised that she was being excluded because she did not speak
Welsh, this woman took action:

> 'I've got a few customers who were speaking Welsh with
> me and I said, "I don't speak Welsh" ... So actually after
> that I have been learning a few words just to keep them
> happy ... I just learn a few words and the main important
> things and just to keep my customers happy I suppose...I'm
> trying to improve my English first and I'm learning a few
> words in Welsh, good morning, good afternoon and how
> are you and things like that.'

This is a good example of BME residents becoming aware of local
'rules' and therefore trying to modify their behaviour to fit cultural
expectations. Interviewees described how they used links to 'Welshness'
other than language to gain greater inclusion in the community. Some
gained acceptance via Welsh spouses and relatives: 'I am married to a
local person, a very local person, for a start I think everybody got to
dispense any sort of racial thing about me' (female, Trinidadian). Another
lady described how for eight months she tried to find a job. When
eventually she got an interview, she explains how she obtained the
job because

> 'My husband – because he went with me. He say I live
> here and told where we live and she said, "Oh I know, I
> know your Mum, I know".This is how everything happens.
> Something more or less like that. Then she say, "Oh can
> you come on Monday?" But it's just me and I am lucky.
> For others I think it's very hard.' (Female, Brazilian)

Other respondents felt that the distinctiveness of racism in Wales was
that it was practised differently by the two main cultural groups living
there. Some respondents felt *more* included by their Welsh neighbours
than by their English neighbours, alluding to aspects of 'tolerance' and
sensitivity. Affirmations such as 'the Welsh are more friendly' (female,
Portuguese), are clarified further by the following interviewees,

> 'The English group unfortunately have the attitude that
> they are the best ... I find the Welsh women they do talk

to me as an equal … the ones who are interested in craft, once they find out that I have got some knowledge they want to pick your brain and they'll come round and talk to you about it. The English ones' attitude is, well you can't know much about it and then you have to prove to them that you do know what you're talking about. It is this superior attitude of everything and every bit.' (Female, Jamaican)

'English people are more closed. Not like Welsh people and Scottish are more friendly or caring to help me.' (Female, Lithuanian)

On the other hand, some minority ethnic residents feel that the Welsh were *less* tolerant and accepting:

'I found most of the Welsh people that I met friendly but they have to stay superficial to you. They ask "Where are you from?", I say "Spain". They say "Oh nice, oh I've been in Spain blah de blah". They ask "Do you work here?" I say "Well yes I work, my husband a doctor" and when they know the basic things, that's it. I never went any further than that. Do you know what I mean? After eight years of living in X most of friends they are not Welsh. They are English, I've got another one who is Scottish, Iraqi, I've got a very good friend from Uruguay. I know Welsh people but they prefer superficial relationship.' (Female, Spanish)

'I definitely think it is worse in Wales because of the Welsh. But yes, it's definitely more here, but also if you think about there is also a resentment in Wales against English people, like they are the true Celts, and the English have taken over their country. Because if go to the Black Mountains it does say, you know, the English took our country, so they are … they resent people not just because of their skin colour, but the actual nationality as well.' (Female, Indian)

And yet others feel that locally resident English incomers are the main perpetrators of racism, albeit perhaps more subtly. One man comments,

'I have come across racism particularly by the English – but it's done in such a way that unless you look very closely you don't even notice it.' (Male, Bangladeshi)

Another lady explains an incident of more blatant verbal abuse:

> 'A English woman she came in (to the café) then I said,
> "Good morning" or something, "Can I help you?" or
> something and then she said, "I would like another waitress,
> you smell like a Paki" and she never saw me before. And
> she said, "Are you deaf as well? – I want another waitress"
> and then my friend look at me and they look at her and
> then she said, "Perhaps she's crazy". They have a lot of
> English here, they are the ones (who) look me up and
> down.' (Female, Bangladeshi)

But the fact that Powys has two main cultural groups, one of which is
made up of recent incomers was also seen as an advantage by some of
our respondents, who felt this deflected racism away from themselves.

> 'I'm not English, so I think the Welsh quite like me!' (Male,
> Greek)

> 'Sometimes I think it is easier to be a foreigner here, than
> it is to be English.' (Female, Thai)

Differences within rural Wales

While there are distinctive elements to rural racism within Wales, our
interviewees also told us that rural racism varied between places, even
within rural Wales. For example, certain interviewees cited more hostile
attitudes within the community of Welshpool, a border town in North
Powys. One man described his experience when moving from
Birmingham to Welshpool to start his own business:

> 'I moved to Welshpool. Now that was a different experience
> altogether. You know I've never seen anything like that –
> every Monday you would guarantee that people go to
> Welshpool and they would fight on the streets and the
> police would literally, would just stand aside and watch.
> And there was not one or two of them, there was groups of
> people, you know. In the restaurant that I had there was
> fighting every night, there was swearing and there was more
> hatred in Wales I felt than there ever was in Birmingham.
> … A lot of trouble. Breaking window almost every other
> day. One person broke the window seven times you know!

seven times! The police were very helpful about it but the local people, all the people there were fights. The older people during the daytime, they were fine. But come at night you would find it was a really violent sort of place, you know. Whereas you would expect that sort of thing in a big city … I can't say that it's characteristic of Wales because I am still in Wales and I am living in Newtown. And this place is totally different than Welshpool. In terms of differences here, people are much more broadminded … the mentality is altogether different.' (Male, Bangladeshi)

Other individuals have suggested that Welshpool is a more hostile place because the leader of the British National Party lives nearby:

'Welshpool there is a problem for me … I read that this is a typical area where the BNP do recruit and I am actually working in an area where there is a major BNP party and that does concern me. Because then you think well, you know they could start to become no go areas.' (Female with children of dual heritage)

'Now that we've got the National Front [sic] place in Welshpool you get people with a lot of attitude.' (Female, Jamaican)

Other respondents thought that hostility within rural Wales varied according to how 'Welsh' an area was, with the cultural and linguistic heartlands being the most hostile of all to people of colour:

'I heard people who are living deep in Wales, in Machynlleth, have you heard of Machynlleth? And they have had bad experiences and the place called Rhayadyr where a family had to leave their business and go because of racial harassment and racial abusement and all those things like that.' (Male, Bangladeshi)

'It's got to bring fear into people's lives and I think that this whole racism thing's mixed up with the way that I class this as the heartlands of Wales. There's a couple of parts of North Wales where you've got the Welsh culture, you've got the Welsh language and the Welsh way of life and they want it preserved and they don't want anything diluting that, whatever it is. Whether it's English or black, it doesn't matter it's diluting and they don't want that. ... this is the heartland. This is predominantly where most of your Welsh is spoken.' (Female, dual heritage)

Interviewer: 'So do you think there are better rural places to live in Wales than others?'

Respondent: 'Yes, I think so, and I would be picking it very carefully ... If I was up right in North Wales, which I wouldn't have, there are people in North Wales that more traditional, more insular. I suppose I chose carefully to where I felt welcome you know, and I felt part of the community.' (Female, Jamaican)

So, while rural racism in Wales is certainly distinctive, we conclude that there is no one racism experienced by all BME people in rural Wales, regardless of who they are and where they live. Rather, there are different rural racisms in Wales experienced differently by different people in different places.

Who perpetrates racism in rural Wales: the Welsh, the English or both?

This second section now turns to our questionnaire results and a different facet of rural racism in Wales and its distinctiveness: whether it is perpetrated by all the population, only by local Welsh people or only by English incomers. Our questionnaire yielded 57 variables for analysis, and to start we extracted two sub-samples from the total using responses to two separate questions to tell us more about the 'local' population. The first sub-sample was people who said they identified very strongly with English identity but not at all with Welsh identity (defined here as the 'English'), and the second was those who identified very strongly with Welsh identity and not at all with English identity (the 'Welsh'). There were 64 people in the 'English' sample and 114 in the 'Welsh' sample. Cross-referencing with a third question allowed us to note that the Welsh sample contained people who were fluent in Welsh (9%), could speak it conversationally (28%), could speak only a few words of Welsh (42%) and could not speak it at all (21%). Clearly in Powys, then, Welsh identity is made up of more than an ability to use the language. Further cross-referencing demonstrated that 66% of the Welsh had never lived outside Wales and 16% were returnees who had moved outside Wales (usually to England) before returning.

Considering now the distinctiveness of racism in rural Wales, Table 2.1 lists those attitude statements with which Welsh and English residents of Powys broadly agree. What this demonstrates is that there is a broad consensus that Britain is a racist country, that this is unlikely to change, that we expect minorities not just to integrate but to assimilate, but that – although Britain may have reached 'its limits' – people are not yet supportive of the concept of compulsory repatriation. All of this lends support to the notion that British culture has engrained within

Table 2.1: Attitudes on which there was broad agreement between English and Welsh respondents

- In Britain there is prejudice against people from India and Pakistan
- Prejudice against Asians is less in Powys than elsewhere in the UK
- In Britain there is prejudice against Black-Caribbean and African people
- Prejudice against Black-Caribbean and African people is less in Powys than elsewhere in the UK
- In Britain there is prejudice against Chinese people
- Prejudice against Chinese is less in Powys than elsewhere in the UK
- There is likely to be more prejudice in five years time than now
- There are a lot of people from ethnic minorities living in the UK today
- The modal number of minority ethnic people living in Powys is 50-100
- There is a limit to how many people of other races and cultures a society can accept
- In order to be fully accepted in British society, ethnic minorities must give up those parts of their religion or culture which may be in conflict with British law
- In order to be fully accepted in British society, ethnic minorities must give up their own cultures
- People belonging to ethnic minorities are so different, they can never be fully accepted members of British society
- People from ethnic minorities are not enriching the cultural life of Britain
- People from ethnic minorities do the jobs which other people don't want to do
- Disagree with the view that all immigrants, legal and illegal from outside the EU and their children, even those born in Britain should be sent back to their country of origin
- Britain has reached its limits; if there were to be more people belonging to racial or ethnic minorities we would have problems
- There are particular ethnic, national or religious groups that I do not feel comfortable mixing with

it a background racism that can trace its roots back to empire and that is reproduced by institutions such as the media and the political and educational systems. These commonalities blanket the whole of the UK.

Beneath this broad consensus, however, are very real differences between the Welsh and the English. These groups appear to differ in both the strength of some of their opinions and their attitudes to specific facets of racism. Table 2.2 therefore draws together the key differences in response between the two samples.

What this suggests is that the English in Powys have both a more jaundiced view of British race relations and are less tolerant of ethnic, racial and cultural minorities. This is further supported by their responses to questions about why they had moved to Powys. Fully, 33% of English respondents said that they had either wholly or partly

Table 2.2: Statistically significant differences in the opinions of Welsh and English respondents

Opinion	Significance level
Welsh think there is less prejudice against Indians and Pakistanis in the UK than the English	0.00
Welsh think there is less prejudice against Black-Caribbeans and Africans in the UK than the English	0.00
English are more likely to think that there are too many people from ethnic minorities in the UK	0.01
English are more likely to think that there is a limit to how many people of other races and cultures a society can accept	0.00
English are more likely to think that ethnic minorities must give up those parts of their religion or culture which may be in conflict with British law	0.01
English are more likely to think that ethnic minorities should give up their cultures	0.03
English are more likely to think that ethnic minorities are so different, they can never be fully accepted members of British society	0.01
English are less likely to think that ethnic minorities are enriching the cultural life of the UK	0.01
English are more likely to think that Britain has reached its limits; if there were to be more people belonging to racial or ethnic minorities we would have problems	0.00
English are less likely to think that racial, religious and cultural diversity adds to Britain	0.03
English are more likely to think that Britain would be better off without its minority ethnic population	0.02

decided to move to a rural setting because few people from ethnic minorities live there, and a further 20% said that this reason hadn't shaped their decision making but had subsequently been seen as an advantage. Moreover, 55% said they would not like to have a minority ethnic neighbour. And, as Table 2.3 demonstrates, 10% said the level of their personal racism was either 7 or 8 on a scale that ran from 1 (not at all racist) to 10 (very racist) (cf. 0.9% of the Welsh). This is entirely in line with the argument that the racism evident in rural Wales is actually English racism, not Welsh racism.

But what of the Welsh in Powys? Do they see themselves as tolerant, and are they actually demonstrably more tolerant? Certainly, as Williams (1995) has argued, the Welsh see themselves as tolerant. Between 80% and 90% of Welsh respondents told us in the survey that Wales was more tolerant of ethnic minorities than either England, Scotland or Ireland (differences significant at the 0.00 level). They also told us that there was less prejudice against Asians, black people and Chinese in Powys than elsewhere in the UK. And, as Table 2.3 indicates, more than three-quarters of respondents said the level of their personal racism was either 1 or 2 on a scale that ran from 1 (not at all racist) to 10 (very racist) (cf. 35% of the English). The Welsh clearly believe they are a tolerant nation, and that rural Powys is especially tolerant.

What is interesting, though, is that this Welsh tolerance appears partial and is not extended to English incomers. This may be seen as reflecting the power-infused ongoing legacy of the English presence in rural Wales. Fully 20% of Welsh respondents in the survey said they would prefer a minority ethnic neighbour to an English neighbour, giving as reasons the belief that English incomers are arrogant and are speculators, and that minority ethnic residents make more of an effort to fit in than English incomers (see Jones, 1993). When asked if there was a particular ethnic, national or religious group that they didn't feel comfortable mixing with, 16% of Welsh respondents said the English, a proportion almost double that of the next least-liked group, Muslims

Table 2.3: Self-rated prejudice on a scale of 1 (not at all racist) to 10 (very racist)

Self-rated prejudice	English (%)	Welsh (%)
1 or 2	35	78
3 or 4	22	17
5 or 6	33	2
7 or 8	10	2
9 or 10	0	1
Total	100	100

(at 8.8%). Clearly, then, the Welsh are not devoid of prejudices and are not *universally* tolerant.

So we are left with an apparent paradox. Why do the rural Welsh, who clearly have prejudices and are capable of intolerance, not direct these at minority ethnic populations, as happens in England? The answer to this paradox probably lies not in inherent Welsh tolerance or notions of *gwerin* communities, but in the uniqueness of Wales and its immigration history, and in opportunity. Robinson (2003) and Robinson and Gardner (2004a) have discussed the uniqueness of Wales, and its long migration history, but opportunity has yet to be considered. Powys has yet to attract a significant minority ethnic population, with the 2001 census recording only 1,086 BME residents in the most sparsely settled county in England and Wales. Even within this small total there is considerable diversity, such that the largest single group ('Other Asians') formed only 21% of the total BME population, and another four ethnic groups each individually formed more than 10% of the BME population. As a result, few of Powys' Welsh residents therefore see or come into regular contact with black or minority ethnic groups in their daily lives. Table 2.4 tabulates the results of three separate questions that asked English incomers, and Welsh people who had lived only within Wales, how much contact they had had with members of the BME population at each of the 374 addresses they had lived in. Statistical testing demonstrated that in every case, the English had had significantly more contact than the Welsh (difference significant at 0.000). For example, only one in three of the English incomers had had no social contact whatsoever with people from minority ethnic groups, whereas the same was true of 80% of the Welsh in Powys. For the large majority of the rural Welsh, then,

Table 2.4: Amount of contact respondents have had with members of the BME population at each of their previous addresses

	None (%)	Some (%)	Frequent (%)	A lot (%)
Socially				
English in England	33	20	25	23
Welsh in Wales	80	11	6	3
At work/school				
English in England	32	17	28	23
Welsh in Wales	71	19	4	7
In the neighbourhood				
English in England	34	18	27	20
Welsh in Wales	80	12	7	1

Note: data relate to the 374 addresses at which respondents had lived.

their professed tolerance is therefore hypothetical, rather than actual. They are expressing opinions about how tolerant they think they would be, were they to have contact with BME people. But where their tolerance of immigrants has been put to the test (in the form of the English or asylum seekers) they are as prejudiced and intolerant as people elsewhere in the UK. For example, even though Powys has received only a small number of dispersed asylum seekers, they were nominated by the Welsh as the least-liked group, followed by the English. And even though Welsh respondents thought there were few BME residents in their county, 19% thought that current numbers were 'too many' (cf. 3% of English respondents who thought the same).

In summary, the claims of Welsh people in Powys that racism in their localities is simply the racism imported by English refugees from multiculturalism, and that they have a fundamentally different attitude to the BME population cannot be sustained. Many of the Welsh people who claim greater tolerance do so in the abstract, having had little opportunity to be racist and little experience of multiracial living from which to form opinions. Moreover, where other ethnic groups (like the English) have moved into their rural communities they have demonstrated a degree of racism that is comparable to that found in other parts of the UK (as was the case when ethnic minorities arrived in urban areas in the earlier part of the 20th century (Evans, 1991)). This should not detract from the attitudes of many English incomers to rural Wales, who are undoubtedly racist and have sought out the area to escape English multiculturalism.

Conclusion

In this chapter we have argued that rural racism in Wales is undoubtedly distinctive from its English, Scottish and Irish equivalents, because of the places within which it is enacted and the unique histories, cultures and demographies that these possess. We have gone further than this, by using quantitative and qualitative methods to demonstrate that there is no single rural racism at work in Wales. Rather, there are a variety of racisms enacted by different groups, for different reasons and manifested differently in different places. Moreover, these impact on different people in different ways.

The clear emphasis on 'difference' that comes through in the findings of this chapter – notably the very wide range of experiences of racism – leads us on to a final note of caution. In short, we feel that there is a danger of both ghettoising and marginalising rural racism. This is manifest in three ways. First of all, in our rush to prove that *rural* racism exists and is a serious problem we are in danger of objectifying it, stereotyping it and foregrounding only those features that distinguish rural from urban racism. Second, any tight bounding of the study of rural racism within the sub-discipline of rural studies runs the danger not only of marginalising our output and diluting its impact but also of navel-gazing. We could simply end up reinventing the wheel if we fail to engage with studies of racism more generally. Third, we are seeking ever-more nuanced accounts of racism: for example rural vs urban racism, rural Welsh racism vs rural English racism, and rural Welsh local racism vs rural Welsh incomer racism. However, this obsession with difference can all too easily distract us from, or blind us to, more profound commonalities that underpin *all* racism, no matter where it is practised (see also Cloke, 1997 for a similar discussion in the context of rural studies).

So, we believe that we should now be looking for ways in which discussions of racism can be drawn together to ensure a holistic view, that becomes more than the sum of the parts, while also still recognising difference. Such a holistic view would draw together the insights of urban and rural studies, the perspectives of the geographer, sociologist, political scientist and psychologist, and the power of multiple methods. And it should recognise the importance of place.

References

Alderman, G. (1972) 'The anti-Jewish riots of August 1911 in South Wales', *Welsh History Review*, vol 6, no 2, pp 190-200.

Chahal, K. and Julienne, L. (1999) *'We can't all be white!' Racist victimisation in the UK*, York: Joseph Rowntree Foundation.

Cloke, P. (1997) 'Country backwater to virtual village? Rural studies and "the cultural turn"', *Journal of Rural Studies*, vol 13, no 4, pp 367-75.

Cloke, P., Goodwin, M. and Milbourne, P. (1995) '"There's so many strangers in the village now": marginalization and change in 1990s Welsh rural life-styles', *Contemporary Wales*, vol 8, pp 47-74.

Day, G. (1989) '"A million on the move"?: population change and rural Wales', *Contemporary Wales*, vol 3, pp 137-59.

de Lima, P. (2001) *Needs not numbers. An exploration of minority ethnic communities in Scotland*, London: Commission for Racial Equality.

Derbyshire, H. (1994) *Not in Norfolk: Tackling the invisibility of racism*, Norwich: Norwich and Norfolk Racial Equality Council.

European Commission (1998) *Racism and xenophobia in Europe: Eurobarometer opinion poll 47.1*, Brussels: European Commission.

Evans, N. (1991) 'Immigrants and minorities in Wales, 1840–1990: a comparative perspective', *Llafur*, vol 5, no 4, pp 5-26.

Evans, N. (2003) 'Immigrants and minorities in Wales, 1840-1990: a comparative perspective' in C. Williams, N. Evans, and P. O'Leary (eds) *A tolerant nation? Exploring ethnic diversity in Wales*, Cardiff: University of Wales Press, pp 14-34.

Evans, N., O'Leary, P. and Williams, C. (2003) 'Introduction: race, nation and globalisation' in N. Evans, P. O'Leary and C. Williams (eds) *A tolerant nation? Exploring ethnic diversity in Wales*, Cardiff: University of Wales Press, pp 1-13.

Fryer, P. (1984) *Staying power: The history of black people in Britain*, London: Pluto Press.

Holmes, C. (1982) 'The Tredegar riots of 1911: anti-Jewish disturbances in South Wales', *Welsh History Review*, vol 11, no 2, pp 214-25.

Husbands, C. (1983) *Racial exclusionism and the city*, London: George Allen and Unwin.

Jay, E. (1992) *Keep them in Birmingham: Challenging racism in South West England*, London: Commission for Racial Equality.

Jones, N. (1993) *Living in rural Wales*, Llandysul: Gomer.

Jowell, R. and Airey, C. (1984) *British social attitudes: The 3rd report*, Aldershot: Avebury.

Magne, S. (2003) *Multi-ethnic Devon: A rural handbook*, Exeter: Exeter Racial Equality Council.

Murdoch, J. and Pratt, A. (1993) 'Rural studies: modernism, postmodernism and the "post-rural"', *Journal of Rural Studies*, vol 9, pp 411-27.

Neal, S. (2002) 'Rural landscapes, representations and racism: examining multicultural citizenship and policy-making in the English countryside', *Ethnic and Racial Studies*, vol 25, no 3, pp 442-61.

Nizhar, P. (1995) *No problem: Tackling race issues in Shropshire*, Telford: Telford and Wrekin Race Equality Council.

O'Leary, P. (1991) 'Anti-Irish riots in Wales, 1826–1882', *Llafur*, vol 5, no 4, pp 27-36.

O'Leary, P. (2000) *Immigration and intergration: The Irish in Wales, 1798–1922*, Cardiff: University of Wales Press.

Osmond, J. (1985) *The national question again: Welsh political identity in the 1980s*, Llandysul: Gomer Press.

Parker, M. (2001) 'Loaded dice', *Planet: The Welsh Internationalist*, vol 148, pp 7-13.

Parry, J. (1983) 'The Tredegar and anti-Irish riots of 1882', *Llafur*, vol 3, no 4, pp 20-3.

Robinson, V. (1985) 'Racial antipathy in South Wales and its social and demographic correlates', *New Community*, vol 12, no 1, pp 116-23.

Robinson, V. (1987) 'Regional variations in attitudes towards race', in P. Jackson (ed) *Race and Racism*, London: Allen and Unwin, pp 160-88.

Robinson, V. (1998) 'Cultures of ignorance, disbelief and denial: refugees in Wales', *Journal of Refugee Studies*, vol 12, no 1, pp 78-87.

Robinson, V. (1999) 'Neither here nor there: refugees in Wales', *Contemporary Wales*, vol 12, pp 200-13.

Robinson, V (2003) 'Exploring myths about rural racism: a Welsh case study', in C. Williams, N. Evans and O'Leary, P. (eds) *A tolerant nation? Exploring ethnic diversity in Wales*, Cardiff: University of Wales Press, pp 160-78.

Robinson, V. and Gardner, H. (2004a) 'Unravelling a stereotype: the lived experience of black and minority ethnic people in rural Wales', in J. Garland and N. Chakraborti (eds) *Racism rurality and community: Contemporary debates and perspectives*, London: Willan Publishing, pp 85-107.

Robinson, V. and Gardner, H. (2004b) *Anybody out there? Minority ethnic people in Powys and their experiences*, Migration Unit Research Paper 18, Swansea: University of Wales Swansea.

Schaefer, R.T. (1975) 'Regional differences in prejudice', *Regional Studies*, vol 9, no 1, pp 1-14.

Smith, S. (1993) Bounding the borders: claiming space and making place in rural Scotland, *Transactions of the Institute of British Geographers*, vol 18, no 3, pp 291-308.

Williams, C. (1995) '"Race" and racism: some reflections on the Welsh context', *Contemporary Wales*, vol 8, pp 113-31.

Williams, C. (1999a) 'Passports to Wales? race, nation and identity', in R. Fevre, and A. Thompson (eds) *Nation, identity and social theory*, Cardiff: University of Wales Press, pp 69-89.

Williams, C. (1999b) '"Race" and racism: what's special about Wales?', in D. Dunkerley and A. Thompson (eds) *Wales today*, Cardiff: University of Wales Press, pp 269-84.

Williams, C. (2003) 'Claiming the national: nation, national identity and ethnic minorities', in C. Williams, N. Evans, and P. O'Leary (eds) *A tolerant nation? Exploring ethnic diversity in Wales*, Cardiff: University of Wales Press, pp 220-34.

Williams, C., Evans, N. and O'Leary, P. (2003) *A tolerant nation? Exploring ethnic diversity in Wales*, Cardiff: University of Wales Press.

THREE

'Let's keep our heads down and maybe the problem will go away'

Experiences of rural minority ethnic households in Scotland

Philomena de Lima

Introduction

Since the publication of Jay's report (1992) *Keep them in Birmingham* and Fife Regional Council's report in Scotland (1991) *Race equality in Fife* and the plethora of reports that have followed, it has at times appeared a long and difficult process to persuade rural agencies and communities to acknowledge, let alone address, racism and racial discrimination. Despite growing evidence of rural minority ethnic households being more vulnerable to racism than their urban counterparts (Rayner, 2001) and calls from a range of agencies and individuals to develop a more strategic approach to addressing rural racism issues (Scottish Council for Voluntary Organisations (SCVO), 1994; Henderson and Kaur, 1999; National Council for Voluntary Organisations (NCVO), 2000), the response by national and local agencies has tended to be slow. Consequently, rural areas have been left behind to catch up with urban areas, given the predominant urban–centred emphasis of research and investment of resources.

The focus of this chapter is on racism and racial discrimination in rural areas of Scotland with a particular emphasis on the Highlands and Islands, and draws on a range of published and unpublished research undertaken by the author between 1999 and 2004.[1] While it is important to acknowledge that the issue of racism in Scotland is highly complex, manifested by the prevalence of prejudice against the English and 'incomers' (Jedrej and Nuttall, 1996; McIntosh et al, 2004) and the persistence of sectarianism,[2] it is important to state at the outset that this chapter is not in a position to address these issues. Having set the context, where the changes in discourses and policies from pre-devolutionary (before 1999) to post-devolutionary Scotland will be discussed (see Scottish Executive, 2003, for information on Scottish devolution), the chapter will:

- Provide a brief analysis of Scotland's minority ethnic groups, particularly focusing on the Highlands and Islands (Orkney, Shetland and the Western Isles) of Scotland.
- Summarise research findings on the experiences of rural minority ethnic households/dwellers, identifying gaps as well as examples of practical initiatives to address issues of racist discrimination and harassment.
- Conclude by highlighting some methodological issues that emerge from researching rural minority ethnic households as well as providing an overview of an agenda that requires to be addressed in rural Scotland.

While it is important to recognise the complexity and controversial nature of concepts such as 'race 'and 'ethnicity', it is beyond the scope of this chapter to rehearse the discourses surrounding their use. The difficulties in drawing boundaries around these concepts is reflected in the debate on the ethnic categories adopted in the 1991 and 2001 censuses and have been well rehearsed (Manwaring, 2002; Back and Solomos, 2003; Gunaratnam, 2003). Based on extensive debates and discussions in Scotland (see Race Equality Advisory Forum (REAF), 2001) the term 'minority ethnic' is adopted in this chapter to refer to 'visible' minority ethnic groups – for example, people of Asian, African, Middle-Eastern origins and so on.

Adopting the term 'minority ethnic' to discuss diverse groups is recognised as potentially problematic. Recognising the importance of taking into consideration the 'specificity' (for example, in relation to how individuals define their ethnicity) of people's experiences, where relevant, references will be made to specific groups in making sense of their experiences. Despite the extreme racism experienced by Gypsy Travellers, lack of space precludes any effective discussion of this group or that of asylum seekers and refugees who are mainly based in urban areas of Scotland at present, with little information available for rural areas. However, given the government's commitment to dispersal this situation is likely to change.

Racism and discrimination: a Scottish overview

'Race' in pre-devolutionary Scotland

Although the debate on the extent to which 'rural' and 'urban' areas are distinctly different continues (Hope et al, 2000), discourses on racism and discrimination in rural areas cannot be understood without considering how these issues have been addressed at a Scottish level in general. Before the election of the first Scottish Parliament in 1999, getting 'race' on the Scottish agenda, let alone on the rural agenda, was a challenge. The tendency had been to portray the prevalence of racism as mainly an 'English problem'. The predominant emphasis in Scotland tended to be on a 'numbers-led' rather than 'needs-led' perspective (SCVO, 1994; de Lima, 2001a). In addition to the emphasis on 'numbers', the neglect of racism in pre-devolutionary Scotland has been attributed to a range of other factors, including the dominance of the national question in Scotland where England is the 'other' (Miles and Dunlop, 1986).

Post-devolution: new opportunities

Following the 1998 Scotland Act, which set out the framework for devolved powers to a new Scottish Parliament, an election was held in 1999 and 129 members were elected to the Scottish Parliament. Although equal opportunities/anti-discrimination and immigration legislative powers are reserved to Westminster, two factors could be seen as potentially important in establishing the foundation for developing a more inclusive approach to equal opportunities in Scotland: the influence of a cross-party group (the Consultative Steering Group) established in 1997 by Donald Dewar, the Secretary of State for Scotland (Arshad, 2000); and the 1998 Scotland Act. The Act adopted a much more inclusive definition of equal opportunities than is currently enshrined in UK legislation, encompassing issues such as social origin and age. It also placed a responsibility on the Scottish Parliament to encourage and ensure that equal opportunities are observed when carrying out its functions (Scottish Executive, 2000, p 13). The Scottish Parliament established a Standing Committee on Equal Opportunities and an Equality Unit, which includes race equality, was also established by the Scottish Executive to deal with policy and governance issues (Arshad, 2002, p 208).

While it is important not to exaggerate the influence of devolution on race equality (for example the Scottish Parliament has no minority ethnic representatives), in contrast to the relative inactivity on racism at a strategic level in pre-devolutionary Scotland, it is important to acknowledge that devolution has resulted in noticeable changes. The overall legislative framework combined with the publication of the Macpherson Report (Stephen Lawrence Inquiry, 1999) and the 2000 Race Relations (Amendment) Act have, together, provided a basis from which race equality issues are being addressed. It is also highly possible that bringing decision making to Scotland has made it easier for previously marginalised groups to have more of a say on policy issues in a way that was not previously possible with a Westminster government that was perceived as remote.

Against this background, a more proactive approach to race equality issues is reflected in a range of policy contexts. For example, the Scottish Executive established a short life group, the Race Equality Advisory Forum (REAF), to provide recommendations on race equality (REAF, 2001). There has also been some legislation addressing 'race' and ethnicity issues in devolved areas such as local government, housing and education (CRE, undated; Scottish Executive, undated). Funding has been made available to help build capacity among minority ethnic groups (Black and Ethnic Minority Infrastructure in Scotland (BEMIS)). Initiatives to address issues of racial inequality in specific sectors such as health, for example, by funding bodies such as the National Resource Centre for Ethnic Minority Health (NRCEMH) have also become more evident. A number of these initiatives include a rural dimension in their work: for example, BEMIS has a development worker based in the Highlands, and the NRCEMH has included rural representatives in its steering group and networks and is developing collaborative work with some rural health boards at a local level (Scottish Executive, 2003; undated).

In a devolutionary context, the importance of a more robust evidence-base for policy making has resulted in increased efforts to redress the information deficit that has existed in relation to a range of issues and groups, including rurality and minority ethnic groups. This has led to commissioning of a range of research by the Scottish Executive and an emphasis on including rural perspectives and evidence (Scottish Executive, undated). One of the first examples of such activity was an audit of research on minority ethnic groups in Scotland. The audit highlighted the predominance of mainly local qualitative research, confirming the lack of robust statistical information and made recommendations for addressing the gaps (Netto et al, 2001).

More recently, at least four other factors have impacted on the debates on racism and racial equality in Scotland and from which rural areas are not immune. First, there are the discourses on the 'population time bomb', which point to a declining and ageing Scottish population and the need to recruit migrant labour to plug labour market gaps (Denholm, 2004). The emphasis placed on recruiting migrant labour and encouraging immigration into Scotland (Scottish Executive, 2004b) highlights the variations in approaches being advocated by the devolved administrations, as well as the potential for conflict between devolved administrations and the Westminster Parliament. With regard to the latter, this has led to calls for immigration matters to be devolved to the Scottish Parliament (Dinwoodie, 2004; *Perth News*, 2004). The second factor is the hysteria generated in the UK and Scottish press about asylum seekers and refugees (Barclay et al, 2003). Third is the prevalence of persistent negative and racist attitudes towards minority ethnic groups (Scottish Civic Forum, 2002; Bromley and Curtice, 2003). Finally, there are the consequences of creating a single equality and human rights commission (DTI, 2004).

Demographic trends

Scottish overview

The lack of robust statistical information on minority ethnic groups in Scotland has been an issue that has persistently been highlighted by research. Against this background, accessing data about Scotland's rural minority ethnic households has been even more problematic, given the lack of clarity on definitions of 'rural' employed as well as the small size of the population.

The two main sources of data on Scotland's rural minority ethnic groups are the 1991 and 2001 census data. The size of the minority ethnic population increased from 1.25% in 1991 to 2% of the Scottish population in 2001. Just over 70% of the minority ethnic population was made up of communities with roots in South and East Asia, particularly Pakistan, China and India, while communities with roots in Africa and the Caribbean comprised 7% of Scotland's minority ethnic population. The largest minority ethnic group were the Pakistanis followed by the Chinese, Indians and those of 'Mixed' ethnic backgrounds (Scottish Executive, 2004a, p 5).

In general, the minority ethnic population had proportionally larger numbers of younger people, and far fewer older people, and were more likely to be unemployed, work longer hours and less likely to rent from the public sector. However, there were also ethnic and gender variations, reinforcing the importance of not treating minority ethnic groups as homogeneous. For example, Africans (47%) and Indians (40%) were more likely to have degrees than (43%) Pakistanis who did not have a degree; and women from Pakistani and Bangladeshi households were most likely not to have been in paid employment (Scottish Executive, 2004a).

Settlement patterns

Since devolution there has been an effort to develop a more consistent urban/rural classification framework, hence providing a basis for understanding settlement patterns (see Scottish Executive 2004a, p 24). However, the small minority ethnic population size in rural areas raises issues of confidentiality and ethics, posing considerable challenges for researchers and policy makers. It also highlights the need for caution in interpreting and drawing conclusions from data sources, such as the census, given the disclosure control measures employed to protect individual confidentiality (see General Register Office for Scotland (GROS), 2003b).

While measures such as combining ethnic categories to ensure confidentiality are understandable, there is, however, a tendency for the diversity within minority ethnic groups to become obscured. More detailed data (for example, on gender, age and economic activity) is presented using a restricted 'simple' five-category classification, in contrast to the 15 categories used in the census (GROS, 2003b).

The 2001 census recorded a presence of minority ethnic households in every local authority and health board area in Scotland (Scottish Executive, 2004a, pp 25-6). However, the Scottish minority ethnic population is mainly urban; 88% living in urban areas, 6% in small towns, and 6% in rural areas. In contrast, 68% of all those in the 'White' category lived in urban areas, a further 14% in small towns, and 19% in rural areas. Sixty per cent of minority ethnic people lived in Scotland's four largest cities (that is Glasgow 31%, Edinburgh 18%, Aberdeen 6% and Dundee 5.2%). The remaining 40% were concentrated mainly close to the larger cities, with smaller percentages being dispersed throughout the more remote and rural areas of the Scottish mainland and islands. The Pakistani community were unlikely to be living in 'remote rural areas' – that is, 'Settlements of less than 3,000 people and with a drive time of over 30 minutes to a settlement of 10,000 or more' (Scottish Executive, 2004a, p 24).

Demographic trends in the Highlands and Islands of Scotland

Just as it is important to acknowledge the diversity among minority ethnic groups, it is also important to recognise the diversity of rural areas in Scotland. For example, the Highlands and Islands of Scotland encompass a range of spatial types from urban areas to remote rural areas and towns (Scottish Executive, 2004a, p 24). An analysis at ward level reveals that, with the exception of one ward in the Highlands, the minority ethnic population formed a small proportion of all wards in the Highlands and Islands. Given the small size of the population more detailed census tabulations use the 'simple' five-category classification described previously. For example, using the 'simple' classification resulted in approximately 50% of the minority ethnic population in the Highlands and Islands being classed as 'Other', consequently masking the diverse ethnicities that may exist among this category (GROS, 2003a).

While minority ethnic households in the Highlands and Islands are widely distributed in the more rural areas, in general, the patterns of settlement are similar to those in Scotland as a whole; that is, they tend to be concentrated in and around the urban, or urban-accessible areas. Apart from slightly different patterns of ethnicity, the Highlands and Islands minority ethnic population share similarities with rest of the minority ethnic population in Scotland, in relation to variables such as age, diversity in ethnic identities and patterns and rate of economic activity and qualifications.

Like the rest of Scotland, the Highlands and Islands minority ethnic share of the population had increased since the 1991 census, from 0.5% to 0.8% in the Highlands, 0.3% to 0.46% in Orkney, 0.6% to 1.06% in Shetland and 0.4% to 0.64% in the Western Isles. However, on the issue of ethnic background, people of 'mixed' minority ethnic background constituted the largest category (between 24% and 27%), differing from the Scottish minority ethnic population, where the Pakistani community was the largest community, followed by the Chinese and the 'Other' category. Those of African and Caribbean origin were in a very small minority across the Highlands and Islands, ranging from one to 90 in number. The range of ethnicities represented in the 'Other' category is potentially very diverse and includes people of many different origins, for example, Middle-Eastern, Eastern Europeans, South Americans, Vietnamese, Thai and those from the Philippines (de Lima et al, 2005). The low number of people in any one ethnic group increases their sense of social and cultural isolation and provides challenges to developing social capacity and social capital in order to influence decisions that impact on their lives.

In addition to diverse ethnicities, minority ethnic groups differ with regard to issues such as educational qualifications and employment patterns. For example, people of Indian and African origin were more likely to have higher educational qualifications, in contrast to those from Chinese, Pakistani and Bangladeshi communities (de Lima et al, 2005).

Just over a third of the Highlands and Islands minority ethnic population were born in Scotland, and just over half (particularly the Indian and Chinese communities) were born outside the UK. Research evidence from a study on access to post-school education opportunities suggested that it is highly probable that this group might experience more difficulties in accessing and interpreting information not just about education but services in general (de Lima et al, 2005).

Experiences of rural minority ethnic dwellers

Rural context: overview

Although much of the following discussion on the experiences of rural minority households draws on research in the Highlands and Islands, evidence based on the CRE rural racism mapping exercise[1] suggests similarities in experiences across rural areas in Britain.

The notion of the 'rural' as homogeneous and a 'good place to live' continues to be deeply embedded in popular culture and acts as a powerful motivator for moving to rural areas, as well as exerting influence on the way in which rural life is perceived (Cloke and Little, 1997). Research on rural migration in Scotland (as in England too) demonstrates that the majority of migrants into rural areas have bought into the myth of the 'rural idyll'. Factors such as 'quality of life' and security are critical motivating factors for migrating in rural areas (Shucksmith et al, 1996; Findlay et al, 1999). Although quality of life issues are also important to minority ethnic individuals: 'Liverpool was a big city ... a lot of noise ... here it is quiet, the air is clear, the scenery is very good' (de Lima et al, 2005, p 93), the two most frequently mentioned reasons for moving to areas such as the Highlands and Islands were employment and personal factors such as marriage/family (de Lima, 2001a).

Since the mid-1990s there has been a growing emphasis on deconstructing the myth of the 'rural idyll', defining the 'rural' as a social and cultural construction that encompasses 'exclusionary qualities' that have to be highlighted and understood (Cloke and Little, 1997). While this emphasis has resulted in a growing body of research and literature in Scotland on, for example, poverty, mental health and youth (Shucksmith and Phillip, 2000; Philo et al, 2002), there is nonetheless a dearth of Scottish rural research and literature that has sought to mainstream minority ethnic perspectives and experiences. The closest Scotland has come to addressing racism in rural areas is in relation to research on 'incomers' and 'anti-English' racism (Jedrej and Nuttall, 1996; McIntosh et al, 2004).

Although more recent Scottish rural literature makes passing references to ethnicity as a potential factor that may frame people's experience of how rurality is experienced, there is a continued failure to include ethnicity as an integral part of research and theoretical discourses (see for example, Shucksmith, 2004). While this might be a reflection of the difficulty of accessing minority ethnic groups, it could also be argued that the neglect of minority ethnic groups in rural research is paralleled by the exclusion of ideas that may be perceived as constituting a challenge to established categories of knowledge in academic discourses. Thus this reinforces the assumptions that 'ethnicity' is 'out of place' in the countryside, reflecting the 'otherness of people of colour' (Agyeman and Spooner, 1997, p 199).

With the exception of one or two local studies (for example, Fife Regional Council, 1991) the first Scottish study –*Needs not numbers* – on rural minority ethnic households was published in 2001 (de Lima, 2001a). It was a qualitative in-depth study of 39 householders in four rural areas of Scotland. The *Needs not numbers* study and subsequent research reveals that the ways in which minority ethnic groups experience rurality is complex. On the one hand, their experiences are similar to those of the general rural population in areas such as access to transport and restricted employment opportunities; on the other hand, like their urban counterparts, they experience similar barriers in accessing services and facilities, highlighting similarities in experiences on a range of issues across the rural/urban divide in Scotland (Stevenson, 2003). Furthermore, the characteristics of minority ethnic groups (that is, in terms of their size, diversity and dispersion), combined with their rural location adds a third dimension to their experience, creating different dynamics and pressures. For instance, rural minority ethnic households have tended to be invisible to the planners and deliverers of services at a local level, and yet, paradoxically, they are highly visible in the local communities in which they live and, potentially, more likely to be vulnerable to racial harassment and discrimination (de Lima, 2001a; Rayner, 2001).

Access to services: numbers rather than needs or 'rights'

Although minority ethnic households and groups face similar challenges experienced by all rural residents, nevertheless service planning and provision in rural areas in particular has both implicitly and at times explicitly privileged the 'economy of scale principle', which has led to service provision that treats diverse communities as if they are homogeneous. This homogeneity is based on treating the views and values of the dominant 'White' majority as the norm, demonstrating a poor understanding of the communities that agencies are seeking to serve as well as an internalisation of the widely held belief that 'given the small numbers there is unlikely to be a "problem" to be addressed'. In addition, when challenged, agencies are not averse to using statistics to justify that they are indeed providing a service to local minority ethnic groups in proportion to their size of population; this does not take much commitment, given the size of some of the groups. Against this background, being heard in rural areas is also a tremendous challenge for minority ethnic groups, given their size, diversity and dispersion.

With a few exceptions, the rural public sector agencies in particular have yet to take a more proactive approach in relation to minority ethnic groups. For example, the study of post-school education reveals that institutions in the Highlands and Islands have not developed effective links with minority ethnic groups and households living in the area and have yet to understand the educational needs of the diverse groups that wish to access further and higher education locally. The lack of priority and commitment in some organisations and areas at a senior management level, and the absence of face-to-face engagement with minority ethnic groups and households among service providers in general, are major contributory factors to their lack of understanding of the diverse needs that exist and a hindrance to making progress on service delivery issues (de Lima et al, 2005).

Although, as previously discussed, it could be argued that the issues in relation to access to services that emerge time and time again from rural research are not confined to rural areas alone, the experiences of rural minority ethnic households are compounded by their size, diversity and dispersion, and the lack of commitment to and public investment in initiatives addressing racial equality (de Lima, 2001a,

2001b, 2004; Netto et al, 2001; Stevenson, 2003). There are at least three recurrent themes that emerge in this context.

First, there is poor access to information and advice. Underpinning much of the poor access to services is a lack of knowledge about relevant sources of advice and information and how to access these. This is compounded by least three factors: language and communication barriers, discussed later; lack of knowledge and skills among provider agencies of how best to address the needs of diverse and dispersed minority groups; and the emphasis on a 'numbers' rather than a 'rights' approach to providing services.

Second, there are language and communication barriers, even among households that have lived in the Highlands and Islands for more than 20 years. The inability to speak English or communicate effectively combined with the lack of English-language learning classes and interpreting facilities in a number of rural areas has a number of consequences. For example, it affects people's ability to access work, services and engage with the wider communities. In the words of a research participant, 'It is like being dumb ... you cannot express yourself, your feelings ... you cannot communicate' (research participant, de Lima et al, 2005, p 86).

Chinese participants in the study on post school education expressed difficulties in attending parents' evenings at school to discuss their children's educational progress. In addition, attending the doctor's surgery was also an issue that was consistently raised by a number of women in particular, who were often accompanied to the doctor by their partners/husbands/in-laws and/or their children. In the event of having to go there by themselves they resorted to using pictures, drawing on sheets of paper and gestures to describe their ailment. In this context, opportunities for misunderstanding and possibilities of misdiagnosis were potentially high and were a cause of much anxiety (de Lima et al, 2005).

Third, there are the difficulties in capacity building, discussed previously, given the heterogeneous and scattered nature of the households. Often rural minority ethnic households are so isolated that they are not always aware of other minority ethnic households in the area and internalise the prevailing dominant ideology: 'that there are not many households like them', and so, they should not expect their needs to be met. The internalisation of this perception could also be part of their survival strategy, which results in minority ethnic households putting up with a great deal, 'fitting into the system', rather than challenging it.

Racial harassment and discrimination

'Let's keep our heads down and maybe the problem will go away' is often a typical response among rural minority ethnic groups, emphasising the prevalence of racism (verbal and physical) and discrimination, as well as expressing an underlying fear of reprisals from the perpetrators if attempts are made to address the issue. The heightened vulnerability of minority ethnic groups to racism (verbal and physical) in rural areas or areas where the population size is small has been highlighted by a number of researchers (Chahal and Julienne, 1999; Rayner, 2001). Racism and discrimination are prevalent in a wide range of contexts, for example, in accessing services, seeking employment and accessing relevant educational opportunities (de Lima, 2001a, 2004). The gap between policy statements and practice at the local level is also a constant theme:

> 'Those in the hierarchy need to demonstrate their commitment to equal opportunity. Organisations pay lip service to equal opportunities. The informal racism is even more difficult than overt racism ... you feel left out ... attitudes need to change in a way that stops excluding certain people. Development comes from recognising difference and doing something about it ... I can relate a lot to Inverness, it is like a town in ... however, underneath the society it is difficult to integrate/interact with people.'
> (Research participant, de Lima et al, 2005, p 94)

In Scotland, the gathering of statistics on racial incidents can most likely be traced to the recommendations arising out of the Macpherson Report (Stephen Lawrence Inquiry, 1999). The main mechanisms for gathering statistics have varied depending on the existing local infrastructure. The CRE rural racism mapping exercise in 2001 found that in a number of rural areas in Scotland, such as Dumfries and Galloway, South Ayrshire and the Highlands, agencies were at the very early stages of developing strategies and partnership approaches to race incidents. The study did not uncover any well-established initiatives in rural areas. There were, however, some multi-agency partnerships that worked in rural areas as well as in urban areas, for example, the Racial Attacks and Harassment Multi-Agency Strategy (RAHMAS), which has been in place since 1993 in central Scotland, and initiatives led by Grampian Racial Equality Council (RAHMAS, 2001; GREC, undated). Both have been critical in developing a multi-agency partnership approach to addressing racist incidens, providing an important mechanism for coordinating race equality initiatives across the area, including a central monitoring system that is used to inform practice.

Caution has to be exercised with regard to interpreting the data on 'racist incidents', due to issues such as under-reporting, variable approaches to disaggregating statistics in relation to urban/rural and improvements in recording procedures. Where data are collected, an upward trend in recorded 'racist incidents' is apparent. For example, police statistics showed a three-fold increase in reported 'racist incidents', from 25 in 1999-2000 to 73 in 2000-01 in the Highlands and Islands (Northern Constabulary, 2001), almost a doubling of 'racist incidents' between 1988-99 and 2000-01 in Lothian and Borders (Lothian & Borders Police, 2001) and similar upward trends in Fife and Grampian (GREC, undated). While these increases may well reflect the existence of better mechanisms for reporting and recording statistics, research confirms that racism (mainly verbal, but also physical abuse) is an endemic feature of rural life which manifests itself in many contexts (de Lima, 2001a; 2001b; Stevenson, 2003; Highland Alliance for Racial Equality, 2004).

While the bulk of racial harassment cases involve verbal abuse, damage to property and personal attacks are also prevalent. For example, RAHMAS (2001, p 3) highlighted that, of the 169 incidents recorded, 106 (63%) occurred within business premises. There was evidence of repeat victimisation and 25 incidents involved physical violence. In addition, there was evidence of under-reporting among some communities, the Chinese in particular. The report also highlighted the potential impact of racist crimes on minority ethnic businesses as affecting the confidence, self-esteem and ultimately the physical and mental health of the victim, contributing to social exclusion and constraints on business growth and development.

Studies of young people and children have shown that racism and bullying is also a feature of their lives. In a small-scale study of young people from minority ethnic backgrounds in the Highlands, most young people felt that there was a gap between policies on equality and the practice of dealing with 'racist incidents' such as name-calling, which young people often felt were not taken seriously by schools (de Lima, 2001b). The majority of young people in the study reported experiencing racist name-calling in primary school, in contrast to a small minority who reported experiencing racism, including physical assaults, at secondary school. For the small minority who reported bullying and racism at secondary school, the experiences were harrowing and difficult and involved both physical and verbal abuse:

> 'There was one guy told me to go back to ... Africa, you don't belong here go back to ... Africa that kind of thing. And saying horrible things about ... Africa you know just trying to annoy me. Say they were doing a topic on Kenya, a real ramshackle house would come past and they'd say "Look there's ... house" and remarks like that.' (Research participant, de Lima 2001b, p 11)

The most common form of harassment was naming calling and many attributed this to being the 'only coloured children at school':

> 'When I was young I thought why do I always get branded as the odd one out you know...because our family was the only coloured family in school you know. They didn't see through the colour you know and I mean I wouldn't say I am dark or anything.' (Research participant, de Lima 2001b, p 18)

For many, these experiences did not continue into secondary school and this was attributed to being bigger and being able to defend themselves, as well as having a set of supportive friends. The challenges of fitting into a system that privileges 'white Scottish' values while attempting to maintain one's sense of self is an issue that many young people from minority ethnic backgrounds grapple with, especially given the small and dispersed nature of the rural minority ethnic population. Luke Sutherland (2004, p 5) for example, reflecting on his upbringing in Orkney, describes his feelings and strategies used to become 'accepted':

> I developed an intense ambivalence about Orkney and its people. On the one hand, I felt very much a native and was treated as such, while on the other, I was denied the possibility of real integration because of my perceived otherness ... I expended all my energy deflecting attention by telling racist jokes and daring more than even the most deranged headcases.

The experience of Luke Sutherland and other minority ethnic young people highlights the challenge of maintaining one's ethnic identity in a context where there may be few or no other people from the same background, leading to cultural and social isolation; this is explored in the following section.

Culture, identity and isolation

Social and cultural isolation are issues that are constantly raised by rural minority ethnic households (de Lima, 2001a; de Lima et al, 2005). A number of factors contribute to this sense of social and cultural isolation. A lack of interest and understanding about other cultures among local communities and the stereotyping that prevails is an issue consistently raised by rural minority ethnic households. Constantly having to explain 'who one is' can be a very tiresome experience for young people who have been brought up in a rural community for most of their lives. The study (de Lima, 2001b) on young people from minority ethnic backgrounds in the Highlands found that the majority did not identify themselves as being an 'ethnic minority', but were frustrated by the way 'others', for example their peers and the communities in which they lived, perceived them:

> 'It's not like we're from Pakistan or anything cos we've only been there like twice and don't really speak it fluently and we're not completely Scottish either ... people expect that you come from another country and that you've just been here like for three years or something ...' (Research participant, de Lima, 2001b, p 13)

At an individual level, the frustration of maintaining one's culture and identity is a recurrent theme:

> 'I would definitely not choose to stay here ... I have been here all my life and would choose to go away as far as possible. It is very hard to keep your identity and your culture. It is nearly impossible, if you want to be accepted you feel forced to be like the others in the main culture. You feel so alone that is one reason why I feel I would like to go somewhere where there are more Asians ... Here in some senses I feel like a foreigner ... I do not feel I fit in. People's society here is so different. I am a Muslim and they do not understand what it is to be a Muslim.' (Research participant, de Lima et al, 2005, p 109)

The importance of community networks, based on a shared sense of identity and solidarity, are some of the factors identified as critical not only in facilitating social inclusion and social capital, but also in maintaining health and prosperity (Wacquant, 1998, cited in Sanderson, 2000, p 131). However, the size, diversity (ethnically and socio-economically) and scattered nature of rural minority ethnic households, combined with the lack of investment in capacity building on the part of relevant agencies, has resulted in the lack of opportunities to develop the necessary 'social capital' that would give households the confidence to engage in civic and community involvement, reinforcing their isolation (de Lima, 2003).

Lack of fluency in English (as discussed earlier) combined with a lack of knowledge of the host communities' cultural traditions as well as inadequate support can make it difficult for individuals to engage in community life, not only exacerbating their feelings of isolation, but also delaying their acquisition of language competency: 'If I was alone it could be so difficult. One because of the language and second because of the culture' (research participant, de Lima et al, 2005).

Furthermore, feelings of social and cultural isolation are often reinforced by living in a small town/village where minority ethnic individuals are often perceived as 'outsiders' and there is a lack of interest and understanding about other cultures:

> 'I know people who have been living here for 10 years and they are isolated ... but this depends also on the individuals. Scottish culture can improve by opening up and helping to understand more foreign cultures.' (Research participant, de Lima et al, 2005, p 98)

The perception that many agencies in rural areas do not demonstrate an ethos that values diversity is a very strong recurrent theme that emerges from research undertaken in the Highlands and Islands:

> 'If they [referring to schools, colleges and institutions in general] don't know about other cultures, they won't value other cultures ... the schools and Scotland as a whole are "culturally illiterate"... if they [adults, teachers, etc.] are culturally illiterate themselves, they are not going to be able to talk and value other cultures are they? They cannot value something they are not aware of.' (Research participant, de Lima et al, 2005, p 109)

Changes in rural Scotland: new initiatives

Despite the predominantly negative picture that emerges from research on rural minority ethnic households, it is important to acknowledge that the situation is gradually beginning to change in rural Scotland. This is in part due to the general contextual factors discussed earlier in this chapter as well as due to the requirements of the 2000 Race Relations (Amendment) Act. Despite evidence (Bromley and Curtice, 2003), which demonstrates consistently negative attitudes towards minorities among a section of the Scottish population, the recent campaign led by the Shetland Island community to stop the deportation of a Burmese family and an Aboriginal Australian woman demonstrates strong community support at the local level (Crawford, 2004).

Since 2000, there has been an increase in activity in areas such as the Highlands due to the allocation of a small amount of funds from national agencies, such as the CRE, the Voluntary Action Fund that administers the Ethnic Minority Grant Scheme (EMGS) and the Home Office (Connecting Communities). Most of these initiatives have led to a number of posts being established to undertake a range of work from developing capacity, addressing racism to supporting victims of racism. The extent to which resources should be invested in developing parallel provision or used to develop provision within the mainstream has yet to be assessed. The initiatives in the Highlands have examples of both; however, it is too early to assess their impact.

Previous research undertaken in rural areas in Scotland (de Lima, 2001a) highlighted the positive benefits (for example, in terms of better access to services) of having dedicated resources allocated to working with minority ethnic households. This was reinforced more recently when, for example, the Chinese community in the Highlands were given an opportunity to contribute to the study on post-school education opportunities through the assistance of a link worker. Having someone the community trusted and could communicate with was crucial in achieving meaningful engagement with the project as well as their views (de Lima et al, 2005). In addition to initiatives being developed at a local level, there are also possibilities for local initiatives to be developed with support from national agencies. For example, the NRCEMH has developed collaborative work with the Western Isles National Health Service (NHS) Board with a view to exploring relevant health issues and setting up a minority ethnic health forum (Scottish Executive, undated, p 45). In this context, short-term secondment opportunities have also been offered to local workers, facilitating a process of knowledge and skills transfer by linking in with projects elsewhere in Scotland (de Lima et al, 2005).

Minority ethnic groups are not passive victims and are increasingly taking steps to address race equality and discrimination issues themselves, even in remote rural areas such as the Highlands. While much of this is based on voluntary activity and the initiative of individuals, these are important first steps in building social capital and the basis for more active civic engagement. For example, in the Highlands, despite the challenge of bringing together scattered households, groups such as the Indian Association have been organising social events such as family picnics and Diwali celebrations. Similarly, the Muslim community in Inverness come together for worship and have managed to negotiate access to a burial ground in Inverness. More recently, some funding has been secured by a Chinese volunteer to help build the capacity of the Highland Chinese community. These are a few of the many examples of initiatives developed by rural minority ethnic households to address their needs.

Methodological issues

Undertaking research on rural minority ethnic households is undoubtedly challenging and there are four key issues that merit specific attention. First, identifying and accessing households given their small size is not only time consuming, but also raises ethical issues of confidentiality and anonymity that have to be addressed sensitively. Building trust is a crucial part of the process, especially in a context where minority ethnic individuals are often wary of becoming involved in research that they perceive as making them more 'visible' than they are already. In this context, taking time to explain the project, the possible outcomes as well as the constraints and demonstrating an understanding of their social context, are crucial in negotiating access. In addition, taking steps to ensure that individuals are not identifiable is vital. This may mean not locating the individuals in specific geographical communities or divulging their ethnicity.

Second, given the demographic features of the rural minority ethnic populations highlighted in this chapter, employing a range of methods (that is, qualitative as well as quantitative) is well suited for researching rural minority ethnic populations (see Creswell, 2003 for discussion on 'mixed methods'). Quantitative information and data-gathering techniques are unlikely to yield meaningful and robust information, unless they are supplemented by in-depth qualitative information. Using a 'mixed methods' strategy enables the researcher not only to maximise the information (in scope and depth), but also provides opportunities for cross-validation and triangulation in a context where the population is small.

Third, with sampling it is important to recognise that given the nature of the rural minority ethnic population traditional sampling techniques are not necessarily appropriate. Against this background, it is important to use a combination of approaches that will maximise the participation of minority ethnic individuals, such as boosting samples, snowballing using services or contacts that are most likely to be in touch with minority ethnic households as well as the use of the electoral roll.

Fourth, there has been a tendency for 'deficit models' to underpin much of the qualitative research, thus resulting in a tendency to portray rural minority ethnic individuals/groups as 'victims' rather than as individuals with a variety of 'assets' that can be built upon. This has also at times led to an inward focus on the characteristics of groups/individuals, instead of examining the ways in which groups may be thwarted in mobilising access to resources by differential access to power and resources. Mainstreaming minority ethnic perspectives in rural policy initiatives and research in general continues to be a challenge and is yet to be effectively addressed. The question of who, and what, can be regarded as falling within the 'legitimate scope' of rural research, literature and policy is highly political, reflecting the privileging of some issues and neglect of others, such as ethnicity.

Conclusion

The experiences of Scotland's rural minority ethnic households are complex. On the one hand, with regard to issues such as access to transport and employment, they share similar experiences with rural communities in general. On the other hand, in common with minority ethnic groups in Scotland as a whole, they also experience racism and discrimination in a wide range of contexts. However, their small size, diversity and dispersion compound their experiences of racism, social and cultural isolation. This is reinforced by the lack of capacity building support to facilitate the development of social capital, which could form the basis for greater civic engagement. These demographic features have also provided an excuse for agencies not to take racism seriously and have resulted in an underinvestment in initiatives and infrastructures to tackle racism and racial equality in rural areas in Scotland.

There are, however, a number of initiatives that offer new possibilities. The proposal to establish a single equality and human rights commission creates new possibilities for the way in which racism and race equality issues might be best addressed. It has the potential to provide a more effective framework for addressing individual needs given the demographic features of the rural minority ethnic population, as well as addressing issues of multiple discrimination and cross-cutting issues such as gender, poverty and social inclusion. Tackling issues of racism alongside other inequalities may provide opportunities for minority ethnic groups to develop strategic alliances across ethnic boundaries, creating a stronger voice as well as recognising the fluidity of identities.

The issue of identity has received renewed focus in the context of a devolved Scotland (Hussain and Miller, 2004). While research suggests there is a tendency for individuals to adopt hyphenated identities (that is, Scottish-Muslim or Scottish-Asian), it is difficult to assess the extent to which rural minority ethnic individuals see themselves as belonging to 'rural communities'. For many adults living in a rural community is perceived as a 'safe' environment to bring up their families but they have little expectation that their children will want to continue to live in rural areas because of what is perceived as the 'monoculturalism' of rural areas and the lack of respect for diversity. As highlighted in this chapter a number of young people constantly referred to the ways in which their ethnicity is used by the majority 'white' community to constrain and shape the way they might define themselves, making it difficult for them to develop a real sense of belonging to rural communities that draws simultaneously on their ethnic background and experience of living in rural areas.

Other recent factors that have helped to raise the issue of ethnicity in rural areas are concerns about the declining and ageing Scottish population, which have led to a wide range of discourses on the best ways to encourage migration into Scotland (Scottish Executive, 2004b). Indeed, migrant workers, recruited to work in the fish-processing, food, textile, hospitality and care industries, are increasingly a feature of rural communities, such as the north-east of Scotland and the Highlands and Islands. Although, the presence of migrant workers in small rural communities certainly poses challenges, it also creates another opportunity to address issues of racism and racial equality, especially given the weak infrastructures that exist in rural areas for addressing the needs of diverse communities (de Lima et al, 2005).

The role of Scottish devolution and the 2000 Race Relations (Amendment) Act in creating new opportunities for both rural and 'race' issues to be examined has to be acknowledged. As discussed previously it has led to an increased effort to mainstream rural perspectives in national initiatives and to research focusing on minority ethnic groups (for example, NRCEMH and BEMIS). In addition, in areas such as the Highlands, agencies have been more willing to invest in initiatives to address racism and racial equality issues and recent local community attempts to stop deportations are all signs suggesting that life in rural areas may be gradually changing for the better for Scotland's rural minority ethnic groups.

Notes

[1] This chapter will refer to fieldwork undertaken as part of an ongoing PhD being undertaken at the University of Stirling as well as to research undertaken by the author as follows: the North Forum on Widening Access, 2003-04, on access to further and higher education among minority ethnic groups in the Highlands and Islands of Scotland, completed in April 2004; a Commission for Racial Equality (CRE)-funded project 'Rural racism: mapping the problem and defining – practical policy recommendations', which took the form of a rural mapping exercise on 'race' issues, submitted to the CRE in 2002.

[2] 'Sectarianism' refers to the ongoing debate on the significance of religious divisions, specifically between the Catholics and Protestants, on Scottish society. See Bruce et al (2004) for a discussion on the subject.

References

Agyeman, J. and Spooner, R. (1997) 'Ethnicity and the rural environment', in P. Cloke and J. Little (eds) *Contested countryside cultures: Otherness, marginalization and rurality*, London: Routledge, pp 197–217.

Arshad, R. (2000) '"a man's a man for a' that": equality for all in Scotland: equality for all in Scotland?', in G. Hassan and C. Warhurst (eds) *The new Scottish politics*, Norwich: The Stationery Office, pp 153–61.

Arshad, R. (2002) 'Daring to be different: a new vision of equality?', in G. Hassan and C. Warhurst (eds) *Tomorrow's Scotland*, London: Lawrence and Wishart, pp 207-21.

Back, L. and Solomos, J. (2003) 'Introduction: theorising race and racism', in L. Back and J. Solomos (eds) *Race and racism: A reader*, London: Routledge, pp 1-28.

Barclay, A., Bowes, A., Ferguson, I., Sim, D. and Valenti, M. (2003) *Asylum seekers in Scotland*, Edinburgh: Scottish Executive Social Research.

Bromley, C. and Curtice, J. (2003) *Attitudes to discrimination in Scotland*, Edinburgh: Scottish Executive Social Research.

Bruce, S., Glendinning, T., Rosie, I. and Paterson, M. (2004) *Sectarianism in Scotland*, Edinburgh: Edinburgh University Press.

Chahal, K. and Julienne, L. (1999) *We can't all be white! Racist victimisation in the UK*, York: Joseph Rowntree Foundation.

Cloke, P. and Little, J. (eds) (1997) *Contested countryside cultures: Otherness, marginalisation, and rurality*, London: Routledge.

Commission for Racial Equality (CRE) (undated) *CRE Scotland*, www.cre.gov.uk

Crawford, A. (2004) 'People of Shetland unite to save failed asylum-seekers from deportation', *Sunday Herald*, 11 April 2004.

Creswell, J. (2003) *Research design*, London: Sage.

de Lima, P. (2001a) *Needs not numbers – An exploration of minority ethnic communities in Scotland*, London: Commission for Racial Equality and Community Development Foundation.

de Lima, P. (2001b) *The experiences of young people from minority ethnic backgrounds living in the Highlands*, Inverness: Highland Wellbeing Alliance.

de Lima, P. (2003) 'Beyond place: ethnicity/race in the debate on social exclusion/inclusion in Scotland', *Policy Futures in Education*, vol 1, no 4, pp 653-67.

de Lima, P. (2004) 'From Land's End to John O'Groats', in N. Chakraborti and J. Garland (eds) *Rural racism: Contemporary debates and perspectives*, Cullompton: Willan Publishing, pp 36-60.

de Lima, P., Mackenzie, J., Hutchison, A. and Howells, K. (2005) *Access to further and higher education among minority ethnic groups in Moray and the Highlands and Islands*, Aberdeen: North Forum for Widening Participation in Higher Education.

Denholm, A. (2004) 'Migrants help boost population figures in Scotland', *Scotsman*, 1 May, at http://news.scotsman.com.

Department of Trade and Industry (DTI) (2004) *Fairness for all: A new commission for equality and human rights, white paper*, Norwich: HMSO.

Dinwoodie, R. (2004) 'Blunkett controls could hinder Scots fresh talent scheme' (2nd edn), *Glasgow Herald*, 8 May, p 8.

Fife Regional Council (1991) *Race equality in Fife*, Scotland: Fife Regional Council.

Findlay, A., Short, D., Stockdale, A., Li, L. and Philip, L. (1999) *Study of the Impact of migration in rural Scotland*, Edinburgh: The Scottish Office Central Research Unit.

General Register Office for Scotland (GROS) (2003a) *Scotland's Census 2001*, at http://www.gro-Scotland.gov.uk.

General Register Office for Scotland (GROS) (2003b) *Scotland's Census 2001, Supporting Information, Version 1*, at www.gro-Scotland.gov.uk.

Grampian Racial Equality Council (GREC) (undated) *Annual Report 2002-2003*, Aberdeen: GREC.

Gunaratham, Y. (2003) *Researching 'race' and ethnicity*, London: Sage.

Henderson, P. and Kaur, R. (eds) (1999) *Rural racism in the UK*, London: Community Development Foundation.

Highland Alliance for Racial Equality (2004) 'Racial incidents report period: May–Nov. 2004', unpublished [available from the author].

Hope, S., Anderson, S. and Sawyer, B. (2000) *The quality of services in rural Scotland*, Edinburgh: Scottish Executive Central Research Unit.

Hussain, A. and Miller, W. (2004) 'Multiculturalism and Scottish Nationalism', *Connections*, Spring 2004, pp 10-11.

Jay, E. (1992) *'Keep them in Birmingham' Challenging Racism in Southwest England*, London: Commission for Racial Equality.

Jedrej, C. and Nuttall, M. (1996) *White settlers*, Luxembourg: Harwood Academic.

Lothian & Borders Police (2001) 'Racist incidents reported', unpublished [available from the author].

McIntosh, I., Sim, D. and Robertson, R. (2004) 'We hate the English, except for you, cos you're our pal: identification of the English in Scotland', *Sociology*, vol 38, no 1, pp 43-59.

Manwaring, R. (2002) 'Tick box marked —?', *Connections*, Autumn 2002, pp 14-15.

Miles, R. and Dunlop, A. (1986) 'The racialisation of politics in Britain: why Scotland is different', *Patterns of Prejudice*, vol 20, no 1, pp 23-32.

National Council for Voluntary Organisations (NCVO) (2000) *Rural anti-racism project report*, London: NCVO.

Netto, G., Arshad, R., de Lima, P., Almeida Diniz, F., MacEwen, M., Patel, V. and Syed, R. (2001) *Audit of research on minority ethnic issues in Scotland from a 'race' perspective*, Edinburgh: Scottish Executive Central Research Unit.

Northern Constabulary (2001) 'Racist incidents', unpublished [available from the author].

Perth News (2004) 'MP takes up Jemima's case', at http://icperthshire.icnetwotk.co.uk.news/, accessed on 1 July 2004.

Philo, C., Parr, H. and Burns, N. (2002) 'Remoteness, rurality, and mental health problems' (draft), Glasgow: Department of Geography & Topographic Science, University of Glasgow, at www.geog.gla.ac.uk/olpapers/cphilo006.pdf, accessed May 2003.

Race Equality Advisory Forum (REAF) (2001) *Making it real*, Edinburgh: Scottish Executive.

Racial Attacks and Harassment Multi-Agency Strategy Partners (RAHMAS) (2001) 'Tackling crime against minority ethnic businesses', bid submitted to the Scottish Executive under the Make our Communities Safer Challenge Competition – 2001/2002.

Rayner, J. (2001) 'The hidden truth behind race crimes in Britain', *Observer*, 18 February at http://observer.guardian.co.uk/_news/story/ 0,6903,439681,00.html.

Sanderson, I. (2000) 'Access to services', in J. Percy-Smith (ed) *Policy responsess to social exclusion*, Buckingham: Open University Press, pp 130-47.

Scottish Civic Forum (2002) *Scottish Civic Forum discrimination survey*, Glasgow: Civic Forum.

Scottish Council for Voluntary Organisations (SCVO) (1994) *Needs – not numbers: Conference report*, Edinburgh: SCVO.

Scottish Executive (2000) *Equality strategy*, Edinburgh: Scottish Executive.

Scottish Executive on behalf of the National Resource Centre for Ethnic Minority Health (2003) *Annual report of the steering committee and the director of the National Resource Centre for Ethnic Minority Health 2002-3*, Edinburgh: Scottish Executive.

Scottish Executive (2003) 'Devolution', at www.scotland.gov.uk/ about/CS/CS-CISD/00016282/devolution.pdf, accessed 17 February 2004.

Scottish Executive (2004a) *Analysis of ethnicity in the 2001 census – Summary report*, Edinburgh: Office of the Chief Statistician, Scottish Executive.

Scottish Executive (2004b) *Fresh talent initiative*, Edinburgh: Scottish Executive.

Scottish Executive (undated) *A review of the Scottish Executive's response to the race equality advisory forum recommendations*, Edinburgh: Scottish Executive.

Shucksmith, M. (2004) 'Young people and social exclusion in rural areas', *Sociologia Ruralis*, vol 44, no 1, pp 43-59.

Shucksmith, M., Chapman, P., Clark, G.M., Black, S. and Conway, E. (1996) *Rural Scotland today*, Hampshire: Avebury.

Shucksmith, M. and Phillip, L (2000) *Social Exclusion in Rural Areas*, Edinburgh: Scottish Executive Central Research Unit.

Stephen Lawrence Inquiry (1999) 'Report of an inquiry, by Sir William Macpherson of Cluny', at www.archive.official-documents.co.uk/ document/cm42/4262/4262.htm.

Stevenson, B. (2003) *Focus groups with minority ethnic communities*, Edinburgh: Scottish Executive Social Research, at www.cre.gov.uk.

Sutherland, L. (2004) 'A boy from the islands ...', *Observer Review*, 14 March, p 5.

Wacquant, L.J.D. (1998) 'Negative social capital: state breakdown and social destitution in America's urban core', *Netherlands Journal of Housing and Built Environments*, vol 13, no 1, pp 25-40.

FOUR

Remaking English ruralities

Processes of belonging and becoming, continuity and change in racialised spaces

Sarah Neal and Julian Agyeman

Britain prides itself on being a multicultural society, yet out here in the countryside, that's far from the truth. I believe that being British means more than owning a British passport. We need to feel confident that we can explore every corner of it. Until then, we'll continue to feel like strangers in our own land.

(Julian Agyeman's closing words from *Countryfile*, BBC 2, 1 August 1992)

Introduction

Local elections in England in May 2002 saw the British National Party (BNP) achieve its best electoral success when three BNP candidates became councillors in Worsthorne, a small, affluent Pennine village. The *Independent* commented on how Worsthorne 'with its village green, Gothic churches, two pubs and clematis-creepered gritstone cottages seems an unlikely outpost of racism' (3 July 2002). However, during the last decade it has becoming increasingly clear that the success of the far right in the rural idyll that the *Independent* describes is not as 'unlikely' as is imagined. While there has been a long tradition of *dis-associating* the pastoral landscape from issues of ethnicity, race and racism, the growing body of empirical and theoretical work evidences the extent to which the English countryside, and the idea of the English countryside, occupies a particular and racially coded place in Britain's 'national story'. The BNP electoral success in the north of England occurred in the same year in which there were widespread local protests against David Blunkett's (the then Home

Secretary's) now-abandoned proposals to create semi/rural-based asylum seeker and refugee centres (Younge, 2002). Although using a more coded discourse of race than the BNP – allegations of racism were mostly denied by the inhabitants of the villages of Newton and Bingham in rural Nottinghamshire (*Guardian*, 24 June 2002) – the residents' response to the Home Office's proposals to turn a disused RAF base into a refugee and asylum-seeker detention centre has been one in which the issue of desirable and legitimate presences in the rural landscape has been at the fore. That notions of race shape this desirability and legitimacy is evidenced in Gary Younge's coverage of the protests. Younge details a poster in a local florist's shop:

> [it] starts with a question: 'Are you happy to have 750 unknown asylum seekers wandering the streets of Bingham? Young men with nothing to do and lots of time to do it?' It ends with the rallying cry. 'Let's all do something to stop it for the sake of our families, children, way of life and community.' The handful who support the centre say they have been shocked by racist comments from lifelong friends. (*Guardian*, 24 June 2002)

The *Guardian*'s interest in resident anti-asylum-seeker centre protests is a reflection of the place of the countryside in the national psyche. The issues of the rural and racism have engaged significant levels of media interest for a number of years now (see Dhillon, this volume). In 2004 Trevor Phillips, the head of the Commission for Racial Equality (CRE) commented that a situation of 'passive apartheid' and 'mutual incomprehension' existed in rural and urban Britain. These comments received intense media coverage. Similarly, more recently, there was a flurry of media interest in the Lake District National Park's attempts to develop initiatives that would make it appeal to minority ethnic visitors. Represented as a story in which guided walks would be abolished as they were only attended by white middle-class visitors there was widespread local protest expressed ('Lake rangers to quit over tours for whites slur', *The Times*, 4 January 2005; 'Lake District ban on "white middle class" tours', *News and Star*, 4 January 2005) and the national park responded by temporarily halting their attempts to address particular absences in the Lake District ('Walks for white middle aged reprieved for now', *Yorkshire Post*, 5 January 2005).

The media's coverage of the BNP electoral success, the asylum-seeker centre protests, Trevor Phillips' comments and the Lake District National Park's policy developments all represent public moments in which the cleavages and tensions that lie at the heart of the racialised constructions of space can be glimpsed. In this chapter we will argue that, while the geographical space of the English countryside has been particularly imbued with a sense of nation, of an 'old England' it has, at the same time, been a space that has always been fiercely contested. In the first part of this chapter we use the concept of 'rural citizenship' to examine the changing contours of the rural and map a racialised landscape in which questions of inclusion, exclusion, legitimacy and authenticity have been particularly struggled over. We argue that in the contemporary countryside these questions are being framed through a fractured narrative of 'rural idyll, rural crisis'. The ways in which the concept of rural citizenship and the discourse of rural crisis inflect and cut across each other is a key concern of the chapter. We use the story of the Black Environment Network (BEN) and empirical data from a recent research project as the lens through which to examine what happens when particular claims to rural citizenship are made in multicultural Britain.

Rural citizenship

In his classic text on citizenship T.H. Marshall argued for a concept of citizenship composed of the triad of civil, political and social aspects within which particular sets of rights were located. Marshall defined the social aspect of citizenship as 'the whole range, from the right to a modicum of economic welfare and security to the right to share the social heritage and to live the life of a civilised being according to the standards prevailing in the society' (1992, p 8). Marshall was writing in the context of the development of the post-war British welfare state but his notion of social citizenship contains sufficient latitude to speak to other, more diverse contexts. While Marshall argued that the education system and social services were the key institutions in the shaping of social citizenship it is also possible to argue that his identification of 'social heritage', alongside welfare institutions, allows a wider theoretical applicability, and is one in which space can be considered as particularly relevant. Spaces become places through a process of their associated heritage and the meanings and values attached to them (see Introduction).

The issues of rights and entitlements to the welfare institutions cited by Marshall immediately raise, as Taylor (1996) argues, the issue of social power. Again rights and entitlements and the entanglements of these with the category of social power are present in a range of claims on citizenship. As rights and entitlement claims by various social groups are fought for and over, then the analytical and political value of the concept of social citizenship becomes rooted in its relational nature and the question of belonging that exists at its core (Lewis, 2004).

Does a widened concept of social citizenship transfer to the contemporary English countryside? It has a relevancy in that it foregrounds issues of who can make a claim on the countryside and what happens when those claims are made and by whom. Rural citizenship can then be drawn on here as a useful concept through which to describe the rights and entitlements to the symbolic, geographic and social spaces that make up rural England. The dynamics of inclusion and exclusion – the workings of social power – are associated with access (in the wider sense of the term) to the rural and what the English rural *represents* are reflections of the tensions surrounding a more broadly conceived Marshallian notion of social citizenship. This is a version of social citizenship that captures more than status, rights, responsibilities and obligations (Lewis, 2004, p 18). It is one that it stresses the 'unequal effects of particular discourses and social practices' (Lewis, 2004, p 18). The notion of a rural citizenship is one that throws into the citizenship 'pot', alongside entitlements, obligations, nation, belongings and conditions, the specificity of symbolic and social spaces. It foregrounds the cultural status of these spaces in dominant national narratives and emphasises their contested status in a multiculturally constituted England. It is the relationship, and the tensions between the denial and affirmation of the relationship, between multicultural social citizenship, multicultural social heritage and particular spaces that is presented in Ingrid Pollard's Wordsworth Heritage 'postcard' picture series.

'After reaching several peaks, Ms Pollard's party stops to ponder on matters of History and Heritage.'

(Wordsworth Heritage by Ingrid Pollard, original in colour)

Giddens (1982) maintains that in Marshall's theorisation of citizenship the central issue of struggle and resistance is elided. Citizenship is of course an unstable and unsettled category and, as Giddens suggests, there is a mutually constitutive relation between social groups and citizen membership. This relation is constantly in play in the intersections between claims for, and practices of, inclusion and legitimacy. In arguing for a specific rural citizenship it is possible to identify 'claiming' processes and the struggles that underpin these processes. One of the most obvious illustrations is the Ramblers' Association's 'right to roam' and mass trespass campaigns of the 1920s and 1930s. Between the two World Wars there was a vibrant and popular movement that demanded access to the countryside for leisure pursuits, especially for the growing activity of rambling, for the urban-based working classes. As access to rural areas was regularly denied by landowners, despite ancient rights of way and footpaths, the right to roam movement became increasingly politicised as ramblers used the tactic of mass trespass to protest.

The first and best-known of these mass trespasses was on Kinder Scout in the Derbyshire Peak District during the 1920s and 1930s. As Darby (2002) argues, the Peak District's location, surrounded by large industrial towns and cities, explains it as a site of political activity. In 1928 3,000 people took part in a trespass and in April 1932 400 trespassing ramblers were confronted by gamekeepers and county police. Six trespass leaders were arrested and charged and five were jailed. Anti-Semitism fused with accusations of communist plots featured in the trial, which received widespread newspaper coverage (Darby, 2002).

The 1932 events sparked off a number of other similar protests that year. Despite the entrenchment of the landowning elites, the mass land trespasses and the Kinder Scout protests played a partial role in the eventual legislative reform and the creation of national parks in the immediate post-war period of 'high' social citizenship. Matless (1998) argues that the 1945 Labour government's receptiveness to ensuring working-class recreational access to the English countryside reflected a prevailing mood that 'knowledge and appreciation of landscape's morphology and history were ... the basis of good citizenship' (Matless, 1998, p 182). The 1949 National Parks and Access to the Countryside Act oversaw the establishment of ten national park areas during the 1950s including the Derbyshire Peak District (see Askins, this volume).[1]

We have detailed the right to roam movement as an example of a claim to rural citizenship. Shaped by urban working-class struggle and resolved in a political moment of classic Marshallian citizenship in which access to 'the rural' was framed through a rights and obligations model seen, for example, in the codes of behaviour for urban visitors to the countryside – it is relevant to the issue of the ethnic–rural relation in two key ways. First, the fiercely contested issue as to who the rural landscape belongs to and, second, the longevity of this contestation. We are not presenting a simplistic argument here that there is a mirroring between working-class presences and black and minority ethnic presences in the English countryside. However, the concept of rural citizenship can be used as the lens through which to excavate older struggles for entitlements to rural spaces and, at the same time, used as a lens through which to view contemporary challenges as to who lives and works in and visits rural spaces and the ways in which the English rural is conceived in social and cultural imaginations. It is to the nature of this challenge that the chapter now turns.

Idyllised and crisis-ised: contemporary rural contexts

The challenges to claiming rural citizenship are particularly acute given the current polarisation in the dominant narratives of what the English rural 'is'. This polarisation is evidenced in the articulations of the rural as a space of idyll and those articulations that stress it as a space in crisis. Despite their apparent contradictions, both of these accounts can be understood as being underpinned by particular senses of nation and processes of racialisation. On the one hand there has been the process of what the cultural geographer Keith Halfacree (1997) has called 'ruralism', that is, the way in which the post-productivist English rural is conceived (and appeals) – in populist cultural terms – as a site of safety, tranquillity, community, anti-modernity, small-scale-ness: an 'old England'. In the post-productivist era agriculture has significantly receded as the dominant mode of economic production. As Hester Lacey playfully but accurately observes in her *Guardian* article 'Furrows and frappacinos' (8 September 2004):

> There are now more estate agents than farmers in rural areas. Property accounts for almost a quarter of all rural jobs, far more than agriculture and fishing combined at 15%. And rural areas are attracting creative and technical start-ups, weightless businesses not tied to location, founded by entrepreneurs who want the good life.

Certainly jobs in the service sector now account for a higher proportion of rural employment than agriculture-related jobs (Countryside Agency, 2004).

In its post-productivist state Halfacree argues that the rural 'opens up as a space for relatively novel actors to stamp their identity on the British countryside' (1997, p 70). This 'ruralism' conception of the countryside has been a crucial driver in its significant levels of repopulation (see Countryside Agency, 2004). It is a conception of the rural that has been problematised for its inherent or *uber* whiteness and for its potency as a symbol, in the collective psyche, of (exclusive) national identity by a number of commentators since the late 1980s (see other chapters in this volume, also Sibley, 1995; Agyeman and Spooner, 1997; Matless, 1998; Neal, 2002; Tyler, 2003; Chakraborti and Garland, 2004).

On the other hand, simultaneously, the countryside is presented as a site of crisis, of which there are two discernible elements. It is necessary to distinguish here between the 'quieter' crisis and the 'noisier' crisis. The quieter crisis relates to a host of rural problems that range through soaring house prices, transport problems, perceptions of escalating crime rates, low levels or shortages of welfare services, police officers, dentists, doctors and the closure or taking over of community resources and amenities – village schools, chapels, post offices, local shops, local pubs – which are all seen to be accentuating social divisions within rural communities and damaging or shifting rural values, traditions and customs. Given the extent of the problems of housing, transport and welfare services in rural areas (Countryside Agency, 2004; Shuksmith, 2004), it is significant that it has been the *idea* of the rural, rather than rural welfare concerns, that has been particularly, and noisily, crisis-ised as the high profile and bitter hunting dispute and, to a lesser extent, conflicts over Gypsy Traveller movement and residential settlement demonstrate (for example, the Gypsy and resident dispute in Cottenham, Cambridgeshire (see Bhopal, this volume) and the burning of a mock Gypsy caravan by some villagers in Firle, East Sussex in 2003).

However, it is hunting that has become the key arena in which the various tensions and pulls on what the rural 'is' have been staged. The discursive terrain on which the hunting dispute has been staked out by those opposed to its outlawing is relevant in two key ways, namely: the construction of a culturally homogeneous rural community that has a rural way of life and which has hunting at its core and the language that has been deployed to campaign against the New Labour government's legislation. The former excavates a notion of rural sameness and consensus in favour of hunting. Dissident rural voices that are raised against hunting are not particularly heard or seen to be present. In constructing a notion of a homogenised, consenting rural community the opposition to hunting is spatially located as urban. Consequently, there is an anti-urbanist discourse running through the pro-hunting arguments. The anti-urbanism of the hunting debate not only provides spatial markers in the debate, it also speaks to the notion of un-Englishness. With its peculiarly rural mixture of order (the hierarchy of the hunt, strict dress code, gleaming horses), anti-order (riders galloping across privately owned land) (Neal and Walters, 2006) and spectacle, hunting represents a particular distillation of a visceral English exotica. It is the urban, the place of bureaucratic anti-rural governance and nationlessness, which threatens the existence of this exotica. Our emphasis on the idea of the nationlessness of the city is important. It is based on the apparent willingness of the urban to threaten 'English rural ways of life' and it is compounded by the city as the stage in which contemporary Britain's multi-ethnicity is performed (Ifekwunigwe, 2002, p 321). The city becomes the place to which Bywater's term 'notion of 'not-ness' (2000, p 11, quoted in Ifekwunigwe, 2002, p 327) can be particularly attached – the urban is not the easy repository of national identity – while, conversely, the rural becomes the landscape in which claims of national 'is-ness' can be pinned (see Introduction).

The process of attaching Englishness' 'is-ness' on the countryside via the hunting debate has not always straightforwardly followed an urban–rural dichotomy. In what Michael Woods (2005) has called 'the strange awakening of the rural' a more complex rural politics has emerged. It is evident in the figure of Otis Ferry,[2] who became the young, public 'face' of the pro-hunt campaign. Otis Ferry, son of the urbane, louche, rock star Bryan Ferry, does not immediately 'fit' with images of rural traditionalism. This more complex politics is also reflected in the campaign language that the pro-hunt lobby uses. This language has 'borrowed' from urban-associated social justice movements/equal rights campaigns. For example, on a motorway drive on the M1 out of London towards the English Midlands and northern England it is quite possible to see huge pro-hunting signs erected in fields bearing the messages 'Fight Prejudice' and 'Fight Prejudice. Fight the Ban'. On the bridges that traverse the motorway, slogans such as 'Fight the Ban' and 'Rural Revolt' are graffitied. Written across the landscape these slogans re-use claims and tie them to a very different set of values and actors.

These new discursive practices for framing rural politics regularly emerged in the series of focus group interviews in Sarah's recent research project that examined identities in contemporary rural England.[3] For example, in one interview with Graham, a Young Farmers' organiser, a very measured assessment of the hunting question was given. What are striking, however, are the parallels with socially and culturally excluded groups that Graham uses:

> *Graham:* 'I think people…it concerns me that people don't understand the countryside … it concerns me – I'm trying to do this carefully because I'm going to use hunting as an example and it's a slightly difficult issue. I don't hunt and I've got no hunting connections … but I think it is an issue where an urban majority is trying to restrict what a rural minority wants to do and at least part of that is about misunderstanding and not fully comprehending what people who are living their lifestyle in a different way are trying to do and at the margin you can argue about the animal rights issue and I understand that but it is also a fact that people who are in rural areas are not well understood by the majority. And it's the same for any minority group, I imagine, that they feel they are not well understood.'

> *Researcher:* 'And do you pick that up, that people feel that they are a rural minority?'

> *Graham:* 'Yes. And people, the hunting issue is something that has very much focused that … people feel at times that their way of life is not appreciated I think, that people are almost trying to stop their ways, the ways they want to carry on.' (Interview, 7 January 2004)

The 'way of life argument' and the hunting debate recur in an interview with Miriam, another Young Farmers' organiser,

> *Miriam:* 'I think the big issue is – and I'm not wanting to go into the arguments about hunting now but what was coming through with the Countryside Alliance … was "This is our way of life and we're wanting to protect it". I think the challenge is, nothing is preserved in aspic, the world is moving on. It was portrayed, rightly or wrongly, as town versus country … It was "This is our way of life, this is our tradition and its our right to continue to do it"

> [but] you've got more people who are perhaps from what is known as the chattering classes, the *Guardian* readers type, moving in and saying "Well actually no we don't agree with this. We want to live in the countryside and perhaps we're the new countrysiders but we don't necessarily want all these traditions" so that sort of came to a head and I don't know quite where it is going now.'
>
> *Researcher:* 'It is interesting that you see these contestations because that's what we are interested in, "who is claiming to be a country person".'
>
> *Miriam:* 'Yes. I mean I would say that there are a lot of people who live in the countryside who are probably not traditionalists but have a great empathy with the countryside.' (Interview, 12 February 2004)

What Miriam flags here are the different claims made on rural space through the emergence of a more diverse rural constituency. This is captured in her description of the 'new countrysiders' (liberal, middle-class migrants) and traditionalists (local rural). Although Miriam does view the hunting debate through the 'way of life' lens, what is notable is her recognition of change and the fact that attachments that those people who move to the countryside feel for the countryside can exist beyond customs such as hunting.

The issue of the changing countryside is one that is particularly contested. Part of this contestedness is based precisely on the 'timelessness' that the rural land and villagescapes appear to offer in the idyllised versions of the countryside. As we and other rural and ethnicity scholars have shown, the appeal of this timelessness can be washed through with notions of nation and national belonging. As Sibley (1995) argues, changes and the presence of problematised 'others' in rural spaces appear to pose dangers to Englishness itself: 'Dominant rural communities in England have at different times identified threatening, abject others in the form of colonial and ex-colonial peoples, nomads, the urban working class and youth cultures. They have all defiled rural space, they have all come from somewhere else' (Sibley, 1995, p 220).

Change in this context thus poses threats to this imagined countryside. However, this process of seeing/feeling changes in rural areas and fearing or lamenting what is lost as a consequence of change has a particular longevity and tenacity in the imaginings of the rural.

Tensions between the notion of the countryside as timeless and unchanging and an awareness of it as a site of change and reconfiguration are not new. As Raymond Williams argues (1979, p 19), anxieties about a changing rural are evident across a range of literatures, for example William Cobbett writing about the English countryside in the 1820s and the happier village of the 1770s or George Eliot's fondly remembered childhood countryside in *The mill on the Floss*. Certainly George (Bourne) Sturt's (1966) writing in 1912, about 'a rural England that is dying out' (cited in Williams, 1979, p 18) and his worries about the arrival in the village of a new middle class or 'villa residents' in the (then) village of Farnham have a remarkable familiarity and resonance with contemporary anxieties and contestations.

In the focus group interviews in Sarah's research project the perception of change in the groups' local rural areas was regularly expressed and this was often accompanied by a remembered happier and safer rural. For example, Charlotte in one of the Devonshire Women's Institute (WI) groups explained how, as a child, 'We always used to walk to school, that's a thing you don't hear nowadays, children walking to school. But it's not safe for them to now' (22 January 2004). Walking and cycling to school was a common memory. For example, this excerpt comes from another Devonshire WI group:

> *Margaret:* 'I used to walk to school and ride my bicycle but you wouldn't let a child now.'
>
> *Someone:* 'We had more freedom when we were young.'
>
> *Margaret:* 'You were safe to walk in the village weren't you years ago? You never had crime in the village.' (1 January 2004)

In the same group as Charlotte, Annette, another group member, remembered how:

> 'Years ago my aunt came down here to stay and, I've got different windows now, but then I had a tiny window and I left it undone, I'd say about 25 or 30 years ago, "well," she said, "aren't you going to shut your window if you're going out?" and I said "No, nothing will happen" but nowadays you wouldn't.'

In one of the Hertfordshire Young Farmers' groups they too nostalgically recalled a vanished childhood:

> *Sheila:* 'There's no country children here anymore. It used to be a close community that we had before.'
>
> *James:* 'You'd go and play in the fields, snaring rabbits, you know, shooting with your Dad and things like that. It was just the way it was.'
>
> *Tracey:* 'But not now. You wouldn't now just let your children go out, go out of your sight.' (24 January 2004)

While there was a certain commonality in expressions of regret and loss of utopian 'traditional' villages and communities, there was also evidence that the change was not always straightforwardly lamented. Often members of the focus groups, especially the WI groups, were members who, as urban migrants, thought of themselves as part of these changes. In some focus groups there was a recognition that new residents in the village had brought with them new energy and through a desire for 'village-ness' had restarted various local societies and events. Like Eliot, Cobbett, Sturt and the members of Sarah's focus groups with their memories of safer villages and their, albeit rarer, recognition of the contributions made by changes in the form of 'incomers', all of these narratives demonstrate what Williams refers to as the 'problem of perspective' (1979, p 20). For Williams this process of recalling and nostalgia is more than 'using the past, the good old days as a stick to beat the present' it is also that 'Old England, settlement, rural virtues – all these mean different things at different times and quite different values are being brought into question' (Williams, 1979, pp 21-2). Following Williams, what we are stressing here is the constant 'becoming-ness' of the rural as it is subject to different claims, desires and values being attached to it. It is to a narrative of claiming entitlement to rural spaces that we now turn.

Claiming rural citizenship

The BEN story

In this section, we examine how the formation and activities of the Black Environment Network (BEN) represented an early attempt to challenge the normative whiteness of the countryside and the urban association of black and minority communities. At the outset, it must be said that the majority of BEN's founders were looking at 'the countryside' as an environmental issue. The crucial factor in BEN taking a more provocative stance through its questioning of nationhood and of Englishness was the influence of Ingrid Pollard's photography (see Kinsman, 1993) and the growing academic and media interest this generated.

In the early 1980s, to talk of race issues in the countryside was to invite quizzical, slightly bemused looks. 'There are no race issues in the countryside' was a typical response. Yet, as Julian taught his geography classes in Carlisle and went on school field-trips to the Lake District, he attracted the attention of hikers and others who would stop and blatantly stare (Agyeman, 1990a). In the mid-1980s, living in London, Julian reflected on this experience of rurality, and, more generally, on the apparent whiteness of the growing environmental movement. He was aware of the growing movement for environmental justice in the USA, fuelled by the landmark 1987 United Church of Christ study *Toxic wastes and race in the United States*, which showed it was predominantly communities of colour and low income that were at disproportionate risk from commercial toxic waste sites being located in their neighbourhoods. This finding was confirmed by later research (Bullard, 1990a, 1990b; Bryant and Mohai, 1992; Mohai and Bryant, 1992; Goldman, 1993; Adeola, 1994). It also led to the coining of a term by Benjamin Chavis that became the rallying cry of many: *environmental racism*. While 'environmental racism' was a powerful focus in the USA, and was seized upon by the civil rights movement, there was not any similar research on disproportionate risk and hazards in the UK. There was, however, Julian's anecdotal evidence and early writings on what became known as *rural racism* (Agyeman, 1989, 1990a, 1990b, 1990c). In some ways, by the early 1990s, rural racism became the UK equivalent of environmental racism. However, there was no civil rights movement in the UK on which to 'hook' the claim; nor a 'justice' frame to align with as in the USA. Black and minority ethnic environmental concerns had to be expressed through 'white' environmental organisations, the majority of which worked very much within an assimilationist agenda. Conversely key racial justice organisations such as the CRE and the Institute for Race Relations (IRR) showed little interest when they were approached about the need to address the intersection between racism, the environment and the countryside. The CRE and IRR did not, during the 1980s, prioritise such issues because they did not fall neatly into any of their programmes, and notions of the 'environment' and the 'rural', a few years after widespread urban disturbances across the country, appeared as irrelevant, somehow *quaint* concerns for minority activists. In this climate, it became apparent that the only way forward was to set up a black environmental organisation.

The opportunity for this came in 1987, European Year of the Environment. The National Council for Voluntary Organisations (NCVO), through their policy and promotions department, asked Julian to chair a project that would fund ethnic minority environmental projects. The scheme was to be called the Ethnic Minorities Award Scheme (EMAS). Allocated £5,000 to distribute, the Committee began inviting applications. It funded 25 projects, of which seven were for countryside trips while other applications related to innovative garden and nature-based projects. This gave birth to the idea of 'cultural gardening', or 'cultural ecology' (Agyeman and Hare, 1988; Agyeman, 1995).

On 30 September 1988, the conference 'Ethnic minorities and the environment: a one-day conference to discuss positive action' was held at the University of London Union. It was organised by Friends of the Earth (FoE) and the London Wildlife Trust (LWT) at the request of Julian, who chaired the planning group. An outcome of the conference was an embryonic BEN. Out of more than 100 delegates, a group of minority delegates including Julian, Ingrid Pollard, Vijay Krishnarayan, Swantee Toocaram, Roland de la Mothe and Judy Ling Wong decided to establish an all-black environmental group to take forward the race and environment agenda. As the conference evaluation reads, 'the black participants expressed great enthusiasm for the unique opportunity to meet in an all-black workshop, and were extremely positive about the setting up of the Black Environment Network' (FoE/LWT, 1989). After the euphoria of the conference, the hard work of setting up an organisation began. Initially BEN was based at Julian's flat in Brixton. Meetings were held at NCVO, Lambeth Council's Planning Department and anywhere that could be found. At the end of the 1980s EMAS had a higher profile than BEN, but by April 1990, BEN and EMAS merged and agreed to work under the name BEN (Agyeman, Warburton and Ling Wong, 1991). In a sense, BEN was the political project, and EMAS was its practical arm. BEN had been given office space by NCVO, in their inner-cities unit. The irony of this was not apparent to Julian at the time, but BEN, whose main profile builder was countryside trips, was put in an Inner Cities Unit because this is where race was 'dealt with'. At the same time, BEN appointed its first director, Judy Ling Wong.

While there continued to be limited interest from the mainstream environmental (FoE and the LWT were exceptions) and 'race' agencies, where there was real interest was in academia and the media, and the two are not unrelated. The work of cultural geographer Phil Kinsman, Ingrid Pollard's photography and Julian's chapter on 'Ethnicity and the rural environment', with Rachel Spooner in Cloke and Little's (1997) *Contested countryside cultures,* all raised the profile of BEN and at the same time informed BEN's political development. BEN began to further (re)frame and articulate its message of countryside access not as an 'environmental' issue, but, echoing the mass trespass protests 60 years previously, as a rights issue. Increasingly central to BEN's approach was an emphasis challenging rurally spaced notions of 'Englishness'. Influenced by Gilroy's (1987) analysis of race as central to British nationhood, Daniels' (1993) work on the power of landscapes as signifiers of national identity and Lowenthal's (1991, p 213) argument that 'nowhere else is landscape so freighted as legacy. Nowhere else does the very term suggest not only scenery and *genres de vie*, but quintessential national virtues', BEN began to stress the issues of, and connections between, environmentalism and the countryside, absences and representations, equity and social justice. In this context what BEN was pushing was that the English countryside represented an exclusive, ecological or white space (Kinsman, 1993; Agyeman and Spooner, 1997) that invokes a sense of 'unease, dread ...' (Pollard, 2004, p 21) for black and minority ethnic populations. Julian and BEN argued that 'the ethnic Other has been constantly redefined and renamed, reinforcing its difference and marginality from a white "norm" which has effectively made ethnic minorities feel unwelcome as visitors to, inhabitants of and workers in, the countryside' (Agyeman and Spooner, 1997, p 99).

BEN's activities and arguments also gathered the interest of the media and in the early 1990s, both the *Guardian* (Coster, 1991) and the *Daily Telegraph* (Deedes, 1992) reported on the issues of the countryside, racism and ethnicity with feature articles (both using the title 'Another country'), as did a variety of local and national broadcast BBC environmental programmes, including *Countryfile*, presented by John Craven. The level and the extent of media coverage given to BEN lent both the organisation and the race–countryside relation a high profile. By 1992 the CRE and local race equality councils were beginning to engage with the concept of rural racism as evidenced by two key reports, *Keep them in Birmingham* (Jay, 1992) and *Not in Norfolk: Tackling the invisibility of racism* (Derbyshire, 1994). The National Alliance of Women's Organisations (NAWO) took a gendered perspective in *Staring at invisible women: Black and minority ethnic women in rural areas*

(NAWO, 1994) to investigate 'rural racism'. Agyeman (2002) argued that these reports 'represented a new challenge to policy makers in the UK, because developing anti-racist messages and policies in multiracial cities where there was at least some support was one thing, but to develop them in "white" rural areas was quite another'. These reports were to become influential in securing racism as an issue on rural service delivery agendas (see Dhillon, this volume).

An organisation worthy of mention here was the then Countryside Commission. From the early days of EMAS/BEN, the commission was, if not enthusiastic, a symbolic supporter of the issue of diversifying rural access. In the commission's consultation document, *Visitors to the countryside* (Countryside Commission, 1991), minority ethnic populations were acknowledged as a group who 'have problems' and 'the problems *they* confront are to do with the countryside being unfamiliar, *apparently unwelcoming*, and difficult to reach or move about in' (Countryside Commission, 1991, p 10, emphasis added). In this highly pejorative explanation the responsibility for access problems is firmly located with minority communities themselves. While EMAS/BEN was involved in the document's consultation process and emphasized the need for a broader conception of the countryside and racialising processes their input was limited. The statement cited earlier was omitted from the final document *Enjoying the countryside: Policies for people* (Countryside Commission, 1992) but in the revised document the only reference to the issues faced by minority groups is a suggestion that the commission's public literature and leaflets needed to make 'positive reference to all sections of society' (Countryside Commission, 1992, p 3). These early commission engagements contrast markedly with more recent work carried out by the (renamed) Countryside Agency. The Agency's *Diversity review: Options for implementation* (OPENspace, 2003) commits central government to·addressing the issue of equity in relation to access to the countryside,

> By 2005, we will carry out a full diversity review of how we can encourage more people with disabilities, more people from ethnic minorities, more people from the inner cities, and more young people to visit the countryside and participate in country activities. Initially, we will do this by seeking their views on what they need to enjoy the countryside. Then we will draw up a plan of action. (HM Government, 2000, p 138)

The extent of the actual difference between *Enjoying the countryside: Policies for people* and *Diversity review: Options for implementation* is questionable – there is still an emphasis on excluded others as rural outsiders needing to be 'encouraged/brought in to the countryside' (see below and Dhillon, this volume) – but certainly the political landscape has shifted. The BEN/EMAS project and its (marginalised) recommendations to *Enjoying the countryside: Policies for people* were developed under Thatcher/Major governments during which there was no policy window for environmentalism generally, let alone *black* environmentalism. In the current political climate when environmental concerns and issues of rural racism have a higher profile, then the *Diversity review: Options for implementation* may represent a different vision, process and product. It is the nature and extent of the changes (and the continuities) in the relationship between the contemporary English countryside, multiculture and exclusion that we now consider.

Passive apartheid or a rural multiculture?

If we recognise that citizenship is, as Giddens reminds us, shaped and formed by the struggles of those who make claims for entitlement then it is possible to argue that the narrative of BEN and other activists, and the presence of black and other minority ethnic rural residents and rural visitors does challenge Phillips' 'passive apartheid-mutual incomprehension' description and establish at least the basis of a multiculturally constituted rural population. In earlier research Sarah argued (Neal, 2002) that the resistance on the part of statutory and voluntary rural agencies to recognising the relevance of race and ethnicity in terms of the areas they worked in and services they delivered was beginning to become partially ruptured and challenged. The familiar announcement of 'no problem here' from the welfare and community agencies that met Jay in the South-West in 1992 was not the kind that Sarah encountered some six years later. Conversely, when she spoke to local authority officers in Farfield they explained how, when they heard the articulation of 'no problem here', they knew that was 'exactly when we do have a problem' (Neal, 2002). This is by no means to suggest that all agencies and service deliverers in rural England are receptive to and actively generating and genuinely pursuing racial equality and socially inclusive strategies in the countryside – although the 2000 Race Relations Amendment Act will be pushing along reform, given its requirements, even in the slower and more resisting rural organisations and service deliverers. However, we would stress the significance of developments such as the establishment of rurally located racial equality councils (for example, Dorset, Cornwall, Devon, Somerset, Lincolnshire, Norfolk) and local authority funding for research into racism and racial harassment in rural Suffolk, Northamptonshire and Warwickshire (Chakraborti and Garland, 2004). Clearly, certain key rural agencies and authorities have embarked on a process in which the issues of racialised exclusion and representation have begun to be addressed. This is evidenced, for example, in the national parks' setting up of the Mosaic Project (see Askins, this volume), in the Countryside Agency establishing its Diversity Review project (see earlier discussion) and in the Forestry Commission (O'Brien and Claridge, 2002) who are beginning a process of consultation and research into developing the profile and work of the commission in ways that will be able to overtly demonstrate a multicultural commitment (see also de Lima and Connolly, this volume).

Again, it is important to stress that these initiatives and interventions are in their early stages and may well be marked out by their fragility and ambivalence – we have seen some of this in the former Countryside Commission's early initiatives and more recently in the Lake District National Park's row (see previous discussion) – and subject to lip service, marginalisation and under-resourcing (Neal, 1998). Certainly, the kinds of initiatives on the part of rural agencies are in an embryonic state in comparison with urban-based agencies and community facilities and the number of incarnations of racial equality, anti-racist, multicultural and valuing diversity policy formations that these have been passed through (Gilroy, 1987; Brah, 1996; Solomos, 2003).

While emphasising these caveats it is nevertheless important to recognise that some shifts have begun to take place. In many ways, the post-productivist rural, that Halfacree argued had opened up rural spaces, is also being shaped by the maturing multiculturalism of England. This multicultural constitution of contemporary England is, of course, a highly conditional one in which, as Ahmed (2000, p 106) argues, 'the "we" of the nation can expand by incorporating some others, thus providing the appearance of difference, while at the same time, defining other others ... (such other others may yet be expelled from the national body)'. Within the conditional, multicultural England, post-Lawrence and Macpherson but also post-September 2001 and July 2005, it is no longer possible to see the categories 'black' or 'Asian' and 'English' as mutually exclusive, although the categories 'Muslim' and 'English' are far less leaky. In this context, the entanglements of multiculturalism mean that the notion of whitened rural spaces becomes more claimed (by some) and, at the same time, increasingly less viable and convincing. In Sarah's project focus group interviews there was evidence of this tension in members' recognition that (their) villages were not currently multicultural but would become more so over time. The different ways in which this recognition was framed is apparent in the following excerpts from the interview data:

> *Jill:* 'The thing about village WIs, we don't have many of the ethnic groups because they don't come to live in the villages. I remember when I went to the Albert Hall, there was Clare Rayner and she stood on the platform and she said "I do think you should make more of an effort to include the ethnic groups, I can't see one face here that isn't white". And she was – and nobody pointed out to her that we once – I don't think we've ever had anybody in the village that – and they would've been invited to join if they had been. But they don't come to live in the villages.'

> *Maggie:* 'No.'

> *Jill:* 'This is it. So we're not really multicultural, we simply aren't.'

> *Deirdre:* 'Well here/'

> *Jill:* [interrupts] '*But we would be if we were given half the chance.*' (Northumberland WI, 23 March 2004, emphasis added)

What is remarkable in this conversation is the professed *desire to be more* multicultural. While this does need to be qualified in the context of Claire Rayner's 'reprimand' to the WI and in terms of Jill's confident assertion of monoculturalism, the implied welcome of multiculturalism is significant. There is a different position expressed in this Young Farmers' interview:

> *Researcher:* 'Do you think the countryside will become more multicultural over time?'

> *Jack:* 'Are we calling the countryside villages or are we calling it just the farms? Because I can't really see farmers becoming more multicultural.'

> *Greg:* 'But farmhouses getting sold off.'

> *Daniel:* 'I think people are bound to come into the country of different ethnic origins. As they do better they will aspire to move to the country the same as [pause] our English townspeople I should imagine. I don't see that there will be any difference.'
>
> *Researcher:* 'And what do you think about that?'
>
> *Tricia:* 'I think it's going to happen anyway isn't?' (Devonshire Young Farmers' Group, 14 May 2004)

This conversation appears to be premised on the *inevitability* of multicultural drift into rural spaces. While farms are identified as distinct by Jack here – and in this way stand as a sort of last outpost of whiteness – there is a recognition that for affluent minority ethnic groups the post-productivist rural will be opened up (see Tyler, this volume). This focus group then proceeds to talk about a South Asian family who live in the village and who are, they explain, 'buying everything' but 'not putting back into the village'. It is this that Daniel claims is difficult: 'It's not that they're Asian it's just their business. I mean you can be an English businessman with the same tactics. I think it's more the business that is the problem than the fact that they are Asian.' The 'putting back into the village' was a discourse echoed in other focus group conversations. It is a response that is rooted in the conditional multiculturalism that was noted above and one that also speaks to a demand for sameness. It is this 'fitting in/sameness' requirement that is present in the following WI focus group conversation:

> *Jackie:* 'We haven't got ethnic people, or if they do, if people do move in, I mean we had, what was she called?'
>
> *Voice:* [after a pause] 'Norma.'
>
> *Voices:* 'Oh yes.'
>
> *Jackie:* 'And she was from Gambia?'
>
> *Voice:* 'I don't know where she comes from.'
>
> *Jackie:* 'But I mean she was wonderful. She fitted right in. She did. She was married to an Englishman. But I think if people do come and live here, generally speaking, there's

always the exception, but they come and fit in with the community because they are so few.' (Devonshire WI, 22 January 2004)

Again this is a rather muddled account of multiculturalism. There is an initial denial of any black or minority ethnic villagers followed by an immediate acknowledgement of multiculturalism captured in the figure of Norma. Norma's foreign Otherness is stressed but then her, and other black and minority villagers', ability and willingness to *fit in* is highly praised. While there may be uncomfortable and problematic dimensions to these conversations, what binds them is the relative *absence* of a denial of an ethnicity–countryside relation. In all three versions (a welcome, an inevitability, a demand for sameness) there is a recognition of a changing rural that will be, or could be, differently constituted. It is, however, the demand for sameness that most particularly binds them. There are again some echoes of the access struggles of the 1930s and the eventual granting of these with the National Parks Act. As Matless (1998) argues, there was an institutional recognition of urban 'recreational citizenship' in the countryside but this was bounded by the conditions and obligations put on urban visitors – most obviously evidenced in the regulation of behaviour in the countryside via the Countryside Code. Similarly, in these focus group conversations, while there may be a welcome and/or an inevitability about an increasing rural multiculturalism, those Others whose presence makes it multicultural will only begin to 'rurally belong' through compliance with a set of rurally constituted conditions and obligations.

Conclusion

Citizenship is reflected in the everyday practices of black and other minority ethnic people visiting and working and living in rural localities in England. Sarah has argued elsewhere (Neal, 2002) that the English countryside cannot be homogeneously conceived of: different areas of rural England need to be recognised as being (geographically, socially, economically) different and diverse. The populist notion of a white countryside is too blunt a notion to be useful. Certainly some areas of rural England are shown through census data (2001) to be almost overwhelmingly, but not completely, white, in terms of the ethnic identity respondents selected. So, for example, Northumberland and North Devon populations were identified as 98.6% white. However, other rural and semi-rural counties of England – Gloucestershire, Suffolk, Norfolk, Berkshire – are more multi-ethnic. Hertfordshire, for example, has a population in which 4.6% of its local communities identify as belonging to minority ethnic categories. What we wish to stress here is, first, that the notion of an all-white countryside is inaccurate. Some areas of rural and semi-rural England have witnessed minority ethnic residential settlement and second, the existence of this small but significant minority rural population needs mainstream political, social and cultural recognition and increasingly so as it increases. Pronouncements like that from Trevor Phillips and the Countryside Agency and the National Parks initiatives compound the notion, and retain a model, of minority ethnic people being urban *visitors* to the countryside rather than being rural residents *living in it* (see Askins, Dhillon and Tyler, this volume). Citizenship claiming is then a process that occurs through the everyday practices of moving to and living in rural and semi-rural England. In one Northumberland WI focus group, Vera, one of the group members, responds to the question about a more multicultural countryside by saying 'It would take a brave one to come into our type of village' (Interview, 13 May 2004). On reading and re-reading this comment in the interview transcript Sarah kept coming back to it. Although constantly troubled at what Vera said, there did seem to be the possibility of reinterpreting Vera's statement in terms of entitlement to citizenship and to the 'thicker' concept of belonging (Crowley, 1999). In some ways Vera's comment can be read as a recognition of the courage that is implicit in the 'non-white' act of moving into an English village, buying a farm, converted barn or renovated cottage. In this interpretation of Vera's observation there is a mirroring of what cultural theorist David Dabydeen[4] has described as the 'outrageous confidence' of black and minority ethnic or non-white populations to be in English rural spaces (see also Tyler and Askins, this volume).

This notion of 'outrageous confidence' exists in a context in which the English rural is discursively whitened and homogenised and in which the issue of rural racism, in a variety of forms, from staring and comments to a lack of service delivery to harassment and violence, is a feature of the countryside (Chakraborti and Garland, 2004). The idea of outrageous confidence speaks to the thicker notion of belonging that we emphasised earlier. In citizenship terms, creating a 'countryside of difference' (Bowling, 2004, p x) is a recognition of entitlement, of a right to *be in* those spaces that have been constructed as symbols of nation and a certain version of Englishness. Belonging, however, is more than the entitlement or right to 'be in'. As Lewis (2004, p 169) argues, belonging:

is a more elusive and less precise concept than that of rights ... 'belonging' points to the associational and identificatory aspects of being a citizen – it is the ways in which we identify and associate ourselves [as well as] the ways in which others identify and feel associated with us.

In this way rural citizenship and belonging are both very much present in Ingrid Pollard's photographic text in which she invites the viewer into the tension between a particular presence, a particular landscape and an accompanying description of 'walking through leafy glades with a baseball bat by my side' (2004, p 23). The ambivalences of presence are evident in the assertion of Wilfred Jones (a Devonshire farmer of African-Caribbean descent and the owner of the Black Farmer Sausage Company), that 'my parents moved to Britain fifty years ago and if, fifty years on, black people feel they cannot go to certain parts of this green and pleasant land then that is a great pity' (*Guardian*, 9 October 2004). Wilfred Jones' own rural presence is, of course, indicative of both a refusal to recognise any such boundaries to citizenship entitlement and a sense of belonging. It is these tensions, confidences and attachments that continue to shape the unfinished, always becoming process of the contemporary English rural.

Acknowledgments

We would like to thank the respondents who took part in Sarah's research project, Dr Sue Walters who conducted the fieldwork and the Leverhulme Trust who funded the research. We would also like to extend our thanks and appreciation to Sue Walters for her invaluable reading of, and suggestions on, earlier drafts of this chapter and to Steve Pile for conversations on rural geographers and representations of the hunting debate.

Notes

[1] The Derbyshire Peak District remains the most heavily visited national park in Britain.

[2] Thanks to Steve Pile for pointing this out in an email discussion on rural spaces.

[3] This 12-month qualitatively designed project was funded by the Leverhulme Trust (2003-04). The data collection was based on a series of focus group interviews with members of local Women's Institutes and Young Farmers' Groups in three different areas of rural England.

The fieldwork also included a number of semi-structured interviews with Women's Institute and Young Farmers' organisers. Dr Sue Walters was the project's full-time research fellow. All the views expressed are the respondents' own and not those of either the Women's Institute or Young Farmers' organisations.

[4] In interview conversation with Julian Agyeman for BBC 2's *Countryfile*, 1 August 1992.

References

Adeola, F. (1994) 'Environmental hazards, health and racial inequity in hazardous waste distribution', *Environment and Behavior*, vol 26, no 1, pp 99-126.

Agyeman, J. (1989) 'Black people, white landscape', *Town and Country Planning*, vol 8, no 12, pp 336-38.

Agyeman, J. (1990a) 'A positive image', *Countryside Commission News*, vol 45, p 3.

Agyeman, J. (1990b) 'Black people in a white landscape: social and environmental justice', *Built Environment*, vol 16, no 3, pp 232-6.

Agyeman, J. (1990c) 'Mind your language', *New Ground*, vol 25, no 26, Summer, p 20.

Agyeman, J. (1995) *People, plants and places*, Tiverton: Learning Through Landscapes/Southgate Publishers.

Agyeman, J. (2002) 'Constructing environmental (in)justice: transatlantic tales', *Environmental Politics*, vol 11, no 3, pp 31-53.

Agyeman, J. and Hare, T. (1988) 'Towards a cultural ecology', *Urban Wildlife*, vol 4, no 3, pp 39-40.

Agyeman, J. and Spooner, R. (1997) 'Ethnicity and the rural environment', in P. Cloke and J. Little (eds) *Contested countryside cultures: Otherness, marginalization and rurality*, London: Routledge, pp 197-217.

Agyeman, J., Warburton, D. and Ling Wong, J. (1991) *The Black Environment Network Report: Working for ethnic minority participation in the environment*, London: National Council for Voluntary Organisations.

Ahmed, S. (2002) *Embodied otherness in post-coloniality*, London: Routledge.

Bourne Sturt, G. (1912 reprinted in 1966) *Change in the vllage*, London: Gerald Duckworth and Co.

Bowling, B. (2004) Foreword, in N. Chakraborti and J. Garland (eds) *Rural racism*, Cullompton: Willan Publishing, pp ix-x.

Brah, A. (1996) *Cartographies of diaspora, contesting identities*, London: Routledge.

Bryant, B. and Mohai, P. (1992) (eds) *Race and the incidence of environmental hazards*, Boulder, CO: Westview Press.

Bullard, R. (1990a) *Dumping in Dixie*, Boulder, CO: Westview Press.

Bullard, R. (1990b) 'Ecological inequalities and the new south: black communities under siege', *Journal of Ethnic Studies*, vol 17, no 4, pp 101-15.

Bywater, M. (2000) 'Englishness, who cares?', *New Statesman* 129 (4480), pp 11-12.

Chakraborti, N. and Garland, J. (2004) *Rural racism*, Cullompton: Willan Publishing.

Cloke, P. and Little, J. (1997) (eds) *Contested countryside cultures: Otherness, marginalisation and rurality*, London: Routledge.

Coster, G. (1991) 'Another country', *Guardian*, 1 June, p 4.

Countryside Agency (2004) *State of the countryside report*, Yorkshire: Countryside Agency Publications.

Countryside Commission (1991) *Visitors to the countryside*, Cheltenham: Countryside Commission.

Countryside Commission (1992) *Enjoying the countryside: Policies for people*, Cheltenham: Countryside Commission.

Crowley, J. (1999) 'The politics of belonging: some theoretical considerations', in A. Geddes and A. Favell (eds) *The politics of belonging: Migrants and minorities in contemporary Europe*, Aldershot: Ashgate, pp 15-41.

Daniels, S. (1993) *Fields of vision: Landscape imagery and national identity in England and the United States*, Cambridge: Polity Press.

Darby, W. (2002) *Landscapes and identity: Geographies of nation and class*, London: Berg.

Deedes, W. (1992) 'Another country', *Daily Telegraph*, 1 April.

Derbyshire, H. (1994) *Not in Norfolk: Tackling the invisibility of racism*, Norwich: Norwich and Norfolk Racial Equality Council.

Friends of the Earth/London Wildlife Trust (FoE/LWT) (1989) 'Ethnic minorities and the environment: a one-day conference to discuss positive action', unpublished conference evaluation.

Giddens, A. (1982) *Profiles and critiques in social theory*, London: Macmillan.

Gilroy, P. (1987) *There ain't no black in the union jack: The cultural politics of race and nation*, London: Hutchinson.

Goldman, B. (1993) *Not just prosperity. Achieving sustainability with environmental justice*, Washington, DC: National Wildlife Federation.

Guardian, 9 October 2004, p 13.

Halfacree, K. (1997) 'Contrasting roles for the post-productivist countryside: a postmodern perspective on counterurbanisation', in P. Cloke and J. Little (eds) *Contested countryside cultures: Otherness, marginalization and rurality*, London: Routledge, pp 70-93.

HM Government (2000) *Rural White Paper: Our countryside: The future – A fair deal for rural England*, London: The Stationery Office.

Ifekwunigwe, J. (2002) '(An)other English city, multiethnicities, (post)modern moments and strategic identifications', *Ethnicities*, vol 2, no 3, pp 321-48.

Independent, 3 July 2002 (at news.independent.co.uk/thisBritain/article).

Jay, E. (1992), *Keep them in Birmingham*, London: Commission for Racial Equality.

Kinsman, P. (1993) *Landscapes of national non-identity: The landscape photography of Ingrid Pollard. Working Paper 17*, Nottingham: Department of Geography, University of Nottingham.

Lacey, H. (2004) *Guardian*, 8 September, (at www.guardian.co.uk/country/article).

Lewis, G. (2004) (ed) *Citizenship*, Bristol: The Policy Press in association with The Open University.

Lowenthal, D. (1991) 'British national identity and the English landscape', *Rural History*, vol 2, no 2, pp 205-30.

Marshall, T.H. (1992) *Citizenship and social class*, London: Pluto (first published 1950).

Matless, D. (1998) 'Taking pleasure in England: landscape and citizenship in the 1940s', in R. Weight and A. Beach (eds) *The right to belong: Citizenship and national identity in Britain, 1930-60*, London and New York: I.B. Tauris, pp 181-204.

Mohai, P. and Bryant, B. (1992) 'Environmental injustice: weighing race and class as factors in the distribution of environmental hazards', *University of Colorado Law Review*, no 63, pp 921-32.

National Alliance of Women's Organisations (NAWO) (1994) *Staring at invisible women: Black and minority ethnic women in rural areas*, London: National Alliance of Women's Organisations.

Neal, S. (1998) *The making of equal opportunities policies in universities*, Buckingham: Open University Press.

Neal, S. (2002) 'Rural landscapes, representations and racism: examining multicultural citizenship and policy-making in the English countryside', *Ethnic and Racial Studies*, vol 25, no 3, pp 442-61.

Neal, S. and Walters, S. (2005) '"You can get away with loads because there's no one here": discourses of regulation and non-regulation in English rural spaces', Seminar Paper presented to Department of Sociology, University of Surrey.

News and Star, 4 January 2005.

O'Brien, L. and Claridge, J. (eds) (2002) *Trees are company: Social science research into woodlands and the natural environment*, Edinburgh: Forestry Commission.

OPENspace (2003) *The Countryside Agency diversity review: Options for implementation*, Edinburgh: Edinburgh College of Art and Heriot-Watt University.

Pollard, I. (1989) 'Pastoral Interludes', *Third Text: Third World Perspectives on Contemporary Art and Culture*, vol 7, Summer, pp 41-6.

Pollard, I. (2004) *Postcards home*, London: Autograph Books, Chris Boot and Arts Council of England.

Shucksmith, M. (2004) 'Young people and social exclusion in rural areas', *Sociologia Ruralis*, vol 44, no 1, pp 43-59.

Sibley, D. (1995) *Geographies of exclusion*, London: Routledge.

Solomos, J. (2003) *Race and racism in contemporary Britain* (3rd edn), Basingstoke: Palgrave.

Taylor, D. (1996) *Critical social policy: A reader*, London: Sage Publications.

Times, The, 4 January 2005.

Tyler, K. (2003) 'The racialised and classed constitution of English village life', *Ethnos*, vol 68, no 3, pp 391-412.

United Church of Christ Commission for Racial Justice (1987) *Toxic wastes and race in the United States*, New York, NY: United Church of Christ Commission for Racial Justice.

Williams, R. (1979) *The country and the city*, London: Chatto and Windus.

Woods, M. (2005) *Contesting rurality, politics and the British countryside*, Aldershot: Ashgate.

Yorkshire Post, 5 January 2005.

Younge, G. (2002) *Guardian*, 24 June.

Part Two:
Ethnicities, exclusions, disruptions

FIVE

Village People

Race, class, nation and the community spirit

Katharine Tyler

Introduction

When I was 10 years old I moved with my family from an ethnically diverse suburb in East London to a small wholly white, predominantly middle-class village in Leicestershire.[1] While growing up in Leicestershire, I travelled each day from my white village to ethnically diverse inner-city schools in Leicester. It is my experience of the spatialisation of race and place between the county and the city in Leicestershire that sowed the seeds of curiosity that led me to do the study discussed here. In this chapter, I draw upon anthropological fieldwork in a suburban Leicestershire 'village' to explore the ways in which the 'village' becomes a stage for the enactment and reproduction of white middle-class cultural homogeneity.[2]

Rural studies scholars have begun to examine the ways in which the scripts and icons that comprise images of the English countryside are intertwined with specifically white middle-class values and lifestyles. After the Second World War, middle-class white city dwellers migrated in increasing numbers to the countryside, seeking a peaceful and respectable way of life, which they perceived to be 'sanctioned by tradition and grounded in nature' (Wright, 1999, p 19). Murdoch and Marsden (1991, p 47) note that by the 1990s, 'the yearning for the rural corresponds in many ways to "Anglo-centricity". Within this space identities are fixed within a white, family centred, increasingly middle-class domain.'

The rural has become depicted as a 'white safe haven', a crime-free zone and a 'retreat' away from what is perceived to be the 'malaise' in English cities often associated with Asian and black settlement (Neal, 2002, p 445; see also Kinsman, 1997).[3] Agyeman and Spooner (1997) and Neal (2002) examine how white middle-class migrants and tourists to the countryside, politicians, the British heritage industry and popular television programmes have drawn upon generations of romantic and nationalist pastoral images to maintain the almost uniformly white constitution of rural England. These writers argue that such idealised images of rural England deny the history of Asians', blacks' and other settler minority peoples' relationships with the English countryside and render 'invisible' the significant minority of 'non-white' residents who live in rural areas (Agyeman and Spooner, 1997, p 202; Neal, 2002, p 445). While 'people of colour' are denied a sense of historical attachment to the countryside, Neal (2002, p 445) reminds us that potent symbols of Britain's colonial past remain inscribed on the English rural landscape, for example, country pubs in the South-West of England are called 'Jamaica Inn'.

Clearly, these scholars successfully draw attention to the force of nostalgic, historic, political and national symbols that contribute to the reproduction of the rural as a white and middle-class domain. However, these studies have not yet been adequately matched by detailed ethnographic accounts that examine how the idea of the rural as a white space is reproduced and maintained by ordinary 'village' people at the local level. This absence is partly due to the overwhelming urban bias in studies of race, racism and anti-racism in the UK.

It is against this background that Nye's (2001) study of the protracted legal dispute involving the International Society of Krishna Consciousness (ISKCON or the 'Hare Krishnas') main centre of worship at Bhakitvedanta Manor is of central importance. In his book, Nye raises some of the key ethnographic themes underpinning middle-class white discourses on racism in rural England. He contends that the legal dispute concerning the 'proper' use of Bhakitvedanta Manor can be interpreted as a struggle in which Asian Hindus fought against what powerful classes of white English people think as the very essence of English life, that is the countryside (Nye, 2001, p 288).

Bhakitvedanta Manor is situated in the heart of an affluent middle-class, white and 'quintessentially' English Hertfordshire village (Nye, 2001, p 51). Nye describes Letchmore Heath as a 'typical' English village where, 'one can imagine men in white flannels playing cricket on the village green, ending their day in the sun at the public house for a warm beer and gentle banter' (2001, p 53). He reports that this nostalgic image of English village life is 'deliberately' and 'ferociously' maintained by the white middle-class villagers 'to keep it distinct from the sprawl, ugliness and noise of nearby London' (Nye, 2001, p 51). The residents felt that the 'excessive' numbers of Asian Hindus visiting the manor was a 'disturbance' and 'disruption' to the village's otherwise 'peaceful' environment. Complaints were made to the local council about the traffic caused by the thousands of devotees visiting the manor (Nye, 2002, p 51). In spite of the middle-class white villagers' protests against ISKCON, Nye (2001, p 296) found few instances of overt racism directed against visitors to Bhakitvedanta Manor. He writes, 'the experience and discourses on racism have worked in more *implicit and subtle* ways' (2001, p 296, emphasis added).

The socio-economic composition of the suburban 'village' in Leicestershire that I studied, and which provides the focus for this chapter, shares similarities with Nye's description of Letchmore Heath. This place is also the home to affluent white middle-class people who, like the villagers of Letchmore Heath, are concerned that their area's 'village' identity will be consumed by the encroaching and ethnically diverse urban cityscape. Picture a place that is a suburb in terms of its residential landscape and close proximity to the city of Leicester rather than a typical English village set in rural landscape away from urban areas. It is in the face of the area's suburbanisation that the middle-class white residents in my study reflexively defend their area's imagined 'village' identity, which is associated with the traditional white rhythms of English village life.

Drawing on this anthropological fieldwork, I have reported elsewhere that middle-class ideas about the 'proper' composition of the 'village' community become apparent in white residents' intolerant attitudes towards the minority of wealthy Asian residents (Tyler, 2003). I return here to this observation in an attempt to develop Nye's analysis of the 'implicit and subtle' constitution of middle-class white discourses on racism. In this chapter, I shall explore the ways in which the middle-class white residents prohibit the minority of wealthy and lower-class Asian inhabitants from participation in the local social, leisure and charitable activities that form the heart of the area's imagined 'village' community.

One framework for tracing these configurations of exclusion is the 'cultural turn' within geographical studies of rural Britain that examine how 'representations of rurality and rural life are replete with ... devices of exclusion and marginalisation' (Cloke and Little, 1997, p 1). Geographers have begun to unpack the incongruity between the nostalgic and national images of the rural community as 'friendly', 'peaceful' and 'caring' with the lived reality that rural lifestyles rest 'upon a degree of intolerance to difference' (Little and Austin, 1996, p 109; see also Cloke et al, 1995). In so doing, these scholars have raised important questions about the paradoxical relationship between the idealised and national images associated with the supposedly harmonious constitution of the rural community, middle-class hegemony, gendered identities and processes of exclusion. Drawing on these writers' insights, my aim is to examine how the distinctively middle-class ideals about the 'neighbourly', 'friendly' and 'caring' constitution of the 'village' community become entwined with the reproduction of white cultural homogeneity.

In what follows, I identify a set of white middle-class discourses and practices that justify the marginalisation of wealthy and lower-class Asian residents from participation in the social networks and activities that constitute the patterns of the imagined 'village' community. I explore the discursive twists and turns that constitute middle-class white residents' apparent 'acceptance' of the Asian family who run and own a shop in the area. Alongside this apparent 'acceptance', I scrutinise the white middle-class residents' perceptions of the supposed 'social isolation' of the minority of very wealthy Asian residents who live in the most prosperous area of the 'village'.

To illustrate the everyday processes of imagining the whitened constitution of the 'village' community, I draw upon the personal testimonies and experiences of middle-aged and retired white residents, that is, residents who are 45 or over, rather than those of younger white adults. The latter are more likely not be over enamoured with the charms of traditional ideals and so are differently orientated to older residents in terms of their lifestyles and cultural attachments. Thus younger residents tend not to have the same emotional investment as older inhabitants in the reproduction of the area's traditional 'village' community, associated with white middle-class norms of respectability and racial intolerance.

At this conjuncture, I must explain my use of the term 'middle-class' to refer to the people that participated in my study. The classed locations of the people with whom I worked reflect the 'internal divisions' that constitute the middle-class in Britain (Vincent et al, 2004, p 231). Sociologists acknowledge that the middle-class is fragmented by a variety of factors that include occupation, education, lifestyle and consumption choices, political preferences (liberal and conservative strands), family structure, cultural tastes and values, economic assets and income (see Butler and Savage, 1995). Sociologists also emphasise the flexible articulation of these elements in relation to individuals' and families' particular identifications. In this regard, some sociologists have concluded that occupation does not neatly correlate with 'social consciousness' and attitudes (see Vincent et al, 2004, pp 231-2 for a review of this debate).

In this chapter I draw upon the racialised discourses of a cross-section of the middle-class in terms of occupation; for example, self-employed builders, wealthy business people and housewives. While my study highlights the internal differences within the middle-class in terms of occupation, material wealth and lifestyle, my account also renders explicit the shared opinions and beliefs that cut across these internal differences.

Butler and Robson's (2003, p 1792) attention to the importance of space and locality in the formation of middle-class identities is particularly relevant to my emphasis upon the 'village' as the site for the reproduction of white middle-class cultural homogeneity. These scholars suggest that: 'Middle-class people identify with neighbourhoods where they perceive "people like us live".' In this vein, Vincent et al (2004, p 233) argue that 'distinctive areas' are 'created with particular ... characteristics' that reflect the internal differences within the middle-class. For these writers it is precisely the way that middle-class people mobilise intra-class distinctions as well as the perceived divisions between class groups that enables them to identify 'people like us' (Vincent et al, 2004, pp 239-40). Accounts of practices of intra-class distinctions and group closure are also played out in the racialised and classed discourses of the middle-class white people from the suburban 'village' discussed here.

Ethnographic research in a suburban 'village'

I shall call the place to which my ethnography refers Greenville. In 1997 I took lodgings with a white family for six months in the area. I took a part-time job in the local pub and regularly attended local activities such as the monthly meetings of the Women's Institute, a national organisation for rural women, and the parish council, the administrative body of a rural village. My participation in these events formed the basis for my understanding of the relationships and social networks that constitute Greenville's imagined 'village' community.

While living and working in the area, I conducted 30 in-depth, semi-structured interviews with a cross-section of white residents in terms of class location, age and gender. The interviews were conducted in people's homes. The central aim of the interviews was to understand white people's perceptions of Asians in their area.

The fact that I could claim belonging to Leicestershire gave my co-conversationalists a certain explanation for why I was interested in their place. My identity as an academic researcher gave me and my work an aura of respectability and even neutrality. My whiteness and middle-class-ness were taken by some residents to be a sign that I would take a middle-class white perspective on the issues discussed rather than take an Asian point of view. I often drew upon my experiences of village life in Leicestershire and the spatial divisions between race and place in the county and the city to help relax those people who were hesitant about discussing their views on race. I did not on the whole challenge white people's narratives that I considered racist. During the course of our discussions it was not clear to me how to deconstruct such comments effectively. My silence was often taken to be a sign of reassurance and agreement. Thus at times within the interviews I worked within the discourses of white privilege and racism that I set out to examine (see also Frankenberg, 1993, pp 40-1).

An imagined 'village' community

Greenville lies only five miles west of the ethnically diverse city of Leicester. The area's close geographical location to Leicester suggests that Greenville is a suburb of Leicester, rather than a traditional English village associated with the rolling countryside of rural England.

The erosion of Greenville's traditional 'village' identity began with the loss of the area's farms approximately 30 years ago with the extension of a major motorway (highway). The development of the motorway has attracted a large influx of middle-class commuters who work in Leicester and other cities in the Midlands region of England. Most of the 4,519 (according to the 1991 census) people living in the 'village' are incomers from Leicester City, other parts of Leicestershire, and more distant parts of Britain. Greenville's population is mainly white. By official census classification, 98.2% of Greenville's population are white, 1.4% are Asian, 0.2% are black and 0.2% are 'other'. There is great wealth in the area. Greenville is home to well-paid professionals and executives, middle management and public sector workers.

The area known as the 'village' consists of an extensive patchwork of suburban-style housing estates and impressive modern designer homes. One of the most prosperous and oldest areas of Greenville is called Greenville Gardens.[4] There are approximately five affluent Asian families living in the wealthy Greenville Gardens area. There is also an Asian family that owns and runs a local grocery shop situated in the heart of Greenville's less affluent residential area.

Greenville is obviously not, then, a typical rural English village. The size of the area's population, its close proximity to the city of Leicester and the area's residential landscape illustrates that Greenville is in fact a suburb of Leicester. It is precisely in the face of Greenville's suburbanisation that my white co-conversationalists are reflexively maintaining their area's imagined 'village' identity and community. My question, then, is not, what do people actually see when they think about their place, but what do they imagine to be there? Moreover, how do my co-conversationalists make their imaginations of 'village-ness' into realities through social interaction and relatedness? (see Cohen, 2000, p 166 for similar ethnographic questions in relation to everyday perceptions of national identity).

Claire is a middle-aged professional woman who moved to Leicester as a student from London with her family some 20 years ago.[5] She explains her perception of the area's ambiguous 'village' identity as follows:

> 'I know that people think that there is a lack of green for a village, but I feel that Greenville captures that country village feeling. People support local things like the Greenville Players [a local amateur dramatics society] and the church activities. The churches are very good at organising charitable events for the old people.'

Sheila also reflects on Greenville's imagined 'village' status and identity. She is a single woman in her 60s and has lived in a small cottage in the area for nearly 40 years. Sheila comments: 'I think that Greenville is still a village but bordering on a suburb, but the community spirit in it is very village-minded. We have got all sorts of things going on ... It is a good and caring community.'

For Claire and Sheila, the idea of 'village-ness' is not a matter of geographical location. Rather, they think that Greenville's 'village' identity revolves around the reproduction of the area's 'community spirit' associated with people's continued participation in local social, leisure and charitable activities. There are numerous community organisations that constitute Greenville's 'caring' and 'village-minded' community. For example, there is a variety of social and sports clubs for retired people who have the time to invest in leisure activities. These include the bowls club, the flower guild, the sewing club, the debating society and the Women's Institute. Younger men and boys can join the local cricket and football teams. Greenville also has a thriving and prestigious golf club whose members are the more affluent of the white villagers. The local churches are key organisations around which people organise charitable activities for elderly residents and youth clubs for adolescent inhabitants.

Involvement in these activities is entwined with the social and moral values of charity, friendliness and neighbourliness. These same sentiments are interwoven into the fabric of nostalgic and national narratives about the structures of feeling that comprise the traditional English village community. Williams (1973, p 30) examines the ways that the scripts associated with 'the rural' in late 17th-century English poetry reflected the wider 'social and moral' values of 'the natural order of responsibility and neighbourliness'. In Greenville, these idealised sentiments and values are felt, made meaningful and experienced by residents in their social relations and networks with each other. This process is a kind of 'banal nationalism' (Billig, 1995) that is so embedded in the intimate details, habits and relationships of everyday life that the sentiments of nationhood become routine and unnoticed flags of identity and belonging.

Middle-class white residents are responsible for the hard work that goes into the organisation of these local activities. Middle-class status in Greenville is partly dependent upon 'material capital' (Bourdieu, 1984), the ability to afford an expensive house in a prestigious environment. However, middle-class status is also reliant upon the acquisition and embodiment of 'cultural capital' (Bourdieu, 1984), which includes a set of culturally appropriate desires, tastes and aspirations for oneself and one's family within the local community. Material capital enhances individuals' acquisition of middle-class status in Greenville. However, money does not substitute for a perceived lack of the tacit cultural knowledge about how to fit into the social networks of community life. This is made evident by my co-conversationalists' perceptions of the very wealthy Asian settlers to the village. These residents have acquired the material trappings of an affluent middle-class lifestyle. However, they are thought to lack the 'cultural ingredients' (Ortner, 2002, p 12) that constitute the appropriate ways of behaving in Greenville's imagined 'village' community.

People's varied participation in the range of local activities reflects differences in age, gender, lifestyle choices and socio-economic location. For example, only the affluent middle-class residents can afford to join the local golf club. Mike, a self-employed builder in his 40s, suggests, 'The golf club crowd seem to think that they are up in the pecking order'. However, people do not need to be wealthy in order to dedicate their time and energy to the organisation of local voluntary activities. Participation in local charity and recreational events brings a sense of personal satisfaction, social recognition and status within the community. Thus, the kinds of social activities that people participate in and the networks of social relations that are formed around these activities become a form of 'cultural capital' in themselves and mediators through which other kinds of capital work on people's lives.

The majority of residents do not, however, participate in the local activities. Madge, a veteran of numerous local activities, comments thus: 'I feel that people who have moved into the village don't always integrate. They tend to use it ... like a commuter place.' For these residents, the area's environment becomes an 'aesthetic backdrop' associated with a quality dwelling in a prestigious environment (Cloke et al, 1995, p 237). As a middle-aged woman who plays no part in the local activities remarks, 'There is a certain snob value living in Greenville, it is a good address'. These residents have a financial and psychological investment in the reproduction of Greenville's 'village' identity. Risks to Greenville's fragile and idealised 'village' community threaten not only the white middle-classes' diverse lifestyles but also the middle-class sense of self (Cloke et al, 1995, p 238). This is exemplified by the ways in which some of my older co-conversationalists felt that the settlement of Asian residents into the area represented one such perceived risk to the reproduction of the area's 'community spirit'.

The Asian shopkeepers and the 'village' community

The most 'visible' Asian family in Greenville is a family that owns a local grocery store. There is a general discourse of 'acceptance' of the Asian shopkeepers based upon their perceived acquisition and self-display of culturally appropriate qualities. This Asian family is thought to be 'polite', 'hardworking' and 'successful' in business and is said to provide a 'useful service' to the community. This discourse of 'acceptance' dovetails with a discourse about the Asian shopkeepers' imagined racialised cultural differences to the white middle-class residents. This racialised differentialist discourse creates absolute and immutable cultural differences between the white residents and the Asian shopkeepers. It is the ambiguous portrayal of the Asian shopkeepers that is dependent upon subtle discourses of racialisation that at times coexist with more crude discourses of differentiation that enables my co-conversationalists to exclude and marginalise this particular Asian family in a multiplicity of ways.

Mike comments on his personal reaction and that of other white residents when the Asian family moved into the local grocery shop. He is in his 40s and owns a building and decorating business. Mike moved from Leicester to Greenville 12 years ago with his family. He is divorced and lives with his teenage children in a modest family house. Mike says:

> 'I remember when the Patels moved in. I thought – great, open all hours … But people said, "Wogs moving into Greenville … We don't want that".[6] They are the same people who will do most of their grocery shopping there … and get charged extra for doing it … They kept saying, "We don't want wogs in Greenville". Why? What is wrong with a coloured guy moving in and doing the village a service, and making money in the process?'

While Mike welcomes this particular Asian family's 'service' to Greenville, he employs two common discourses about Asian shopkeepers: they are 'open all hours' and they 'charge extra'. His belief that the Asian shopkeepers 'charge extra' implies that they are disingenuous in their business practices. Mike continues by explaining how he perceives the shop to be run:

> 'The Patels are a typical example … They have got the female dominancy situation … She's at the till while I go down the cash and carry. The lad finishes school and he stocks a few shelves up, very nice. It wouldn't work in a western culture, you know. My wife at the till while I went down the cash and carry … That is why I am in admiration of their culture, because they are family group orientated … They will prosper and they do respect their parents and they will study. They will have all the prime jobs in this country, I am convinced of it. While, we are still wringing bloody mops out and wearing knotted handkerchiefs on our heads going down Skegness [a seaside town in England] … The Indians, they have had to work hard because they have come to a totally different country, a lot of them poorish. They have got nothing to lose and so the only way for them is up.'

Mike's emphasis upon this family's origins being outside England enables him to construct the idea that there is a racialised cultural boundary separating 'us' from 'them'. Mike thinks that the Patels are a 'typical' example and so they become an 'ideal bearer' of Asian cultural practices and values (Blommaert and Verschueren, 1998, p 96). He admires what he perceives to be Asian values and cultural practices. Mike thinks that they are family-orientated in business, their children work hard at school and respect their parents, and wives are subservient to their husbands. By contrast, Mike's single-parent family represents the contradictory 'western' attitudes and cultural components of individualism, the loss of family values, youthful deviance and liberation from patriarchy. Mike's static and conservative image of Asian culture becomes a projection for his idealistic vision of male dominance and respectful children. Such a traditional way of life will guarantee Asians' economic success and social mobility.

Mike also portrays a stereotypical and quaint image of the English. The English are perceived as daft and ridiculous in 'wearing knotted handkerchiefs' and 'wringing out mops'. Mike's stereotype of the English simultaneously commends but also denigrates the commercial and entrepreneurial aspects of Asians' economic prosperity and hard work. On the one hand, the Patels are thought to charge their white customers 'extra' and their business success is imagined to be dependent upon the exploitation of family labour. On the other hand, the English are believed to favour the good old-fashioned and solid working-class values of steadfastness, honesty and clean living. Mike's self-ridicule of the English evokes an image of deviant Asians stealing the economy from the naive English. Thus, the wearing of handkerchiefs and going to Skegness is an extension of English tradition to the point of self-mockery and not a transformation of it. In other words, Mike's critique of English culture actually reinforces and reifies the normalcy of English-ness that he is seeking to invert and mock.

Paul and Janet also reflect upon the Asian shopkeepers in Greenville. They are a couple in their 50s and have lived in Greenville for about 25 years. When Paul's business became successful, his family moved from Leicester to a spacious bungalow in the affluent Greenville Gardens area. Paul and Janet reflect upon the way that they think that the Asian shopkeepers are an asset to the area:

> *Paul:* 'The local shops here are wonderful. They have taken over the grocery shop, which is superb.'

> *Janet:* 'Yes, they always remember our names. I only went in there once and then the next time they said hello. They are so polite.'

> *Paul:* 'The English used to be a nation of shopkeepers. Well, they beat us hands down. They are so polite and friendly. They are brilliant.'

This particular Asian family is thought to be 'polite and friendly'. In this regard, they are believed to fit into the socially accepted values of decorum and neighbourliness associated with the norms of Greenville's community. Like Mike, Paul admires the Asians' financial and business success. However, both Paul and Mike see Asians and whites as pitched in competition with each other over who will be the owners of the English economy. For Paul, they are now 'the nation of shopkeepers', whereas 'the English used to be'. For Mike, Asians will have 'all the prime jobs in this country'. This is, in effect, a variation on what Nye (2001, p 296) identifies as, 'a common white middle-class British fear that an "Asian family" in a street will lower prices because of the fear of "swamping" and mass influx of other Asians'. In this instance, the Asian shopkeepers evoke ideas about the wider English-Asian diaspora's supposed 'takeover' and control of the English economy to the detriment of white English people. Thus the adjectives of 'brilliant' (Paul) and 'admirable' (Mike) are ambiguously positive and negative descriptions of Asian-ness. Asians are admirable in their economic success, their hard work and their politeness. However, these socially accepted characteristics do not allow 'them' to be incorporated into the invisible moral bonds that constitute the imagined national community. That is, Asians' supposedly different 'origins', racialised cultural practices and their admirable but also potentially threatening business success restricts them to economic pockets of service.

One afternoon after my meeting with Janet and her husband, I had tea with Janet and her friend, Louise. Janet's friend was in her 50s, like Janet. Louise moved to Greenville Gardens as a teenager with her parents. When she married, Louise left the area to live with her husband in the South-East of England. They returned to Greenville approximately 10 years ago. Louise perceives the Asian shopkeepers in Greenville as follows:

Louise: 'I have never been in the Asian shop.'

Janet: [wanting to agree with her guest] 'No I have only been in twice.'

Louise: 'Asians act a bit sly, they try to get their end up [the implication here is that Asians try to do well in business through deceitful practices]. My husband dealt with a man from India and he said that we have got all the low caste rubbish here. The higher caste ones are still in India. A few years ago the *Leicester Gazette* [local newspaper] said that 75% of muggings are done by coloureds.'

Janet: 'It is true that more of the snatchings … on the streets are done by Asians.'

Louise: 'Well I'm not keen … The problem is that they are demanding so much and that causes friction. They come here and they do not accept our way of life.'

Paul and Mike's portrayal of the 'polite', 'brilliant' and 'superb' Asian shopkeepers is transformed into the belief that Asians are 'low caste rubbish', 'sly' in business and unfair beneficiaries of advantage. Janet's inconsistent portrayal of this family illustrates that it is not realistic to expect individuals to be constant in their views on racial and cultural differences. It is precisely this ambiguous portrayal of the shopkeepers, that melds subtle discourses of exclusion with the not so subtle, that enables my co-conversationalists to maintain the belief that they are racially tolerant, while rendering this Asian family outside the norms of respectability that constitute the imagined 'village' community.

Wealthy Asian inhabitants and the discourse of 'social isolation'

The Asian residents who live in the most prosperous area of the village have acquired the material trappings associated with an affluent middle-class lifestyle (Tyler, 2003). However, they are thought not to have developed the socially commended neighbourly and friendly attitudes associated with the rhythms of the 'village' community. By contrast to the Asian shopkeepers, the wealthy Asian residents are believed to isolate and so cut themselves off from the local social networks. This discourse of 'social isolation', once more, enables my co-conversationalists to evade and ignore the subtle and the not so subtle processes of exclusion that render the Asian inhabitants on the margins of 'village' life.

Simon explains why he thinks the wealthy Asians do not participate in the community activities. Like Mike, Simon is a self-employed builder with his own business. He has lived in Greenville for over 20 years. Simon lives with his second wife in a modest house on a suburban-style housing estate in the centre of Greenville. He describes his perception of the wealthy Asian residents' relationship to the 'village' community thus:

'They tend to keep themselves to themselves … They have tended to build fences and electric gates around the big houses, which is something we never saw in the past … I don't think that they do fit into the village community. Where we would tend to socialise in the village hall, we like to stay together as a community to belong to groups, to belong to bowls, and we like to enjoy ourselves. You don't seem to find Asians doing that ... The Asians here don't seem to look for free time – it's work for them. They have got to earn and I am sure that is their upbringing in another country because they were brought up on a meagre upbringing, on very little money and food, whereas we lived better. We have lived in better times and we treasure our spare time to do what we want to do.'

Simon's belief that the Asians' impoverished 'origins' in 'another country' motivates them to earn money resonates with Mike's understanding that Asians, 'have come to a totally different country, a lot of them poorish', and that, 'they will prosper'. These narratives of origin and settlement to England place the Asian residents outside the English nation into a time and place symbolised by a lack of security and economic prosperity. Such narratives of settlement are implicitly dependent upon the 'art of forgetting' (Bauman, 1997, p 53) Britain's colonial past and Asians' ongoing struggles with white dominance. Simon thinks that the Asians' compulsion to work truncates them from the community ethos of friendship and sociality. Thus, the electric fences and gates that surround the Asians' houses not only disrupt the seemingly timeless and tasteful milieu of Greenville Gardens, but are also signs of the wealthy Asians' apparent 'social isolation' from the 'village' community.

In his explanation for why Asian women do not socialise with other residents, Mike, whom we have already met, draws upon a discourse about the hierarchy of class and race distinctions:

'I don't think they do get involved because I don't think they want to ... They have got their nice BMWs stroke Mercedes stroke people carriers thing, which to them is a symbol of status. If you get a Mercedes, you have cracked it. You are half way up the ladder sort of thing. In the same way with the houses the more security you can put around it ... And if you get the fences and big metal gates ... and security cameras you have made it ... Even when the women are picking the children up from school, I have noticed that they sit in their car and they wait for their children ... Whether or not they feel inferior or in a higher-ranking position to the other women, I don't know. It might even be their personal choice.'

Mike has observed that the wealthy Asian inhabitants not only have Mercedes and BMWs, which are prestigious cars for white people, but they also have their own status symbols – people carriers and excessive security around their houses. Mike and Simon's racialisation of status symbols illustrates how any aspect of social life can potentially become transformed into a marker of racialised cultural difference. Blommaert and Verschueren (1998, p 93) make the pertinent observation that, 'Whatever the migrant may be or do, it is always getting culturalised, a process which contributes significantly to the abnormalisation of the foreigner'.

Mike's emphasis on female residents' gendered location as mothers highlights the way that women tend to be the primary carers of children in Greenville, which facilitates their involvement in local activities for children. In the same way that Mike thinks that the members of the golf club believe themselves to be 'up in the pecking order', wealthy Asian women might imagine themselves to be superior to the less wealthy white female residents. Thus, he wonders if Asian women have acquired the superfluous sense of self-esteem and social arrogance that he associates with the wealthy white residents. Alternatively, Asian women might think that their racialised cultural differences to white women render them inferior and so they lack the necessary confidence required to take part in the rhythms of 'village' life. Either way, the perception remains that it is Asian women's 'personal choice' not to socialise with other mothers and so Mike evades and dissolves the inequalities between whites and Asians in Greenville.

At times, Asians are momentarily present at Greenville's 'village' activities, only to disappear in an instant, until the next time they make their presence felt. Sue, a member of an informal debating group for local women, explains the group's reaction to a speaker from an Asian women's group based in Leicester. Sue has lived in an impressive Victorian mansion in Greenville Gardens for 17 years. She moved to the 'village' with her family from London. Her husband is a retired businessman. Sue describes the ethnic composition of her women's group as follows:

'We did have an Asian girl come a few times. She was not a regular because she found it difficult to get here. She lived a bit of a way from here. We felt that she fitted in well – it [that is, her ethnic identity] did not affect our

> relationship at all. This is a very white village – there are
> only about three Asian families here ... No problems have
> arisen in our group and no one would feel differently to
> anyone. In fact, I find it a bit boring. It would be better if
> we had say Scottish and Asian people in the group, we
> could all benefit from that ... Actually now I think of it we
> did have a speaker once from an Asian women's group. I
> have to say we all thought this – she was very bitter. There
> was a barrier up before she even started. But I do not think
> that they are different.'

Sue rejects the significance of racial, ethnic and national differences.
Writers on the formation of white ethnicity have argued that the
denial of racial and ethnic differences can paradoxically facilitate
racialised constructions (Frankenberg, 1993, p 143; Solomos and Back,
1995, p 122). Sue believes that the predominantly white and English
constitution of Greenville is 'boring', bland and culturally neutral.
However, she thinks that the attitudes of the Asian visitor and temporary
club member are the source of potential antagonisms. By contrast to
the temporary Asian club member who was thought to 'fit in', the
Asian speaker's 'bitter' disposition was felt to be unnecessary and
inappropriate in the face of the white club members' open, accepting
and tolerant approach to race. Thus people who are perceived to be
racially different are considered to be acceptable only in so far as their
attitude to race enables their 'coloured-ness to be bracketed and ignored'
(Frankenberg, 1993, p 147).

Simon, Mike and Sue emphasise their racially tolerant and open
attitudes towards the wealthy Asian residents and visitors to Greenville.
This apparent 'acceptance' of Asians is pitched in opposition to the
Asians' perceived preference and choice not to become involved in
the social networks that constitute the imagined 'village' community.
This discourse of 'social isolation' negotiates and manages the
incongruity between the ideal that Greenville's community is 'friendly',
'caring' and 'neighbourly' with the reality that those who are perceived
to be racially different are excluded by a culture that represents them
as inappropriate.

Conclusion

Neal (2002, p 457) perceptively argues that 'the dominance of whiteness
and the pervasiveness of the pastoral idyll' are defining characteristics
of rural racism. The specifics of my ethnography suggest that nostalgic

images of the whitened constitution of the traditional English village community are interwoven with a specifically older white middle-class discourse and aesthetic. I have examined how the dominant national scripts of the 'rural community' as 'friendly', 'neighbourly' and 'caring' are racialised when articulated and negotiated by ordinary 'village' people at the local level. In so doing, I have explored the ambiguous coexistence of subtle and the not so subtle portrayals of racial differentiation that comprise a set of white middle-class discourses.

My co-conversationalists' racialised discourses are overwhelmingly framed by senses of nation. In this regard, my co-conversationalists merge their particular reflections upon the Asian inhabitants in Greenville with their ideas about the wider Asian-English diasporas' relationship to the English nation. When they think about the Asian shopkeepers' business success and the prosperity of the wealthy Asian inhabitants, the people with whom I worked summon up stereotypical images concerning Asian settlers' imaginary 'takeover' of the English economy to the detriment of white English people. They are also reminded of Asians' supposedly 'backward', 'impoverished' and different 'origins' that lie outside the white English nation. In this way, the English nation becomes associated with a purity of tradition and an ancestral claim to territory that displaces and denies Britain's racially heterogeneous colonial past. The effect of this discourse is to render the minority of wealthy and lower-class Asian inhabitants not only on the margins of the imagined 'village' community but also outside the white English nation.

While my aim has been to make visible the unmarked category of white ethnicity that often remains 'invisible in its dominance' and displaced through multiple processes of 'power evasion' (Frankenberg, 1993), the silence of Asian residents' views on the 'village' community provides an important avenue for future research. Nye (2001, pp 74-7) reports the case of Chandra Vadivale, the only middle-class Asian settler to a village in Oxfordshire. Nye notes that Vadivale's daily interactions with his middle-class neighbours were amicable. However, his neighbours complained to the local council about Vadivale's use of an outhouse in his garden as a Mandir (a Hindu temple of worship). The neighbours made complaints about the high levels of noise twice a year at festival times, when up to 150 guests gathered in Vadivale's garden. Some neighbours even found the smell and smoke from food and spices burnt in ritual sacrifice intolerable. From Vadivale's perspective there was no difference between having the scale of visitors to his house for an act of worship and holding a summer garden party, which was a common occurrence among white middle-class households in the village. He also believed that the smell of burning spices emitted from the ritual sacrifice was more 'wholesome' than the smell of 'roasted pig meat' on barbecues in his neighbours' gardens (Nye, 2001, p 75). Such ethnographic insights into middle-class Asian people's experiences and perceptions of their relationship to the village community need to be documented and examined in much greater detail if the representation of the rural as a white domain is to be dismantled.

Acknowledgements

I thank Sarah Neal and Julian Agyeman for their excellent and encouraging comments on a draft of this chapter.

Notes

[1] The county (region) of Leicestershire is situated in the East Midlands area of England, and the city of Leicester is approximately 100 miles north of London.

[2] In order to highlight the ambiguous and imaginative 'village' status of the area under review, I use scare quotes when referring to this place as a 'village'.

[3] I use the term 'Asian' in this essay to describe settlers to Leicester from South Asia and South Asians who came to Leicester from the former east African British colonies between 1968 and 1975. I use the term 'black' to refer to settlers from Africa and the Caribbean. I use these terms because they are the ones used by my co-conversationalists. I also use 'Britain' to refer to England, Scotland, Wales and Northern Ireland and 'England' to refer to the English.

[4] Place names outside and within Greenville are fictional.

[5] All residents' names are pseudonyms.

[6] The term Wog is said to be an acronym for Western Oriental Gentleman.

References

Agyeman, J. and Spooner, R. (1997) 'Ethnicity and the rural environment', in P. Cloke and J. Little (eds) *Contested countryside cultures: Otherness, marginalisation and rurality*, London: Routledge, pp 197–217.

Bauman, Z. (1997) 'The making and unmaking of strangers', in P. Werbner and T. Modood (eds) *Debating cultural hybridity: Multi-cultural identities and the politics of anti-racism*, London: Zed Books, pp 46-58.

Billig, M. (1995) *Banal nationalism*, London: Sage Publications.

Blommaert, J. and Verschueren, J. (1998) *Debating diversity: Analysing the discourse of tolerance*, London: Routledge.

Bourdieu, P. (1984) *Distinction: A social critique of the judgement of taste*, trans by R. Nice, Cambridge: Cambridge University Press.

Butler, T. and Robson, G. (2003) 'Negotiating their way in: the middle-classes, gentrification and the deployment of capital in a globalising metropolis', *Urban Studies*, vol 40, no 9, pp 1791-809.

Butler, T. and Savage, M. (eds) (1995) *Social change and the middle-classes*, London: UCL Press.

Cloke, P. and Little, J. (1997) 'Introduction: other countrysides?', in P. Cloke and J. Little (eds) *Contested countryside cultures: Otherness, marginalisation and rurality*, London: Routledge, pp 1-18.

Cloke, P., Phillips, M. and Thrift, N. (1995) 'The new middle-classes and the social constructs of rural living', in T. Butler and M. Savage (eds) *Social change and the middle-classes*, London: UCL Press, pp 220-41.

Cohen, A.P. (2000) 'Peripheral vision: nationalism, national identity and the objective correlative in Scotland', in A.P. Cohen (ed) *Signifying identities: Anthropological perspectives on boundaries and contested values*, London: Routledge, pp 145-69.

Frankenberg, R. (1993) *White women, race matters*, London: Routledge.

Kinsmen, P. (1997) 'Renegotiating the boundaries of race and citizenship: the black environment network and environmental and conservation bodies', in P. Milbourne (ed) *Revealing rural 'others'*, London: Pinter, pp 13-36.

Little, J. and Austin, P. (1996) 'Women and the rural idyll', *Journal of Rural Studies*, vol 12, no 2, pp 101-11.

Murdoch, J. and Marsden, T. (1991) *Reconstructing the rural in an urban region: New villages for old? Countryside Change Working Paper 26*, Newcastle: University of Newcastle.

Neal, S. (2002) 'Rural landscapes, representations and racism: examining multicultural citizenship and policy making in the English countryside', *Ethnic and Racial Studies,* vol 25, no 3, pp 442-61.

Nye, M. (2001) *Multicultural and minority religions in Britain: Krishna consciousness, religious freedom and the politics of location*, Richmond: Curzon Press.

Ortner, S.B. (2002) 'Subjects and capital: a fragment of a documentary ethnography', *Ethnos*, vol 67, no 1, pp 9-32.

Solomos, J. and Back, L. (1995) *Race, politics and social change*, London: Routledge.

Tyler, K. (2003) 'The racialised and classed constitution of English village life', *Ethnos*, vol 68, no 3, pp 391-412.

Vincent, C., Ball, S.J. and Kemp, S. (2004) 'The social geography of childcare: making up a middle-class child', *British Journal of Sociology of Education*, vol 25, no 2, pp 229-44.

Williams, R. (1973) *The country and the city*, London: Hogarth Press.

Wright, P. (1999) 'An encroachment too far', in A. Barnett and R. Scruton (eds) *Town and country*, London: Vintage, pp 18-34.

SIX

New countryside? New country

Visible communities[1] in the English national parks

Kye Askins

The question of identification is never the affirmation of a pre-given identity, never a self-fulfilled prophecy – it is always the production of an 'image' of identity and the transformation of the subject in assuming that image ... identity is never an *a priori*, nor a finished product; it is only ever the problematic process of access to an 'image' of totality. (Bhabha, 1986, pp xvi–xvii)

Introduction

The 2001 census re-confirmed that England *is* a multi-ethnic society. Indeed, there has been much recent debate regarding ethnicity and difference, multiculturalism, cosmopolitanism, hybridity and multiple identities within academia, among policy makers and across the wider public realm in the UK. The Parekh Report (2000), in particular, addresses the complex political and social issues surrounding identity, citizenship, difference, cohesion and equality (see also Alibhai-Brown, 2001; Kundnani, 2001). However, these debates are invariably connected to the urban sphere, while the dominant representation of the English countryside continues to portray a racialised (white) country scene as a symbol of idyllic innocence and, crucially, as repository of a 'true', originary Englishness (Short, 1991; Matless, 1998). That is, the English countryside continues to be interpreted as the 'real' England for 'real' English people, in a construction that appropriates 'real' as 'white', excluding a range of groups from accessing the countryside, both physically and emotionally (Cloke and Little, 1997; Milbourne, 1997). The perceived absence of 'ethnic minorities' in rural spaces – as visitors, residents or in its symbolism – continues to belie the description of English society as multi-ethnic (Agyeman and Spooner, 1997).

There is, then, a substantial gap between the burgeoning discourses of multi-ethnicity, and the 'traditional' institutional representations and social understandings involved with rural public space. Visible communities are often theorised, researched and written as 'rural others', in recognition of the structural inequalities and cultural prejudices that non-white people face in English society, which both constitute and are reinforced by a dominant racialised version of the countryside. This chapter is not intended to challenge the paradigm that calls for greater examination of the racisms affecting visible communities in rural spaces, in the effort to tackle those racisms and the exclusions they sustain. However, I want to come at the issue from another perspective, because there is a danger that if we *only* focus on visible communities *as* 'rural others', we reconstruct people from non-white backgrounds as *always already* marginalised in the countryside. Such categorising denies visible communities' own claims to rural space and national identity. To disrupt the dominant understanding that 'real' Englishness is tied up with a 'rural idyll', and that both are white, involves not just an examination of racism in the countryside, but demands rethinking Englishness itself.

The chapter draws on quantitative and qualitative research concerning visible communities' perceptions and use of the English national parks. Questionnaires were conducted with people from Asian and African-Caribbean backgrounds in Middlesbrough and Sheffield[2] (referred to as the 'urban survey'), which asked about the North York Moors (NYM) and Peak District (PD) national parks specifically, and the wider countryside more generally. Six focus group interviews and 20 individual in-depth interviews with visible communities were undertaken to explore perceptions in more detail.[3] Participant observation during day visits to the national parks, organised for focus group interviewees, allowed the study to test perceptions in context, as did involvement with the Mosaic Project, a three-year initiative co-managed by the Council for National Parks and Black Environment Network, which facilitated residential trips to national parks for visible community groups. A visitor questionnaire survey across the NYM and PD (referred to as the 'visitor survey') was also completed.[4]

The national parks of England and Wales were originally designated under the 1949 National Parks and Access to the Countryside Act. This legislation was the response to pressure from the 1920s onwards, from groups concerned about rural recreation, access and landscape protection (for example, the Ramblers' Association, the Youth Hostel

Association), demanding free access to privately owned rural areas for the general public, in particular the urban-bound working classes. In 1932, a mass trespass on Kinder Scout (an area in the Peak District) was staged to highlight the social exclusion of lower socio-economic groups from the countryside, and in 1945 the Dower Report finally recommended the designation of national parks, which should be 'extensive tracts of beautiful and wild countryside which would provide scope for open air recreation' (Dower, 1945). The national parks currently work to 'twin purposes', adopted in the 1995 Environment Act's review of national parks and wider conservation policy:

- to conserve and enhance the natural beauty, wildlife and cultural heritage of the national parks; and
- to promote opportunities for the understanding and enjoyment of the special qualities of the parks by the public.

The initial proposal for this research arose from concern among national park management that visible communities were absent from the parks, and uncertainty as to how to tackle this issue in terms of their duty to 'promote opportunities' to the public. The study, though, revealed a far higher number of visitors from visible community backgrounds than had been anticipated, and this chapter is an attempt to think through the implications of visible community *presence in* the national parks. The focus, therefore, is on visible communities who *are visiting* the national parks. Those voices speaking of exclusion from a racialised English countryside are missing from this account, but it is important to hold onto the exclusions they describe, as the chapter will implicitly argue throughout.

The chapter is divided into two main sections. The first addresses the concept of resistance, and considers visible community challenges to a mythologised absence in the countryside through both their *presence in* the rural and their *desire to be present*. It also examines the vulnerability of such contestation, and the ways in which power relations enable hegemonic society to limit and recuperate visible community resistance to dominant discourses and practices. In particular, I explore the ways in which entanglements between ethnicity, gender, socio-economic and generational positions affect visible community visitor patterns, and unpack how the construction of stereotypes, based on visual recognition and socialised understandings of (absolute) difference, is caught up in these entanglements.

The second section is concerned with visible community 'claims' to the countryside that go beyond resistance, and focuses on the variety of ways in which rurality may be implicated in, and/or extricated from, national identity formation. The diversity of identifications encountered in the research disrupts any 'easy' reading of attachment and belonging in the English countryside, and points to the need to think identity and belonging *relationally*; to be inclusive of visible communities' heterogeneous positions and perceptions of their 'place' in the countryside, and the countryside's 'place' within national identity. However, I caution that relational understandings must also incorporate the materiality and history of power relationships if they are to be transformative rather than simply descriptive.

Limited/ing resistance

> Essentialised notions of 'blackness' or 'Asianness' ... are imploded through the intervention of alternative or transruptive discourses – the potential for more than a transitory transformation remains, however, uncertain. (Alexander, 2000, pp 145-6)

In the urban survey, a quarter of the questionnaire respondents in Middlesbrough and a third of those in Sheffield stated that they *had visited* the NYM or PD at some time. Additionally, 8% of the visitor survey respondents identified as coming from non-white backgrounds. These statistics are somewhat problematic due to methodological concerns[5] ('8%' almost certainly overestimates the situation), but what both sets of figures show is that visible communities are certainly not absent from the English national parks. The qualitative data also supports visible community presence in the countryside, with over half of the individual interviewees describing personal experiences as repeat visitors to the NYM/PD, for example:

> *S9:* 'I'll go to see a good view and stop and usually there's an elderly couple there and I have a chat with them ... I'll go for a drive just 10 ... 15 minutes and you're there it's so peaceful ... and calm and it relaxes me ... I come back more motivated.' (Individual interview in Sheffield: male, 55-64, Black British)[6]

In addition, one of the focus groups had visited the NYM together prior to taking part in the research:

F2: [talking about bad weather] 'At least we enjoyed it …
it didn't stop us enjoying it.'

F1: ''Cos we like to go in groups don't we? … you know
it's better … it's like more socialising you get together …
you take your food along you have a picnic there … it's
like a day out for …'.

F5: 'We should be going go to the countryside more'
[general chorus of 'yes']. (Focus group in Middlesbrough:
nine females, aged between 25 and 64, variously identified
as British Asian, Pakistani, Pakistani English)

Most notably, socio-economic position emerged as central to
perceptions and use of the national parks. The majority opinion among
respondents to the urban survey was that national parks are middle-
class spaces, an opinion supported throughout the interviews by
statements to the effect that higher socio-economic positions enable
access to the countryside, and lack of money prevents visits:

'I don't go all that often sometimes take my son … we'll
have a drink, buy a souvenir but it's expensive out there
though … and going there too the cost puts you off.' (B1,
individual interview in Middlesbrough: male, 25-34, British
Asian)

The impact of socio-economic position was further evidenced through
visible community visitor patterns, in particular *how and where* people
accessed the rural. Taking the 'how' issue first, it is instructive that
many Mosaic Project participants believed that they would not have
visited the national parks without the intervention of Mosaic, and
discourses concerning lack of opportunity *because of class position* were
prevalent. For example, a women's group visiting the NYM for three
days clearly desired to visit the countryside *'at least three or four times a
year would be good'*, but identified lack of community group funding as
the key barrier, reinforced by the women's low income and lack of
private transport. 'Lack of finance' echoed throughout the research:

S5: 'I get funding for each trip wherever I can … but it, it
really is the biggest problem … we would go do many
more visits to countryside if we could get the money to
take the groups … the lack of money to get transport …

minibuses … that is the only thing stopping us.' (Individual interview in Sheffield: male, 25-34, British Pakistani)

This quote also highlights a common discourse among respondents, namely that visible community visits to national parks are (always) undertaken in large groups. Indeed, extended family/community group trips were generally conceived as either organised by community leaders or facilitated and led by expert bodies (the national parks, Mosaic Project), and visible community trips to the countryside often described not only as requiring grant funding, but also in the context of targeted projects or specific initiatives.

A gentle stroll in a national park

Where people choose to go was also framed in part by economic positions – visible communities tended to visit the periphery rather than venture deeper into a national park. Dovestones, on the fringe of the PD close to Oldham, sees mostly working-class visitors including families and groups of young men from Asian backgrounds, while Bakewell, a 'honeypot' market town near the centre of the PD, receives mostly middle-class white visitors. The *proximity* of Dovestones to the place of residence of substantial Asian communities enables access for those visible communities who identified lower incomes as preventative to going further into the national parks.

In foregrounding a lack of financial means as the main factor limiting trips to national parks, people rarely linked economic position to ethnicity. However, there are two key issues regarding how socio-economic position influences visible communities' access to the countryside. The first is that visible communities are over-represented in the lower classes: 77% of 'ethnic minorities' live in the 88 most deprived wards in the country (Commission for Racial Equality, 2004) – a statistic resulting from structural power inequalities in England, grounded in historical colonial attitudes towards visible (racialised) difference/inferiority (Donald and Rattansi, 1999), and reiterated by the ongoing failure of policies and strategies aimed at improving 'race' equality and relations (Bourne, 2001). Economic barriers to visiting the countryside, therefore, unequally affect people from Asian and African-Caribbean backgrounds.

The second issue is that the impact of socio-economic positions on visiting national parks *does not preclude* the possibility that perceptions of exclusion and a sense of 'otherness' may *also* be involved in visible communities' choice of group size and destination. That is, alongside lack of funds to go in communal groups beyond the periphery of the national parks, an understanding of the rural as unwelcoming may also influence staying closer to spaces of everyday experience, and being among people from similar backgrounds. Moreover, these two issues are interconnected, and suggest that *resistance against* ethnic stereotyping may, at the same time, be limited by the same processes involved in producing those stereotypes in the first place.

Similar issues are raised when exploring generational difference. While national parks' own visitor surveys invariably indicate high numbers of visitors over 65 years old (NYM, 2003), in the urban survey 56% of visible communities in this age group stated that 'lack of interest' inhibited visits above anything else. Tellingly, there were proportionally higher numbers of individuals on lower incomes among the 65-plus visible community respondents than across other age groups, and older participants described having little interaction with society beyond local visible community networks. Support and friendship were drawn through long-term relationships with individuals from similar (often the same) backgrounds, who had arrived in England at roughly the same time and experienced decades of more open racism than their younger relatives; majority opinion among the older respondents was that they would receive a negative reception in rural areas.

Lack of interest in visiting national parks was also clearly evident among 15-24-year-olds in the urban survey.[7] Those who visited the countryside did so to take part in specific activities such as kayaking, archery, canoeing (physical and 'exciting' activities), but not 'just' for a walk or 'to look around the towns'. This echoes the national park experience of young people generally – the late teens and early 20s are often described as 'the missing years' in national park visitor profiles. More pertinently here, younger visible community respondents' perceptions and experiences of reception in the English countryside ranged from racist comments to quite the opposite:

> *F4:* [discussing a recent youth group trip to the NYM] 'There are people there so … it's not, not what I thought like it would be like …'
>
> *Facilitator:* 'What do you think of the people?'
>
> [Everyone talks at once.]
>
> *Facilitator:* [to F3] 'Did you say you think people there are unfriendly or—'
>
> *All:* '—NO'
>
> [The group are very loud and definite about this.]
>
> *F3:* 'They're all nice.'
>
> *F2:* 'Very friendly.'
>
> *F4:* 'Yeah … everyone was nice.'
>
> *All:* 'YEAH'
>
> *F1:* 'It's just that there's just not much facilities, that's why everybody's nice because there's only a few people living there … but if more people lived there it'd become more more unfriendly [as in the city].' (Focus group in Middlesbrough: eight young females aged 13-16, all identified as Pakistani)

For this group of young women, from working-class backgrounds, the rural was synonymous with friendliness *because* of the small numbers of people living there, whereas the city was constructed as unfriendly and hostile. This understanding defies the stereotype of small, close-knit rural communities suspicious of all strangers, especially those most visibly different, commonly described by older visible community participants.

Gendered perspectives resonated across the research too. Despite previous visits and a desire to return, many women described a lack of confidence in their ability to access the countryside independent of wider community organisation and national park input. They explicitly linked this to having limited knowledge of the areas and no experience of organising trips to rural places themselves, but also highlighted safety issues:

> *S3:* 'A lot of people don't have cars I know there are a lot of people that do but ... I mean ... women that might just want to take off for the day with the kids their husbands might have the car and not them so ... but they don't want to use the buses it's too much hassle ... you don't know what's gonna happen I mean it could break down or, or ... there could be trouble.' (Individual interview in Sheffield: female, 25–34, Black British)

This woman was not alone in attaching a degree of fear to being in the countryside, or in outlining a need for specific initiatives/support to enable/encourage her to visit a national park. Among men from Asian and African-Caribbean backgrounds, lack of confidence and safety issues were far more muted, and financial issues highlighted as the predominant barrier to accessing the countryside (as discussed previously). Men also stressed a need to be together within familiar groups, but they placed emphasis on doing what they wanted to do because *they chose to*, not as part of specific projects or initiatives: the key message was one of self-determination. Within such discourses, singular importance was placed upon visiting the rural as a way of reiterating and strengthening (ethnic) group bonds. Gender differences, however, emerged through the study as closely linked to class position: among middle-class visible communities visiting national parks, differences between women and men were far less perceptible, as we shall see later in the chapter. In this way, gender positions are also caught up in the entanglements between class and ethnicity that can serve to limit resistance.

(Dis)placing the stranger

Thinking about the examples offered so far in this chapter, what I want to highlight is the continual push-and-pull between rural presence and limiting factors that was played out through the research. Barnor Hesse's (2000, p 17) conceptualisation of resistance attempts to capture this ongoing interplay between challenge and subjugation. He uses the term 'transruptions' to describe: 'interrogative phenomena that, although related to what is represented as marginal or incidental or insignificant ... nevertheless refuse to be repressed. They resist all attempts to ignore or eliminate them by simply recurring at another time or in another place' (Hesse, 2000, p 17). Visible communities' presence in the national parks can be described as a transruption to the dominant construction of the countryside as a white/racialised space. While actual presence in the rural was often limited by physical and emotional barriers, a refusal to be repressed was evidenced *in* that limited presence as well as in the more constant *desire* to go to the countryside.

Thinking about such transruptions in the context of this research, it is necessary to address the 'visibility' of non-white people in rural England. Sara Ahmed's understanding of 'the stranger' is useful here. Ahmed (2000) writes that 'we' actually recognise 'the stranger' not as someone unknown to us, but as already constructed *as different*. That is, people unknown but recognised as the same as 'us' go unnoticed, but someone recognised as unknown *but different* is always identified as a stranger. Such identifications are tied up with the history of previous encounters/experiences between 'us' and 'them' attached to this moment of recognition. Moreover, they are entangled within socialised understandings of the previous encounters between 'our' group and that of the stranger. Crucially, stranger stereotypes incorporate ideas of potential threat, but it is through unequal power structures and notions of territorial ownership that these constructions lead to social exclusion based on visible difference.

With this in mind, Ahmed goes on to question the assumption that we can have an ontology of strangers: that it is possible for anyone to be a stranger (unknown), because strangers *are presumed known* via the social construction of stereotypes. She argues that such productions of difference should be theorised through: 'thinking about the role of everyday encounters in the forming of social space ... Such differences are not then to be found *on the bodies of others*, but are determined through encounters between others; they are impossible to grasp in the present' (Ahmed, 2000, p 9, original emphasis). Ahmed's concept of 'the stranger' as always already socially produced foregrounds the historicity and materiality of social relations embedded in the imagery of stereotypes, moving us beyond simplistic notions of visible difference. To accept the figure of the stranger as simply present conceals the antagonistic social relations that produce the stranger as a figure in the first place, and how 'the stranger' comes into being through the 'marking out' of space, bodies and 'terrains of knowledge'. (Re)cognition cannot be based on the very present encounter, then, but on perceptions built up over time as to who has the authority to be in a particular space.

Thinking visible communities as 'rural others' attempts to take into account the relationships of social antagonism between white and non-white people in the English countryside, and as a political signifier retains its potency. But it also risks a focus on difference that reproduces boundaries. The irony is that emphasis on otherness may normalise a homogenised majority, even while trying to destabilise that majority: the very act of naming *as* 'other' can return visible communities to marginalised positions and perpetuate power imbalances. 'Visible communities' is an attempt to encapsulate the social antagonisms Ahmed describes without privileging the idea of *minoritised* otherness, though it can be argued that the focus on visibility traps this term in the same paradox. To deconstruct this 'always already' othering, then, we need to rethink the recognition of others in ways that shift emphasis away from the majority/minority binary. The examination of 'whiteness' is crucial in this project (see hooks, 1992; Bonnett, 2000; Ware and Back, 2002 – and other chapters in this book). However, interrogating heterogeneity within the 'white' ethnic category must be alongside consideration of differences within visible community categories, if we are to work towards more equal recognitions.

Returning to the idea of transruptions, foregrounding the socialised histories of encounters between 'others', and the power relations involved, helps us to think through the issues caught up in limited/ ing resistance more carefully. As Ahmed warns: 'There is a failure to theorize, not the potential for any system to become destabilized, but the means by which relations of power are secured, paradoxically, *through this very process of destabilization*' (1999, p 89, original emphasis). She reminds us that differences that threaten the 'system' may be recuperated by the hegemony to retain its position, since it has the power to do so. This power allows it to understand and promote transruptions *as displacement from social norms*, reclaiming the tactics of resistance within a structured ontology – often designating them as negative outcomes of social change. Thus examining strategies of resistance must also address the 'complex social and psychic mechanisms for dealing with such tactics' (Ahmed, 1999, p 90), in order to better understand and dismantle processes of social and spatial exclusion. Three key recuperation tactics are briefly considered here.

First, the *ongoing denial of visible community presence* in the rural, by a majority of countryside agencies and in the dominant public psyche, is one such tactic. Media representations, for example, consistently reiterate 'ethnic minorities' as missing from the rural environment (*Guardian*, 2004; Radio 4, 2004). Second, visible community individuals who visit the countryside are perceived as *not 'normal'* within 'their' ethnic group, and their actions as differing from majority visible community practices. As exceptions to the rule, their challenge can be brushed aside: if a visible community 'norm' remains different to the white majority, visible communities remain outsiders in the countryside, and not 'really' English. This discourse was common among white respondents in the visitor survey, but also among many visible community interviewees:

> *S4:* 'No nah it certainly, black families and that type of thing [going to the countryside] ... it's unheard of ... but it's national park stuff and all that type of stuff potholing and all that type ... it's not what black people do.' (Individual interview in Sheffield: female, 35-44, Black British)

> *S8:* 'In my experience I've seen a black guy or a black woman with a rucksack rigged up for walking me I just looked twice [...] because you know black folks and rucksacks aren't ... and a sleeping bag and all the rest of it

Enjoying activities in the countryside

AIN'T what we DO [laughs] ... but in fact I've done it.'
(Individual interview in Sheffield: male, 35-44, Black
British)

Third, emphasis on the *actions* of visible communities *as different from social 'norms'* is employed to imply different behaviour *as* absolute ethnic difference. The stereotype of visible community absence from the countryside shifts to describe visible communities who are present as *behaving differently*: only visiting in large extended family groups, not wearing 'appropriate' (read 'normal') clothing for walking, and so on. This production retains visible communities as essentially different through contrasting the behaviours of white and non-white groups, maintaining the power-laden binary and, in eliding *action* with *the body*, re-inscribing difference as ontological fact.

I have so far explored some of the ways in which visible communities *contest* being positioned as 'rural others', but also how interconnections between ethnicity, gender, age and particularly class can serve to *limit* presence in the rural. In an ongoing interplay between challenge and suppression, transruptions continue to challenge hegemonic beliefs, especially in terms of the desire to visit the countryside, but remain caught in the dominant–minority binary. However, the transruptive was also surpassed, and it is to more transformative issues that we now turn.

Claiming the countryside/claiming the country

Across the quantitative and qualitative research, some visible communities claimed the English countryside through constructions of place and identity that denied the recuperation of presence in the rural as marginal. Beyond limited resistance, these actions/accounts destabilised the 'white rural' myth by claiming identifications with Englishness that were connected to being in, and being comfortable in, rural space. This is *not* to say that the rural was automatically, therefore, considered central to national identity, or nationality personified through the rural: connections between nation, ethnicity and rurality were complex and shifting, and visible community claims to Englishness and/or the English countryside context- and person-specific.

As outlined previously, socio-economic position was a key factor underlying people's ability to visit national parks (regularly). Middle-class identities were generally open and fluid, and cultural practices similarly hybrid and multiple. These practices included 'traditional' activities associated with particular ethnic groups, as well as incorporating not-connected-with-ethnicity occupations. Within interview discourses, the latter practices were ostensibly framed around knowledge issues, the privilege of having time for leisure, access to private transport and disposable income. In the following quote, the practice of rural recreation as prevalent among professional work colleagues is described:

> *S7:* [talking about being non-white in the countryside] 'So I feel comfortable yeah but something that I'm very aware of ... and what I notice is that you know a hell of a lot of social workers in the countryside [laughs] ... you know it seems to be a really specific group of people ... and like on Sunday in Grindleford you go there and you just meet so many people that you know [laughs] ... so I think sort of it is it can be very one dimensional, you know, the people that go out into the countryside ... very middle class.' (Individual interview in Sheffield: female, 25-34, mixed race (white and African Caribbean) English)

This woman experienced the rural as a place for specific groups, 'very one-dimensional', but the principal frame of reference was class rather than ethnicity. She believed that her position as middle class had the greatest influence on her day-to-day life and practices, and her claim to belonging in the Peaks was centred on feeling part of English society through her work, her engagement in the local community where she lived and a 'diverse social life'. Moreover, she did not consider her position as *being against the 'norm'* for visible communities, but understood visible communities to be represented across all classes and other social positions.

Similarly, another interviewee explained that she did not perceive herself to be marginalised in the countryside in any way. This second woman identified as English and was a regular visitor to national parks with her husband and children *because* the rural was a central component of their English identity, and countryside recreation was part of her family's cultural practice. At the same time, her Indian ethnicity and Sikh religion were also important to her self-identity. Her sense of belonging in the English countryside was attached to a secure identity that was nevertheless plural and fluid – moreover, this identity was secure because its pluralism and fluidity stemmed from a middle-class position that distanced her from dualistic constructions of self as marginalised by a dominant other.

Numerous other examples of the rural as inherent within

constructions of (their) Englishness point to the evolving nature of visible community identity in England. However, the majority of visible communities who visited the countryside understood and related to their English identity via a different set of values. Consider a situation observed during a Mosaic Project visit to the PD. A group of six young men from Asian backgrounds, aged between 15 and 19, were crossing a road, when a passing car slowed down and the three young white male occupants shouted 'Pakis go home!' in a threatening way. The visible community young men, whose parents had all moved to England from India, responded by smiling and shouting back 'Yes we are!' and 'We are home!' in an affirmative, non-aggressive manner. In doing so, the group were claiming the space they were in, both countryside and country. In addition, they were subverting the very act of naming: they identified themselves as Indian, British, English and Asian, and various configurations of these depending on context, but rather than challenging the term 'Paki', they claimed their visible difference as positive identity, *intertwined with their Englishness*, refusing to be marginalised.

For these young men, their ethnicity was folded through their nationality. In later discussion, the group articulated their sense of belonging in the countryside via a rights-based discourse ('we are English therefore we have the right to be in all English space'). This was combined with attachment to, and a sense of being comfortable

Family outing

in, the rural, fostered through regular trips to the national parks as part of family life, but they did not consider English rurality as inherent to their national identity. The latter was rarely singular and highly ambivalent, with country of birth and ethnic background the main factors in ongoing negotiations with nationality.

Throughout the interviews, 'being English' was most commonly connected to being born and growing up in England, followed by claims to national identity through ownership of a British passport:

> *Facilitator:* 'How do you identify your nationality?'

> *S8:* '… um … for me I was actually born here … now my home is here and it's all I know … I'm not sure how to answer that … no it's being … born here really, it's on my passport that's it [laughs].' (Individual interview in Sheffield: male, 35–44, Black British)

This man believed that white English people hold the countryside to be important as part of their national identity, but he did not 'engage with it in that way', nor did he perceive that his cultural practices had anything in common with 'your average English culture'. As a consistent visitor to the countryside, though, he identified closely with what he described as the 'spirituality' of rural environments. He was also open to the possibility that his opinions might change over time as he reassesses his identity:

> *S8:* 'Um and I think even me calling myself Black British you know that that's only happened in the last five years really … I mean it's been a transition really from um … West Indian … to Afro Caribbean to now I feel quite comfortable with Black British … but it's not happened overnight it's been a 20-year journey, 23-year journey … and it, it isn't over.' (Individual interview in Sheffield: male, 35–44, Black British)

While constructions of national identity drew heavily on discourses that featured birth and experiences of growing up in England, specific *values* were also important to how visible communities envisaged English nationality, and these values were embedded in the political and human rights realms rather than in any physical place.[8] Most notably, ideas surrounding freedom of speech and movement, and liberty and choice, were key to what English identity represented. In addition, safety (from crime and health risks) and security (in terms of a stable future) were listed as valuable components of Englishness, together with access to a state education system and health services, and a diverse employment sector. Furthermore, for those (predominantly middle-class) visible communities that identified with Englishness in the ways described here, the construction of the countryside as inherent to (white) Englishness was *not* an emotional barrier to visiting national parks, because it was irrelevant:

> *B2:* 'Feeling this sense of attachment ... belonging or not isn't the issue ... no being SEEN to belong isn't even the issue ... if I want to go there [the countryside] I go there for the reasons I go there for ... belonging doesn't come into it.' (Individual interview in Middlesbrough: female, 35–44, British Indian)

Alternatively, the importance of rurality within nationality was stressed as cross-national and cross-cultural. One participant, citing the 'tradition' of the rural in imaginations of Chinese nationality, queried the production of the countryside as *only* inherent to Englishness, and highlighted a commonality between constructions of English and other national identities. Indeed, the importance of countryside to many participants was discussed through notions of Indian, West Indian, Pakistani and Ghanian identities, for example. This allowed individuals to develop attachment to the English countryside via connections between one rural landscape and another, and research participants discussed visiting places that reminded them of countries of (parental) origin. The Lake District and Peak District, in particular, were often linked to both the Himalayan foothills and the Blue Mountains in Jamaica. Such links went beyond the visual sense, too, with people describing sounds and smells as indicative of other places.

Yet another perspective questioned the importance of the countryside within dominant perceptions of English national identity itself:

> *B7:* 'I think the English don't have any value for the countryside ... they only talk of it if ... they talk of lots of things like Americans talk about apple pies and family but they have no family or apple pies all they have is McDonald's ... similarly I think the English use ... countryside ... queen, these things when they are in when it suits them ... but most of the time I've never seen half the English I've met who live in the town never have been to the country ... but it's a nice myth of the past ... it's handy you know

> like I would say Taj Mahal or something but I'm not bothered about the Taj Mahal ... you know I think it's more a nostalgic thing the countryside ... it's always there in the back you pick it up to show you're English.' (Individual interview in Middlesbrough: female, 45-54, Indian)

This woman's claims to the countryside were through her love of nature and being in natural surroundings, she regularly walked in the NYM, and described a sense of belonging there and attachment to the area. She believed that the rural is a symbol wheeled out only when nationality needs to be explained, but has lost its relevance in modern-day England: a tactical device to denote a national identity that it is easier to leave unexamined.

Towards new imaginations: national identity and the rural

What this chapter can only briefly highlight is the wide diversity among visible communities encountered in the research, regarding the ways in which the rural is (not) imagined in constructions of Englishness, drawing upon different heritages, experiences, cultural values and social positions. As such, it is not possible to correlate attachment to the English countryside, or a sense of belonging in the rural, with identification with Englishness – neither is Englishness itself a singular or fixed construct. This suggests the need to rethink ethnic and national identity/ies, and re-examine different models of constructing/seeing selves and strangers. Here I want to draw specifically on the work of Elspeth Probyn, whose central argument regarding how we think about space, belonging and identities is:

> that the outside ... is a more adequate figure for thinking about social relations and the social than either an interior/ exterior or a center/marginal model. The notion of outside supposes that we think in terms of 'relations of proximity', or the surface, 'a network in which each point is distinct ... and has a position in relation to every other point in a space that simultaneously holds and separates them all'. (Probyn, 1996, p 11: citing Foucault, 1987, p 12)

She poses the term 'outside belonging' *against* categorising tendencies, and to incorporate the movement that the *wish to belong* carries: 'to consider more closely the movement of and between categories'

(Probyn, 1996, p 9). Working at the level of *desire to* belong sidesteps the 'actualities' of belonging or not, or being seen to belong or not, and works against constructions of identity as fixed within an ontology of the visual given. Desire proposes the notion of a continual *becoming* of identity, rather than static identification. This model is helpful in theorising the complex and various claims to the English countryside and Englishness made by visible communities, and, in holding white communities' identifications and becomings on the same surface, it enables us to displace the dualistic 'norm'/'stranger' construction.[9]

It can be argued that theorising the social as a surface, in terms of an outside, leads to a relational model that does not allow for any recognition of the structural inequalities that do violence to 'minority' groups, consideration of power struggles, or acknowledgement of the oppression that constantly threatens agency. However, my aim here is *not* to sweep these issues aside, but to contend that these inequalities must be *held in tension* with a new way of looking that tries to realign the power geometries. Probyn (1996, p 12, original emphasis) writes that this can only be done if the surface is understood, *not* as an object, but as a *process*: 'as a way of configuring the lines of force that compose the social, lines of force that are by their very nature *deeply* material and historical'.

Thinking relational identities and becoming as a process opens up the possibility of unpacking 'the stranger' by moving away from bodily recognition, while at the same time holding the central role of visual recognition in identification, and the exclusionary processes it is implicated in, in this surface too. 'Outside belongings' allows for a project of Englishness always in construction, fluid and negotiable, that draws on people's own conceptions of and desires to identity – without ignoring

This land is our land

that those identities exist politically as well as personally. It suggests that the rural can continue to play a role in national identity construction and becoming, not as an exclusionary phenomenon but alongside (on the outside with) various imaginations of Englishness.

I want to restate here that visible community voices speaking of racialised exclusion from the English countryside were present in the research, and there is a need to interrogate processes of exclusion and racism in rural areas, and examine how 'rural others' are (re)produced, in order to disrupt those very productions. But there is also a need to disrupt the construction of visible communities as 'others' in the countryside, and to envisage use and imaginations of national parks and rural space – by visible communities and white communities – in ways that circumvent any allusion to a 'norm'.

This chapter has been suggesting that there are ways of being in the countryside that refuse an objectifying gaze, and inscribe desires and identities that refute dominant presumptions and stereotypes. In rejecting an ontology of the 'other' as recognisable in the present, we are forced to consider historical social relations between groups (and across space) as inherent in the structuring of hegemony, and in its ability to recuperate resistance against it. Thinking identity and belonging as becoming (as desire to become) in a more relational way – crucially *together with* the processes of dominance that impact on these identifications and desires – offers a way of disrupting ingrained positions, and may move us closer towards renegotiating social relations. As the Parekh Report (2000, p 8) clearly states, a genuinely multi-ethnic England needs to re-imagine itself: 'The key issue ... is one of English identity and how previous conceptions of English identity have excluded so many people who live in and richly contribute to English society.'

Exclusion from rural space may be equated with an entrenched dominant Imaginary that constructs Englishness as implicit in a racialised rurality. Addressing such exclusion requires English society to rethink and redefine its *identity as a nation in inclusive ways*, allowing for multi-ethnic and multicultural belongings that incorporate diverse visible communities alongside diverse white communities. The research points to the multiple, hybrid and fluid ways in which visible communities recognise themselves as English, and the variety of connections through which they construct a sense of belonging in and attachment to the English countryside. *Englishness* must be recognised as *not only white*, if the entrenched Imaginary is to lose its relevance: 'As the writer Andrea Levy says: "If Englishness doesn't define me, redefine Englishness"' (Alibhai-Brown, 2001, p 258).

Acknowledgements

First and foremost, I thank all those individuals who gave their time and energy to participate in the research. I am also grateful to Rachel Pain and the editors for their constructive and supportive comments on an earlier draft of this chapter. The research was funded through an ESRC CASE PhD studentship, award no. S42200034003, with the NYM as CASE partners.

Notes

[1] Terminology: I use the term 'visible communities' (after Alibhai-Brown, 2001) to describe people of Asian, African and Caribbean backgrounds. This is to avoid the homogenising tendencies of the term 'black' (Modood, 1992) and the power-laden term 'minority'. It is not intended to reify or fetishise physicality/phenotype, nor to deny the power inequalities endemic in English society, but is used as a political signifier to highlight that these inequalities are commonly grounded in perceptions of inferiority/threat attached to visible difference from a white 'norm'.

[2] This part of the research involved 310 respondents in Middlesbrough, 296 in Sheffield.

[3] The interviews were equally divided between Middlesbrough and Sheffield.

[4] For this part of the methodology, 295 questionnaires were completed in the NYM, 300 in the PD.

[5] In brief, 'random sampling' was skewed by potential respondents' dis/interest in the survey themes: many white visitors declined to participate in the survey, while the majority of visible community visitors approached agreed to take part.

[6] Interviewees were asked to 'tick boxes' regarding gender and age, but to describe their identity without a list of choices in front of them. They are represented in the chapter by letters/numbers attached during analysis to ensure anonymity.

[7] 52% in this age bracket stated lack of interest as the main reason that they did not visit national parks; 29% identified lack of knowledge of the parks as key barrier.

[8] That is, cities were not simply substituted for countryside as emblematic of Englishness.

[9] Furthermore, the acceptance of no desire to becoming a certain identity (or being in a certain place) can be incorporated in this outside. This opens up the possibility of not wanting to be in the rural through personal choice, rather than absence as always already reduced to exclusionary processes and practices.

References

Agyeman, J. and Spooner, R. (1997) 'Ethnicity and the rural environment', in P. Cloke and J. Little (eds) *Contested countryside cultures: Otherness, marginalization and rurality*, London: Routledge, pp 197–217.

Ahmed, S. (1999) '"She'll wake up one of these days and find she's turned into a Nigger": passing through hybridity', *Theory, Culture & Society*, vol 16, no 2, pp 87–106.

Ahmed, S. (2000) *Strange encounters: Embodied others in post-coloniality*, London: Routledge.

Alexander, C. (2000) '(Dis)entangling the "Asian gang": ethnicity, identity, masculinity', in B. Hesse (ed) *Un/settled multiculturalisms: Diasporas, entanglements, transruptions*, London: Zed Books, pp 123–47.

Alibhai-Brown, Y. (2001) *Mixed feelings: The complex lives of mixed-race Britons*, London: The Women's Press.

Bhabha, H.K. (1986) 'The Other question', in F. Barker, *Literature, politics and theory*, London, Methuen, pp iii–xviii.

Bonnett, A. (2000) *White identities: Historical and international perspectives*, London: Pearson.

Bourne, J. (2001) 'The life and times of institutional racism', *Race & Class*, vol 43, no 2, pp 7–22.

Brah, A., Hickman, M.J. and Mac an Ghaill, M. (eds) (1999) *Thinking identities: Ethnicity, racism and culture*, Hampshire, Macmillan.

Cloke, P. and Little, J. (eds) (1997) *Contested countryside cultures: Otherness, marginalization and rurality*, London: Routledge.

Commission for Racial Equality (2004) (www.cre.gov.uk, accessed 12 April 2004).

Donald, J. and Rattansi, A. (eds) (1999) *'Race', culture and difference*, London: Sage Publications.

Dower, J. (1945) *National parks in England and Wales*, Cmnd 6628, London: HMSO.

Foucault, M. (1987) *Maurice Blanchot: The thought from the outside*, trs B. Massuni, New York, NY: Zone Books.

Guardian (2004) 'Countryside retreat', 28 January 2004.

Hesse, B. (ed) (2000) *Un/settled multiculturalisms: Diasporas, entanglements, transruptions*, London: Zed Books.

hooks, b. (1992) *Black looks*, Boston: Southend Press.

Kundnani, A. (2001) 'In a foreign land: the new popular racism', *Race & Class*, vol 43, no 2, pp 41-60.

Matless, D. (1998) *Landscape and Englishness*, London: Reaktion Books.

Milbourne, P. (ed) (1997) *Revealing rural others: Representation, power and identity in the British countryside*, London: Pinter.

Modood, T. (1992) *Not easy being British: Colour, culture and citizenship*, Stoke-on-Trent: Runnymede Trust and Trentham Books.

NYM (2003) 'Social inclusion: a special report from the 2003 National Park Society Conference', *Voice of the Moors*, vol 74, no 2, pp 9 17.

Parekh Report (2000) *The future of multi-ethnic Britain*, London: Profile Books.

Probyn, E. (1996) *Outside belongings*, London: Routledge.

Radio 4 (2004) *You and Yours*, broadcast 21 April 2004.

Short, J.R. (1991) *Imagined country: Society, culture and environment*, London: Routledge.

Ware, V. and Back, L. (2002) *Out of whiteness: Color, politics, and culture*, London: University of Chicago Press.

SEVEN

Visions of England

New Age Travellers and the idea of ethnicity

Kevin Hetherington

Introduction

This chapter consists of reprinted material from Kevin Hetherington's book *New Age travellers, vanloads of uproarious humanity* (2000).[1] Drawn from two chapters, the edited extracts presented here scrutinise the particular formations of New Age Traveller identities in Britain in the 1980s and 1990s. Hetherington examines the processes of these identity constructions and in doing so reveals how notions of ethnicity, class and rurality are redrawn and intersect to produce a very different narrative of belonging to, and desiring to be in, rural spaces. It is a narrative that incorporates processes of bricolage and performativity and privileges the countryside as the terrain in which these take place. However, in this narrative the countryside is more than simply the place in which composites of identities are rejected and remade. The countryside is itself at the heart of the identity-formation process. But this is not a countryside that corresponds with the dominant, (secondspace) rural imaginary. Rather it is a countryside that is interpreted as a space of freedom and resistance.

Authenticity, ethnicity and identity

In fixing a sense of self-recognition, belonging and membership, identities are about trying to simplify what is often a much more complex set of relations. Identities are never singular. More often they contain a mix of different identity positions that have developed a sense of unity over time (Hall, 1990, 1992, 1996). New Age Travellers are no exception. When they form their identity they do so by identifying with a series of other identities, some of which they see in a positive way and others more negatively. The choice of identities with which they associate themselves is not, however, a random one. Their identity can be seen as hybrid, similar to a collage in appearance, but one that is organised around an identification with others who have in some way come to be associated with the ideas of authenticity and marginality. In particular, Travellers adopt an identity that brings together a series of disparate 'ethnic' identities that share one thing in common: their marginalised and often oppressed status within society.

An important source of identity for Travellers is that associated with nomadism; in particular they draw on identities linked with what they perceive to be a traditional Gypsy way of life (Okely, 1983). Given the significance of living on the road to their lifestyle, how Gypsies look, how they dress, the types of dwelling they live in, the history and the myths associated with being a Gypsy or a tinker or a wanderer are all used as borrowed sources when Travellers live out their own identities. While there may well be respect for earlier forms of nomadism, this is not the only source, and it is not adopted in a complete way. Added to it are other sources. One in particular has to do with an approach to nature. Many Travellers have a strong awareness of environmental issues and adopt what can be described as a 'Deep Green' attitude of living on the land. Native peoples, especially certain First Nation Americans, are seen as an example of a people who have such a reverence for the earth and are then taken as a source of inspiration. Another can be seen in the nomadism of other traditional cultures. A further nomadic influence, while not of an ethnic kind, is the circus. Circus entertainers and showmen are traditionally nomadic and have a very distinctive style associated with their kind of theatre. Many Travellers draw on this too.

Nomadism, however, is not the only source in the shaping of this identity. The strong links with youth sub-culture, first the hippies of the 1960s, then the punks and Rastafarian styles of the 1970s and more recently with the rave culture of the 1990s have all left their mark on the outlook, attitudes and style that Travellers adopt when trying to create a sense of who they are (McKay, 1996). These influences are brought together in varying compositions to create a set of tribal identifications out of which an individual sense of what it is to be a Traveller can emerge.

New Age Travellers are not, therefore, a distinct group with a single identity. The issue of ethnic identity is not, however, insignificant. The nature of this lifestyle and the related process of identification is highly eclectic, creating what we might see as an elective and pastiche ethnicity, drawing on sources as diverse as youth cultures, Eastern mysticism, Native American traditions, environmental and pacifist beliefs, identification with the communalism of the Diggers and Levellers during the English Civil War, Gypsy lifestyles, commune living, the medieval mountebank and circus entertainers, stylistic elements from Rastafarianism such as dreadlocks, Celtic paganism, Arthurian legends of Avalonia and earth mysteries beliefs. Of course, not all of these can be described as ethnic identities. Rather, they are the sources out of which a new, achieved ethnic identification is created. The main characteristic of such a series of 'tribal' influences is the syncretist way in which they are fused together to create a series of elements that make up recognisable identities that are then attributed an ethnic status.

The body plays a particularly important part in this process of identity making. The body of the Traveller is one that is represented as marginal. In many cases, Travellers adopt a style for the body that can be described in one of two ways: as 'authentic' or alternatively as 'grotesque'. In the first case, such a Traveller will commonly wear brightly coloured clothes drawn from a variety of sources that would again include orientalised influences, a romanticised image of traditional Gypsy styles of dress and images from the circus. Such a bodily means of identification might also be expressed through various so-called 'ethnic' styles of clothing and jewellery, along with New Age accoutrements such as talismans and crystals, expressing a concern with spiritual healing and bodily well-being. Tattooing, especially the use of Celtic designs, will also be common among both men and women. There is here a strong identification with the dispossessed and marginal peoples of the world and their cultures.

The other type of embodiment is one that is associated with a cultural tradition known as the grotesque (Bakhtin, 1984). This style of embodiment can be associated with the image of dirtiness and can be summed up by the idea of an embodied style that seeks to express a culture of resistance through dirt. It should be stressed, however, that, contrary to popular belief, not all Travellers dress in dirt. For some the alternative is an embodied attempt to express a culture of authenticity. For others, the so-called 'tinker tan' is nothing more than a sign of the general practicalities of life on the road without immediately available washing facilities, which means that one will inevitably get dirty. But for those who adopt a grotesque body and make it central to their identity, a group generally known as crustics, dirt is a positive means of tribal identification. As one Traveller told me,

> 'Some of the young crusty types have obviously gone to lots of trouble to look as dirty as they do. I mean, I could not change my clothes and not wash for a year and I still

> wouldn't look like that ... They've obviously studied it. It's
> an image, it's cultivated, cultivated crustiness.' (Interview)

In taking an anti-aesthetic to extremes, such Travellers, or crusties, are likely to dress in old combat fatigues, boots and perhaps have long, matted, dreadlocks. Body piercing, henna-dyed hair and tattoos are also increasingly used by Travellers. This grotesque style can be interpreted as an embodied expression of opposition that signifies a rejection of all that is associated with conventional ways of living. Marginal identities like those assumed by many Travellers, it is suggested, are in part produced by the adoption of a marginal embodiment, one that is outside conventional standards, as is shown through the associations with either the circus or dirt, both of which, of course, are central to the idea of the carnivalesque (Bakhtin, 1984, ch 5).

The embodied identities that are produced can be described as eclectic 'monstrosities'. This involves the mixing of genres and inversions of the high/low hierarchy of the body within the carnivalesque. This process of identity transformation is one that requires the use of the body in ways that are in some way out of place, 'excessive' or which challenge social norms. Through such forms of embodiment and identity, Travellers find a way of ordering their social world. This ordering conveys social messages about the position of this person within a terrain of conflict: that between rejected centrality and affirmed marginality. We have two body representations here but they both play with the same themes: carnival, grotesque, freedom, dispossession, and a nomadic culture of travel. Such an identity is all about change. It is about getting rid of a previous identity and of assuming a new one under such conditions that are associated with the Traveller lifestyle. It is all about becoming someone different. Such a move is made by adopting extreme shifts away from the social norm.

Uncertainty, ethnicity and identity

I describe Travellers as blank figures in the English countryside (Hetherington, 2000). At one time they were an unknown group who were underdetermined within the categories of identity that we associate with English rural life. Their identity was seen as dangerously different, not because it was other in the sense of being the antithesis of all that Englishness or even Britishness stood for, but because it was visibly hybrid and uncertain; a made-up identity that claimed authentic ethnic status for itself. That underdetermination helped to create conditions in which Travellers could be seen as folk devils or scapegoats, and between 1985 and 1986 at least, their convoy formed the focus of a moral panic that was partly resolved by the introduction of clauses to criminalise their way of life in the 1986 Public Order Act, a process that was continued with the 1994 Criminal Justice Act. The response to the underdetermined is often some form of overdetermination and part of that process is simplification. To name is to simplify. It is to try and define a group as deviant and to subject that group to social control (Becker, 1964). Despite the attempts to label Travellers, they have always seemed able to evade elements of that labelling and to retain a degree of uncertainty that allows them, in the very nature of their identities, to give others *the slip*. This is something that can be seen in local council responses to Travellers and the problems they have with identification, labelling and in making identities stick.

During the course of my fieldwork among Travellers, I contacted a county council in southern England and asked to interview a representative about their experiences with New Age Travellers. This was a county that had seen some of the most significant and widely reported conflicts with Travellers. My initial letter had been addressed to the 'press and public relations officer' at the council. I did not know whether such a post existed but it seemed a reasonable assumption to make at the time as an appropriate office with whom to make initial contact. After a short while I received a reply from the chief public health officer at the council, who informed me that he dealt with 'Gypsy matters' and that he was happy to be interviewed on the subject of New Age Travellers.

It became apparent during the course of the interview that the council adopted a different policy towards New Age Travellers as compared with other Travellers such as Gypsies. Gypsies were provided with sites and facilities under the rules then in existence that were set out in the 1968 Caravan Act. In particular, the council was obliged to provide them with sites where they could live in their caravans as well as basic toilet, water and sewerage facilities. New Age Travellers, however, were excluded from this provision within this county. County council policy was to evict them wherever possible and to have them escorted, under police supervision, out of the county and into a neighbouring one. I asked why there was this different attitude towards Gypsies and Travellers. The answer was not that Travellers caused trouble whereas Gypsies did not but rather that Gypsies were true nomads who had a culture based around travel, whereas Travellers were not true nomads but interlopers on the Gypsy lifestyle. True nomads here implied that they had been living this way of life for 'a long time' and that their way of life had an authenticity to it that was grounded in some sense of ethnic origin by birth. They were seen to be on the road for legitimate reasons and not out of choice in the way that Travellers were perceived to be. A 'long time' was defined in council policy at the time as more than five years.

No doubt when this policy was first adopted in the 1980s it was effective in being used to exclude those who had just begun life on the road as Travellers. The problem, however, was that by 1992, when this interview was conducted, there were New Age Travellers who had been on the road for more than five years. Indeed, some had children who had been born into this way of life and had not known any other. I asked if this made a difference as to whether they were allowed to stay in the county, and was told that it did not. The way that the council overcame this problem was simple. When the council was unable to apply its five-year rule, it decided to remove people on the basis of whether they *looked* like Travellers or like Gypsies. It was their appearance and their lifestyles that determined whether or not they were allowed to stay; they were taken as signs of either an authentic and legitimate travelling status or a bogus one.

Under law, then, the council had to provide facilities for Gypsies. In order to meet the required provision for *real* Gypsies it used criteria to try and judge ethnic origin and legitimacy. For people who were known to be Gypsies or who were born to Gypsy families this was not a problem, for they were deemed to be Travellers by ethnicity. Those who looked like New Age Travellers, or who led a New Age lifestyle, were deemed not to be authentic nomads; they were there by choice rather than birth. For Traveller children this did not matter either; they had been born into something inauthentic rather than ethnic and were therefore not a vehicle for a family to describe themselves as legitimate Travellers.

Clearly, then, naming and being able to visually determine a person's ethnicity were the means by which the council set out to determine who was entitled to provision under the law. The council used this means to try to establish fixed categories such as duration of time on the road as signs of a particular identity. This is not uncommon. We all judge by appearances. Indeed, appearances tell us a good deal if we know how to decode the way signs are used in dress (Sennett, 1986). But such judgements can also be used in spurious ways as a source of discrimination, even as an attempt to justify it. When anomalies occurred, as they were beginning to do by 1992, those names and categories no longer fixed things in the required manner. Under those circumstances the council had to fall back on judgements based on perception, intuition and some past experience. The main issue for the council was not just that it did not want New Age Travellers in its county but that the boundaries as to how one defined a New Age Traveller were slippery and changing, both as time and routine meant that this started to become an established way of life and also as fashions and styles changed. The council started down the route of formal classification and identification, but when that did not work it went on appearance, hunches and guesswork instead.

To understand what is meant by the term New Age Traveller as an identity rather than simply a lifestyle it is necessary to consider the hybrid, slippery and underdetermined attributes that constitute this way of being seen both by oneself and by others. Key to the Traveller identity is a relationship between perceptions of what is authentic and what is inauthentic. These judgements can be loosely mapped on to a relationship between the idea of ethnicity and the idea of class. This relationship between ethnic identity and authenticity is not only an issue for local councils, it is also central to the way that many New Age Travellers address the issue of identity. That identity, as this example suggests, is a contested, uncertain and slippery one. In the eyes of many – including county councils, the police, government and the media – Travellers are not authentic. Their identity lacks a grounding in what is perceived to be the real grounds for a nomadic identity: ethnic status determined by kinship over a long period of time. Instead, they are seen as illegitimate frauds whose identity has no ground in any of the constituent parts of ethnicity: kinship, locality, religious affiliation, shared cultural tradition or any other source that provides a commonsense understanding of what ethnicity is all about.

It should be noted that a recognition in commonsense understanding of ethnicity as authentic does not stop discrimination, as many Gypsies and other ethnic minority members find to their cost on a daily basis. However, it is their culture and their ethnic status, seen as real, that are often discriminated against rather than their claims to an ethnicity as such. Indeed, racism relies on categories of identity that are seen as real or essential in order for such discrimination to take place at all. Fears of miscegenation, cultural hybridity and change rely, in the minds of racists, on the idea that the authentic and essential character of an identity is under threat from some alien source that is equally essential but at the same time the expression of all that is Other and different (Said, 1991; Hall, 1992, 1996).

New Age Travellers are a source of anxiety for many people because of the alien character of their lifestyles and their look, but they are not seen as an authentic ethnic Other against which to discriminate. The fear and hostility directed towards Travellers is perhaps an expression of something else. In the minds of many they are seen as interlopers on the idea of ethnicity; people for whom ethnic identity has become a matter of choice rather than birth. Such an idea challenges the very concept that identity has a grounding in some essential and incontrovertible source. The idea that it can be made up on the spot is an underdetermined and uncertain position and one that is perceived as a source of threat because it cannot be dealt with satisfactorily in the usual forms of labelling and identification.

For Travellers themselves, their identity is a chosen one that has been made up through the development of a particular style, set of values and lifestyle practices, but that does not mean that it is seen by them as in any way lacking authenticity. Travellers do not identify with any one ethnicity but through a hybrid mix of different identities, with *the idea of ethnicity* itself, and that is both a problem and a source of anxiety to those who see ethnicity in ideas of essential biological/cultural and racial characteristics. Travellers are not discriminated against because of who they are, but because they represent the unknown and perhaps because of what they reveal about the hybrid and uncertain nature of ethnic identity, authenticity and choice.

The categorisation and naming problems that Travellers create for people and the potential anxieties they can produce are re-grounded or normalised in a very specific way: through issues of social class. For many people the ethnic status of Travellers may be an inauthentic pastiche, but their social class origins are seen as real enough. These origins are very much seen as being wealthy and middle class. This justifies the populist rationale that Travellers choose to make themselves homeless and should therefore not be entitled to state financial support. I suggest, however, that wanting to see all Travellers as middle-class people from comfortable homes has as much to do with questions of identity and origins as it does with state benefits. Only those who are authentic might be tolerated and only then if they adapt to suit the majority population. But visibly to stand out and assume an identity that is grounded in ethnic claims that were seen to have been invented quite recently is anathema to British ways of thinking about identity (Strathern, 1992). The hiatus and uncertainty that they created within the public imagination was resolved by attempts to detect a spurious class origin that did not provide legitimacy to this group, but on the contrary was used as an argument to openly discriminate against them.

In order to understand the identity claims that Travellers are making and the responses to them, these issues of ethnicity and class have to be analysed. For those opposed to Travellers, their authentic identity resides in their class origins rather than their ethnic origins. For

Travellers, what gives them a sense of identity is their attachment to certain ideas about ethnicity and authenticity and an apparent classlessness. What makes matters more complicated, however, is the way that class is indeed enmeshed within these claims, though not in the simplistic ways discussed above. For the British public and media, Travellers are seen as a threat because they are different. That difference is characterised by its underdetermined and uncertain qualities. An attempt to resolve this uncertainty is made by overdetermining the Traveller identity by seeing it as nothing more than a mask for a class identity. For Travellers, on the contrary, it is the denial of class, seen as an inauthentic source of cultural origins and experience, that leads them to seek refuge in the idea of ethnicity as a basis for their new identities.

Spaces of identity

To better understand the identity and tribalism that Travellers have created and the nature of the responses they have generated, we need to locate them in the social space that they have made their home. The identity that I have described here is one that has emerged against the idea of suburbia and of the life associated with it. Travellers are to be found far away from suburbia in rural and often remote areas, especially during the summer months. Wales, Highland Scotland, Devon and Cornwall, the so-called Celtic fringe, are popular locations for travel. So too was the West Country in England, an area rich in prehistoric sites and associated, in places such as Glastonbury, with an aura of pagan mystery. However, travel in this area became increasingly difficult after the dissolution of the convoy in 1986, although it did not disappear altogether. Neither did the opposition to Travellers. It is still common, as I write in 1998, to see the entrances to farm fields across England blocked with old bits of farm machinery in order to stop Travellers or ravers trespassing onto land either to park up, or, less common these days, to hold a festival.

The idea of identity that I have discussed here is also expressed through an attitude to the landscape. The Celtic fringe, pagan sites and the unspoilt English countryside are the antithesis of the idea of suburbia. They are, in particular, the spaces of an earlier, largely forgotten British ethnicity waiting to be reclaimed. The ideas of identity and of a constructed ethnicity are mapped out in a distinct way of seeing the landscape. The spaces that Travellers occupy are spaces of identity. They are created through the production of identity. Not only are identities created through the practices of festivals and travel in the countryside, but the imaginary geography of the rural is also a source in the making of this identity. It is the margins, the mysterious and forgotten parts of the British Isles, with which Travellers identify. This is homologous with their imagined ethnic status.

However, others identify with the same landscape, but they often see it differently. Their understanding of such places may well be at odds with those of Travellers. The extreme negative populist response to New Age Travellers has been sanctioned by the authorities ranging from central government, the police and county councils to English Heritage and the National Trust. All have sought to exclude, remove or criminalise the Traveller way of life. In doing so they too have drawn on representations of the landscape in which they see Travellers as having no part. This landscape is an imagined geography that is also associated with the idea of ethnicity – an ethnicity defined by a white Englishness. For others such as Travellers to come in and claim it as the space of an alternative ethnicity, and a made-up one to boot, has, I believe, been the real source of anxiety and conflict that has surrounded New Age Travellers. The image of pastoral England, of a picturesque landscape that represents social stability and tranquillity, is one that has developed in Britain, especially in England, over the past two centuries. It is made most visible when it comes under threat. That representation is drawn upon to exclude Travellers. They in turn have often had an ambivalent relationship with such an understanding of the countryside. Drawing on other traditions, associated with ideas of mystery and spirituality in particular, they have constructed an alternative representation of the landscape.

In the next section I explore the relationship between Travellers and this landscape. The social space that is generated around Travellers is a contested one. Some of the key elements of this conflict can be seen in particular around the site of Stonehenge that was so important to many Travellers during the time when this way of life first emerged. The idea of the rural as an authentic contrast to suburbia is also significant but so also is the different way that an idea of authenticity is used to support competing interpretations of the rural landscape. Finally, the space that we call home has been significant in the conflicts surrounding Travellers. In looking at the identity of Travellers I want to set it against the making of such a social space and to look at its significance to a more general understanding of identity at the end of the 20th century in England, in the rest of the British Isles and increasingly in a wider European context as well. Rarely is the English countryside seen as a site of ethnic conflict. In the past, conflict has largely been to do with class access. The ordering of the representation of rural England is one that is based upon issues of class. To introduce ethnicity is to introduce a blank figural element that has to be resolved in other ways. Ethnic conflict in Britain is usually associated with the imaginary geography of the inner city. It is in the spaces of the inner city that the uncertainties surrounding, ethnicity, migration, national identity and social change are generally articulated. New Age Travellers take those uncertainties into the countryside; they take uncertainty into the heartland of what is assumed to be the stable ground upon which a sense of English identity is established.

Landscapes of freedom

Travellers create an identity around the idea of ethnicity that is based upon a predominantly lower middle-class experience that seeks to reject a class identity by adopting an ethnic one that comprises a collage of marginal ethnic identities. At a glance, it would be easy to suggest that Travellers favour the rural over the town and that they have developed a way of life solely around that position. It is certainly true that the rural is important for most Travellers and that many of them prefer to live or to be on the road in rural areas than in towns. It is also the case, however, that certain urban areas have also become important for Travellers as well as for those who identify with the Traveller identity, even if they do not actually travel on a regular basis. The types of space that Travellers tend to identify with cannot be seen simply in terms of rejecting the urban over the rural. It is a particular representation of the urban as routine, mundane and without the opportunity for self-expression that is rejected:

> 'I started travelling later than most I suppose, but we're all doing it for the same reason – to escape from society. I went to art school until I was twenty, travelled round for a bit hitch-hiking and that … I got married to a woman who already had kids. The trap. No work, no nothing. We lived in a council house in Ashton-under-Lyne. Trashton-under-Slime we called it.' (Rico, in Lowe and Shaw, 1993, p 132)

In rejecting the idea of suburbia, Travellers are not simply rejecting the town for the country but a class experience as well as a dominant form of English identity. This would be easy for those Travellers who are Welsh or Scottish, as they could draw on national identities that are already in some ways seen as oppositional to an English identity.

For the most part, however, Travellers do not look to other national identities in the construction of their own but to groups like Gypsies, nomads or 'first nation' peoples who have one thing in common: they have no national identity in the modern sense implied by the ideas of nationalism. They have an ethnic status but it is not attached to the territoriality of any nation-state.

The idea of nomadism is premised upon an absence of a national identity and a national sense of belonging. It is a territorial identity in which 'territory' is freed from the associations of nation and can be connected to other kinds of spatial myth-making. But to identify with the position of the nomad is not to reject the idea of national identity altogether. Travellers identify with the idea of national identity *in absentia*. The very fact that they choose to be ethnic nomads in the country of their birth (and of course there will be examples of Travellers born in other countries, so I generalise on the basis of the majority here) would suggest that they have to deal as much with the experiences of insiderness as outsiderness. They are trying to get away from class and national identities by adopting ideas of ethnicity and nomadism that are seen as unbounded, and free from national and class characteristics and traditions. Class and nationality are the Other to the identity they are trying to create. The making of Travellers' identities, therefore, does not emerge through ignoring ideas of national identity but is expressed through a process of negotiation with ideas of class and national identity and trying to transform them into something else (Hall, 1990, 1992, 1996).

One example of this is when Travellers identify with marginal groups within English history. In their writings, poems, line drawings and the small publications that have been generated over the years by Travellers and their supporters, a pervading sense of being in conflict over competing understandings of what it is to live in England prevails. Images of sacred sites, old drovers' lanes, ancient woodlands, areas of unspoilt wilderness and open vistas over countryside with a few villages are common in the way that Travellers represent the landscape. Two kinds of images that are especially common are those of groups of Travellers in the process of being harassed by the police and of idealised images of peaceful Traveller sites and festivals set in an unspoilt rural environment with just a whiff of wood smoke wafting over the scene (Garrard et al, 1986; Earle et al 1994). There is also psychedelic imagery mixed in with Celtic symbols, line drawings of Travellers at rest and endless images of Stonehenge with the sun rising over it as if signifying a new dawn.

If early on, in the days of the free festivals and the convoy, open conflict around access to land and to sites such as Stonehenge was common, Travellers increasingly insist that they want no trouble and just wish to be left alone to live their own lives as they choose. Such a claim often takes the form of a desire to have a space in which to live and to be free to choose how to live:

> 'Even though I've just got a couple of small caravans to live in I don't think I'd swap it for a four- or five-bedroom house with a view of a town. Surroundings, your outside space, is just as important as your inside space in my view. I've lived in Wales, right on the top of hills where you can look round three hundred and sixty degrees and not see anyone. That feeling of space and privacy to me is worth a lot.' (Jay, in Lowe and Shaw, 1993, p 132)

Such statements are often couched in terms of challenging the perceived state of servile obedience by the Travellers' Other, the urban and especially the suburban dweller:

> If you live in a city you depend on thousands of other people to provide your needs. The city is a complex and ultimately fragile life support system. People who live in cities live like battery hens cramped, exploited and sick. If you live on the road, life is hard but ultimately you bear the responsibility for providing for your own needs. There is a great dignity in this. This is where the threat to the state lies. What many Travellers are saying in living the way they do is: 'We don't need you. Just leave us to live our lives in peace'. (Rosenberger, 1989, p 34)

The first element that contributes to the place myth of the rural that Travellers have created is thus around this idea of the countryside, symbolised especially by the open road or field, as a space of tranquillity and freedom. This is not that far removed from the romantic idea of the rural idyll. It differs in one important respect from the mainstream idea of arcadia, in that it is based in an idea of individual freedom rather than a sense of organic community and acceptance of tradition and hierarchy. We know that Travellers value a strong sense, if not of community then of communion and fellowship found in such things as festivals, convoys and acts of pilgrimage to sites such as Stonehenge. This sense of belonging, however, does not in any way undermine the importance of individual liberty, expressed in the form of having a space for oneself to be able to live and develop as one chooses. Rather, such a sense of communion provides the solidarity and support for individuals to develop as individuals (Hetherington, 1998).

Traditions of resistance

The second element that lies behind the place myth that Travellers construct of the rural is the idea of the countryside as a space of resistance. Travellers know that other nomadic people in Britain have always had a hard time and encountered local opposition. They have had to be resourceful in finding sites on which to live, as have Travellers. Alongside the local council caravan sites that, since 1968, were provided for Gypsies, there have been long-established illegal sites that Gypsies have used, sometimes for considerable periods of time. Drovers' tracks, green lanes, bits of common land, as well as some fields that have long been used to park up, have provided sites for Gypsies and other Travellers. They are all identified with and sought out by Travellers.[2] If historic sites are hard to come by, Travellers have attempted, with little success and a great deal of conflict, to continue this tradition by creating their own. Finding farmers who will let them park on their land, using bits of wasteland, common land, unused council-owned land and, significantly, land that has been under dispute by other competing parties are some of the ways that Travellers have tried to create their own sites.

In doing this they have created a great deal of opposition not only from landowners, the police and councils, but also from local people. Such conflict has often taken the form of court orders to remove them and then eviction by the bailiffs, aided by the police. Sometimes this eviction has been resisted; more often it has meant being moved on and the search for an alternative site. As a consequence, the roadside lay-by has often been another site where Travellers are to be found, more out of necessity than by choice. In supporting what they do, and in trying to resist local harassment and eviction, Travellers have often sought to locate themselves in a long-standing historical tradition of claiming access to the countryside. As well as Gypsies, working-class ramblers and plot-landers are other sources of inspiration. So too have been urban squatters. But above all, historical examples, associated with the demands to be given access to common land, have been the main source of inspiration; in particular the Diggers of the English Civil War are most commonly invoked as ancestors to this tradition of claiming rights to common land.

This tradition emphasises the idea of reclaiming the land for the dispossessed. Sometimes this idea is articulated through a critique of the concept of land ownership; at other times, among more environmentally aware groups, of curbing the harmful effects of contemporary industrial society upon nature and the countryside. In resisting ideas about land ownership and restrictions on movement and settlement on sites within the countryside, Travellers place themselves in an invented tradition of popular English protest (Hobsbawm and Ranger, 1983). This has its origins in the early modern Enclosure Acts whereby common land was claimed by landlords and enclosed as their property. Local traditions of asserting commoners' rights as well as illegal encampments by religious communities, Gypsies, tinkers and other nomads are seen as part of an English tradition of protest, and many Travellers like to see themselves as a continuation of that tradition:

> Green Lane [near Salisbury] was an example of a successful land squat that lasted for nearly 100 years – one woman, Gran Saunders, was born and died there. When finally taken to court in 1980 the longest surviving resident had been there 17 years. Green Lane started as a Gypsy site during the 1880's though towards the end there were more self-styled hippies than tinkers. The final tally in 1980 was 330 people living in coaches, caravans, shacks and tipis. (*Ideal home survival guide*, n.d.)

To reiterate, in describing such a tradition as identifying with a form of Englishness, I am not suggesting that Travellers identify with a nationalist view. Rather, the emphasis is on the importance of the idea of an ethnicity that has been suppressed within the hegemonic forms that make up English identity today. It is the ethnic rather than national character of what England is, or was, imagined to be that interests many Travellers. In particular, it is those groups who have been marginalised within English history, and who have resisted that marginalisation who are seen as making up a tradition with which Travellers associate themselves. They draw on these English traditions to give legitimacy and a sense of history to what they are doing. Thus they also engage with the idea of England in order to try and erase it as a national idea from their way of life.

In the case of both of these senses of the rural as a space of freedom and a space of resistance, this distinctly English tradition, represented by a historical lineage of groups who have identified with the road, the fair and the common, gives these ideas a sense of authenticity. But this is only half of the story: there are two other elements to be added before we get the full picture of the place myth of the rural that Travellers have developed. A third component can be added to the place myth of the rural that many Travellers believe in. Alongside these notions of a space of (authentic) freedom and a space of (authentic) resistance we should add that the rural is also seen as a space of mystery. In particular, this more spiritual element is shaped by another very English tradition known as the earth mysteries tradition.

Earth mysteries and the countryside

The term 'earth mysteries' generally refers to the study of ancient sites from a standpoint which is, at the outset, critical of modern science and its way of interpreting the landscape. Earth mysteries practitioners adopt what may be described as a holistic approach to understanding the landscape that draws on ancient folk ways, pagan and spiritual forms of understanding rather than those of a more rationalist and scientific kind. It seeks to interpret the landscape by uncovering sources of energy, 'secret' alignments and forgotten practices embedded within it. It sees the landscape as a space of ancient wisdom that has been lost to modern knowledge. Only the initiates who know the secret practices are able to gain access to this wisdom. Through such practices as dowsing, ley-line hunting, numerology, rediscovering folklore and customs associated with particular sites, the earth mysteries tradition aims to challenge the ways in which the landscape is understood through more rational and instrumental means associated with archaeology, planning, the heritage and tourist industry as well as by commonly held ways of looking at the countryside through ideas of arcadia, idyll and the picturesque. Earth mysteries believers seek to find in the landscape forgotten practices of knowing and understanding both the natural and the social. The earth mysteries approach seeks to value forms of rejected knowledge that have been lost in the post-Enlightenment world of modern scientific practices and readings of natural processes (Webb, 1974).

It would be unfair to suggest that all New Age Travellers share a belief in the practices and the epistemological claims of earth mysteries researchers. What they have in common is an understanding of the rural landscape as a space full of mystery and discovery and a sense of the countryside as a place of authenticity that challenges the predominant ways of regarding the countryside as a site defined by agribusiness; tourists, commuters or scientists.

It is the case that many Travellers have adopted a place myth of the rural as a space of mystery, and that sense of mystery plays a significant part in shaping the identity of Travellers. For most Travellers, the countryside is not a rural arcadia expressed through images of pastoral peace; rather, it is a place of mystery, in which the sacred is reinvested into the landscape through a syncretist paganism and holism. The role of travel as a quest for meaning, small-scale community and self-discovery, and of festival as a source of freedom and invention, take place in such an imagined mysterious landscape, which provides a backdrop for these practices. This understanding of the rural landscape stands in contrast to ideas that inform the representation of rural arcadia for many country dwellers and tourists. They too may share a romantic view of the countryside based on culture having tamed and cultivated nature, turning it from a wilderness into a garden. In contrast, the place myth of Travellers wishes to turn the countryside, if not into a wilderness, into a place where wilderness and a sense of the sublime might be found and nature restored to itself by revealing its power and mystery. Their authenticity and mystery is not that of the English country garden.

Opposing England

The fourth element in this place myth is the idea of exile from the English countryside. Through continual eviction, local opposition to their presence and legislation against their way of life, many Travellers have recently begun to seek what they see as refuge outside Britain:

> 'Think I started the Big Exile during the winter of 1990–1991. It was a question of self preservation. Just had to go at any cost. Been travelling abroad before, but this was real desperation. Woke up one morning with pigs on my left and scaggies on my right. That was it. Spent a lot of time fighting both. Had to get out. It's important not to let them think that they have you, just by taking your rig off you a few times. I've had sixteen years of that. Have to keep out there.' (Dianne Campbell, in Dearling, 1998, p 11)

This process of Travellers leaving Britain has accelerated since the Criminal Justice Act came into force in 1994. There are now probably at least as many, if not more, Travellers from Britain living and travelling in mainland Europe as there are remaining in these islands. To some extent the provocative spirit of resistance that focused on Stonehenge and other festival sites between 1984 and 1992 has given way to a decision to give up on England altogether and the continual hassles one encounters by being a Traveller in this country. This is not to say that Travellers do not encounter similar problems in other countries, especially with the police, customs officers and other officials (Dearling, 1998). But there are differences. Laws of trespass are different, rights of access vary, local people respond differently to groups whom they regard as exotic and a little strange but not as threatening, as they have been seen in the counties of southern England. This may be put down to different local traditions, patterns of land ownership, attitudes towards the land and to migrant and nomadic people, or it may be a lack of familiarity with the lifestyles of Travellers, the fact that they now generally travel in small groups and that there is no local memory of convoys of hundreds of vehicles moving around in the summer, surrounded by conflict and almost hysterical media reporting as was the case in Britain in the mid-1980s. It is also significant that other nations have different ways of representing the countryside and it may be that Travellers do not present the same threat there as they do to the predominant view of the English countryside.

All the same, mainland Europe is not seen as some kind of utopia. It is more a space of exile from one's preferred home, from which one has been excluded. The tradition of persecuting nomads, Gypsies, as well as Jews, is one that has a dreadful history in Europe. But despite this, and perhaps because of their novelty value, Travellers have sought refuge in France, Spain, the Scandinavian countries as well as in parts of Eastern Europe (Dearling, 1998). The same things that were sought in Britain – space, freedom and a natural environment in which to live as one chooses – remain.

Even before this physical exile from Britain began, Travellers already viewed the English countryside as a space of exile and lived in it as such. In particular, they often chose to live on sites that were in exile not only from the picturesque heartland of the English countryside but also from the suburban life of the town. The old droves, ancient pagan sites, remaining bits of common land, upland or moorland areas in Scotland, Wales and Cornwall all stand in opposition to the comforts and routines that have come to characterise living in England, whether town or country. To live in such places, to celebrate festivals there, to treat some of the more significant sites as shrines, is not only to live on the margins because there is nowhere else but to see such margins as a space of exile: a space either of retreat from one's homeland or a more overt rejection of some of its dominant myths. These are the spaces of a negotiated, achieved ethnicity. Travellers, in adopting such sites, lived in England *in absentia*. Their way of life identified with an idea of England from which they saw themselves exiled.

Conclusion

Travellers live in a country that they identify with *in absentia*. They have constructed a place myth of that country by identifying with elements of its imaginary rural geography in order that they might reject its predominant class and national senses of identity. In choosing to live in exile as nomads in one's own country and to see such a way of life as a challenge to all that one's home represents is to valorise the idea of the margin as the basis of one's identity. I have suggested here that the place myth of the English countryside that Travellers have created consists in seeing the rural as an authentic space. That sense of authenticity is expressed in four ways: through myths of freedom, resistance, mystery and exile. Around these ideas Travellers have come to create a set of place myths: about the urban and the rural, about sacred sites, the road, common land and so on that are implicated in the ways that they live. Through the construction of such place myths we can see how issues of space and identity are co-constructed in relation to one another. There is an affinity between the types of spaces that Travellers have chosen to live in, how they see them, how they constitute them through their practice, as well as how they see the ones they reject. Their sense of themselves, both individually and collectively, their sense of ethnicity, of belonging and of marginality are expressed not only through the practices of their daily life, theft rituals, their homes and the way they dress, but also through their place myths about the countryside and about England.

Notes
[1] Hetherington, K. (2000) *New Age travellers, vanloads of uproarious humanity*, London: Cassell. Reprinted with the permission of the publisher, The Continuum International Publishing Group.

[2] Rarely does this go the other way. Most Gypsies detest Travellers. Like the settled population they hate the dirty look, the mess that is associated with their sites and their involvement with drugs. They also blame Travellers for the hostility they experience from local people. They believe that Travellers have given nomadism a bad name.

References

Bakhtin, M. (1984) *Rabelais and his world*, Bloomington, IN: Indiana University Press.

Becker, H. (1964) *Outsiders*, New York, NY: Free Press.

Dearling, A. (1998) *No boundaries: New Travellers on the road (outside Britain)*, Lyme Regis: Enabler Publications.

Earle, F., Dearling, A., Whittle, H., Glasse, R. and Gubby (1994) *A time to travel? An introduction to Britain's newer Travellers*, Lyme Regis: Enabler Press.

Garrard, B., Rainbow, J. and McKay, A. (eds) (1986) *Rainbow village on the road*, Glastonbury: Unique Publications.

Hall, S. (1990) 'Cultural identity and diaspora', in J. Rutherford (ed) *Identity*, London: Lawrence and Wishart, pp 222-37.

Hall, S. (1992) 'The question of cultural identity', in S. Hall, D. Held and T. McGrew (eds) *Modernity and its futures*, Cambridge: Cambridge University Press, pp 274-316.

Hall, S. (1996) 'Who needs identity?', in S. Hall and P. DuGay (eds) *Questions of cultural identity*, London: Sage Publications, pp 1-17.

Hetherington, K. (1998) *Expressions of identity*. London: Sage Publications.

Hetherington, K. (2000) *New Age travellers, vanloads of uproarious humanity*, London: Cassell.

Hobsbawm, E. and Ranger, T. (eds) (1983) *The invention of tradition*, Cambridge: Cambridge University Press.

Ideal home survival guide (nd), no publication details available.

Lowe, R. and Shaw, W. (1993) *Travellers: Voices of the new age nomads*, London: Fourth Estate.

McKay, G. (1996) *Senseless acts of beauty*, London: Verso.

Okely, J. (1983) *The Traveller Gypsies*, Cambridge: Cambridge University Press.

Rosenberger, A. (1989) *Festival eye*, London: Festival Eye.

Said, E. (1991) *Orientalism: Western concepts of the Orient*, London: Penguin.

Sennett, R. (1986) *The fall of public man*, London: Faber and Faber.

Strathern, M. (1992) *After nature*, Cambridge: Cambridge University Press.

Webb, J. (1974) *The occult underground*, La Salle, IL: Open Court.

EIGHT

Issues of rurality and good practice

Gypsy Traveller pupils in schools

Kalwant Bhopal

'We try to integrate Traveller children, try to treat them like everyone else, with the proviso that we have to treat them differently.' (Marie, teacher at South Hall Village School)

Introduction

In the mid-1960s Tony Boxall (1992) took a striking series of photographs documenting the changing lives and fortunes of Gypsy Travellers in the Kent and Surrey countryside. These were notable for the levels of access obtained by Boxall, who had no previous connection with the Gypsy Traveller community, and also for the insight his pictures opened into a time of great change within the community. These were changes from a lifestyle that centred around horse-drawn transport to more conventional cars and vans and the changes undertaken by many families from a primarily nomadic lifestyle to one that was often settled.

Today Gypsy Traveller[1] groups remain marginalised and excluded. They experience overt racism and this often contributes to their levels of achievement and attendance in schools. Turner (1999) has highlighted the treatment of Gypsy Travellers not only by government but also by society at large. Turner indicates that the challenge for the government and the media in reporting Gypsy Traveller activities is to address the real issues within the nomadic world of Gypsies, such as the need for secure accommodation, education, literacy and an acceptance of a different way of life which is nomadic. Recently New Labour has begun to take the plight of Gypsy Travellers seriously. This has resulted in the publication of a 'Travellers Strategy' to discuss problems arising from unauthorised camping as well as general policy and service development issues for Gypsy Travellers, which includes the role of educators (Local Government Association, 2003). Prior to 2005 there had also been tentative signs within the media of a more complex understanding of how perceived problems of Gypsy Traveller lifestyles are driven by inadequate government policy. The BBC's recent analysis of residents' anger at a site in Cottenham, Cambridgeshire, presented a picture of both local residents and Gypsy Travellers united against the local council's exercise of planning regulations (Casciani, 2004). Even more surprising, perhaps, is a report on the National Farmers' Union (NFU) Countryside website (NFU, 2004) that covers a similar story in a village outside Chichester and refers to the Cottenham approach as a practical way forward; if not exactly sympathetic to the Gypsy Traveller cause, it is certainly not overtly hostile. However, this is not, of course, to underestimate the extent of hostility regularly expressed by local residents towards Gypsy Traveller communities. The incident in the village of Firle in the Sussex Downs in which a mock Gypsy Traveller caravan was set on fire testifies to the continuing anti-Gypsy Traveller sentiment in rural and semi-rural areas of contemporary Britain. More recent right-wing media coverage of Gypsy Traveller communities has seen a further retrenchment and an increasingly extreme anti-Gypsy Traveller rhetoric, as demonstrated in the *Sun* newspaper's 'Stamp Out the Camps' campaign.

This chapter will explore aspects of good practice in a mixed comprehensive school in a rural village. It will argue that the rural setting has an effect on anti-racist strategies, issues of segregation and integration and curriculum content for Gypsy Traveller pupils. It will highlight the need for policy makers to consider the racism faced by many Gypsy Traveller pupils in developing innovative practice to meet the needs of pupils with nomadic lifestyles that present significant challenges to educators and local education authorities (LEAs).

Gypsy Travellers, ethnicity and culture

Although many Gypsy Travellers now live and work in urban environments, and have done so for several generations, they are often understood to 'belong' within the countryside. This perception is often a romanticised image associated with horses and picturesque wagons, a recent example in *Country Living* magazine (Thomas, 2003) includes a set of photographs that show ornately decorated horse-drawn wagons, cast-iron kettles hanging above an open fire and 'characterful' faces. Sibley (1981, 1986) has argued that positive accounts of Gypsy Traveller culture are presented within these romanticised terms and that where Gypsy Travellers stray from these 'authentic' ethnic rural images they become seen as deviant, dangerous and undesirable (see also Hetherington, this volume). These 'romantic' accounts do not address vast parts of Gypsy Traveller culture, such as the differences between different groups of Gypsy Travellers throughout Europe and the history of Gypsy Traveller diaspora, differences in language or the violent continuing persecution of Gypsy Travellers in Europe.

In the UK a small number of Gypsy Travellers are tied to agricultural work throughout the year, many more are involved, often for cultural or sentimental reasons, in seasonal agricultural work that they combine with other trading (Acton and Kenrick, 1991). The attachment to the rural environment within Gypsy Traveller culture also materialises in the importance of horse fairs, (notably at Appleby, Stow-on-the-Wold and Barnet), and the large gatherings at certain race meetings (Okely, 1983).

Among Boxall's photographs are a number that provide an exceptional glimpse into the world of Gypsy Traveller children, in particular a sense of mimicking the postures, stances and sensibilities of their parents from an early age. They speak volumes about the differences in cultures experienced by these children in comparison to their contemporaries from both the town and the countryside; these children appear singularly at ease within the harsher environments generated by a transitory lifestyle. The 1990s marked a significant shift in the expectation for these children with the introduction of the first specialist education provision for Gypsy Travellers by LEAs (Acton and Kenrick, 1991).

Differences in culture that marked out Gypsy Traveller children were mirrored within the school setting. These differences become apparent as markers both in the perception of Gypsy Traveller engagement with the educational institution and in the relations between Gypsy Traveller children and their peers. In the first case there is a resultant discrimination as dominant non-Gypsy Traveller culture fails to address the needs of a minority culture. Gypsy Travellers consequently are less successful in terms of the educational institution. In the second case the inherent difference becomes the basis for racist name-calling and bullying. Both of these trends will be examined more fully in this chapter.

Gypsy Travellers, rurality and education policy

There is no research that has specifically attempted to explore the issue of good practice in relation to rurality and whether the countryside can affect good practice and what it means in terms of racism for Gypsy Traveller pupils in schools. However, while managing a DfEE project (Bhopal et al, 2000) examining successful approaches to Gypsy Traveller education it became apparent that the rural environment was a factor in determining their experiences of education.

While there is now a significant body of emerging literature and research on the issues of ethnicity, exclusion and racism in the countryside (for example, Agyeman and Spooner, 1997; Cloke and Little, 1997; Neal, 2002; Chakraborti and Garland, 2004; contributors in this volume) there is still relatively little *social policy-centred, welfare site-specific* research on the ways in which racism and exclusion impact on welfare provision and delivery in rural areas. For example, in their review of the potential of challenging racism through education, Broadhurst and Wright (2004, p 161) argue that 'because of the dearth of investigations into racism in education in the rural this has necessitated the use of findings from urban environments where research has been much more plentiful and insightful'. In its analysis of qualitative data from in-depth case-study research, this chapter directly addresses this absence and reveals some of the complexities and lacunae in educational policy-making and implementation in relation to ethnicity and educational experience and achievement in rural settings.

Rurality and education

Research that has looked at Gypsy Travellers in the countryside has not focused on the spatial relation of Gypsy Travellers to their communities. The Cambridgeshire Travellers Review (2003) argues that priorities within education and training include establishing the vocational needs of young Gypsy Travellers and identifying suitable programmes and educational opportunities. At the same time, disruption to school-based education is a key issue for Gypsy Traveller pupils as some pupils are not in one location long enough to have their needs properly identified. The Review further states that the main barriers to attendance at secondary schools are thought to be bullying, teacher expectations, lack of transport and parental disapproval of secondary education (see also Dorset County Council Gypsy and Traveller Policy, 2002). This research does not attempt to discuss the contextual and spatial location of Gypsy Travellers in the countryside and how this affects aspects of good practice, racism and equal opportunities.

There has always been some conflict between Gypsy Travellers and settled communities, but as the nature of life in the countryside has changed, particularly as employment in farming becomes less secure, the tensions have become more pronounced. This situation has also been influenced by the 1994 Criminal Justice and Public Order Act. Sections 77 and 78 gave local authorities new powers to deal with unauthorised encampments and removed obligations to provide official sites. The legislation was accompanied by the Department of Environment guidance, which restated earlier advice advocating tolerance in eviction policies in respect of Gypsy Travellers and drew attention to the wider obligations authorities might have to Gypsy Travellers under other legislation. Local authorities were advised to liaise widely with health, education and welfare services (Bhopal et al, 2000).

Policy approaches

There is no specific UK-wide policy on Gypsy Travellers. However, in 2001, the Scottish Parliament's Equal Opportunities Committee published a report that called on public bodies to treat Gypsy Travellers as a distinct ethnic group until such time as a legal test case provides official recognition under the 1976 Race Relations Act (Scottish Parliament, 2001). Many areas have been tackled by the report, including education. There is also an emphasis on the monitoring of anti-bullying strategies, which should include Gypsy Travellers as a separate ethnic group, as well as on the systematic monitoring of education services to measure progress in meeting targets for the educational attainment and inclusion of Gypsy Traveller children in schools. The Commission for Racial Equality (2001) has also welcomed and given support to the Scottish Equal Opportunities Committee (2001) on its inquiry into Gypsy Travellers and its conclusion that Gypsy Travellers should be regarded as a racial group for the purposes of framing legislation and policies relating to public services.

Schools, colleges and LEAs now have a statutory obligation to promote racial equality. The 2000 Race Relations (Amendment) Act that came into force in 2002 places a new statutory duty on public bodies, including schools, to eliminate unlawful discrimination, to promote equality of opportunity and to promote good relations between people from different racial groups. These duties are enforceable, whatever the ethnic composition of the school or college.

There is no systematic national data on the size and nature of Gypsy Traveller communities. What data there exists are fragmentary and incomplete. Gypsy Travellers are, however, recognised as a minority ethnic group in the UK under the 1976 Race Relations Act but are not listed separately for enumeration purposes as part of national census data collection. Consequently, there are no reliable figures on the numbers of Gypsy Travellers and different sources give markedly different estimates. The cohort of Gypsy Traveller children within the Department for Education and Skills (DfES) and OFSTED figures over the past few years mainly relate to Gypsy Traveller children who are semi-nomadic. A relatively small number of children are thought to come from Gypsy Traveller backgrounds where families have 'settled' into houses either temporarily or permanently. However, there are no national or regional data on the numbers of 'settled' Gypsy Travellers. The estimates range widely from 100,000 to 350,000 (Bhopal et al, 2000). It is therefore difficult to assess the numbers of Gypsy Traveller children. Figures collected from a recent DfES data collection exercise show that there are 42,879 Gypsy Traveller children in England (Minority Cohesion Team, 2003).

Funding

Funding for specialist education for Gypsy Traveller children has undergone continuous change since the 1988 Education Reform Act established funding for Traveller Education Services. There have been five changes in funding. The 1990 Education (Grants) (Travellers and Displaced Persons) Regulations, established under section 210 of the 1988 Education Reform Act, empowered the Secretary of State to pay a grant to LEAs in support of expenditure to promote and facilitate the education of Travellers irrespective of age. Section 488 of the 1996 Education Act replaced section 210 of the 1988 Act, forming the Section 488 Specific Grant for Traveller Education. From April 2000 the grant was merged with the Ethnic Minority Achievement Grant to form the Ethnic Minority and Traveller Achievement Grant (EMTAG) falling within the Department's Standards Fund. From April 2001 the grant was de-merged from EMTAG to become the Traveller Achievement Grant (TAG) but was still part of the Standards Fund. From April 2003 the TAG was merged together with other smaller grants, along with additional funding, to form the Vulnerable Children's Grant (VCG). The VCG allows LEAs to allocate funding based on local needs and to provide coherent support across a range of vulnerable children, including those from Gypsy Traveller backgrounds (Minority Cohesion Team, 2003).

Funding for Gypsy Traveller children goes to the Traveller Education Service (TES) within the local authority to support the provision of specialist peripatetic teachers, classroom assistants, specialist education welfare officers, distance learning resources and staff training. The TES work closely with their local education authority and schools with the aim of helping improve levels of attendance and achievement and raising awareness and understanding of Gypsy Traveller children and their culture within the educational community.

Good practice

Later in this chapter I will describe some research that places an emphasis on developing innovative practice to meet the needs of children and young people whose lifestyles present practical and cultural challenges to service providers, in particular looking at a school that is praised by OFSTED for successfully providing education to a rural Gypsy Traveller community. Addressing the educational disadvantages of Gypsy Traveller children is a matter of urgency to ensure that individuals can enjoy their full human rights and equality of opportunity. This demands that policy makers be aware of the diversity that exists within the Gypsy Traveller diaspora. The way that policy makers view Gypsy Travellers shapes how policy towards them is formed and implemented. The current lack of success of Gypsy Travellers in mainstream education reflects a long history of governments failing to adopt appropriate and effective policies towards Gypsy Travellers in general. This failure is rooted in the reluctance of policy makers to appreciate the history and circumstances of the Gypsy Traveller population. There has been the tendency for this group to be seen as the 'problem' (Save The Children, 2001). It is unusual to indicate that the 'problem' may be the result of personal or institutional racism or ill-advised policies. Often the policies and practices directed towards Gypsy Travellers have been derived without any consultation or involvement of the users. A long-term commitment is needed on the part of local governments to resource reforms aimed at ending discrimination adequately, also to ensure that proper systems are in place to monitor and evaluate the outcomes effectively. Consultation and involvement of parents and children is the most effective means of identifying barriers to attendance and achievement and of developing strategies to address them (Save The Children, 2001). The whole school community must be involved in developing strategies to address racist bullying, and physical and verbal abuse. Where good practice has been developed, this should be shared across schools and educational authorities. Decisions taken at a local governmental level have direct significance for Gypsy Travellers, especially in the field of education.

Local authorities usually have the primary role in allocating resources and monitoring the quality of educational provision.

Gypsy Travellers and achievement in schools

The poor participation rate and low levels of achievement in education by Gypsy Traveller children have been a matter of serious concern for over 40 years. This period has also seen a significant growth in the literature (Plowden, 1967; Swann, 1985; Liegeois, 1987). Individual published reports and other inspection evidence provided the background to a formal statement in the form of an OFSTED report in 1996, *The education of travelling children* (OFSTED, 1996). The report detailed the progress made by schools and defined good practice. Serious concerns about the education of Gypsy Traveller children were expressed relating to issues of access, attendance and achievement: 'Access to school for secondary aged children remains a matter of grave concern. There are possibly as many as 10,000 children at this phase who are not even registered with a school' (OFSTED, 1996, p 45). In 1999 OFSTED published formal evidence on the education of Gypsy Travellers. While pointers to good practice were described, the general conclusions of the report confirmed serious concerns of previous reports: 'Gypsy Traveller pupils are the group most at risk in the education system. Although some make a reasonably promising start in primary school, by the time they reach secondary level their generally low attainment is a matter of serious concern' (OFSTED, 1999, p 18). Kiddle (1999) also provides an analysis of the changing relationships between Gypsy Travellers and schools and the real and/ or imagined impact on both cultures. This identifies the difficulties of gaining a satisfactory education and the importance of schools to be responsive to the needs of Gypsy Traveller children whose pattern of attendance may well be affected by the dictates of a nomadic or semi-nomadic way of life.

The publication of attendance league-tables has resulted in an increased reluctance for schools to accept Gypsy Traveller children (NATT, 1999). Although there is an emphasis on schools being more inclusive, this highlights the imposed institutional discrimination faced by nomadic communities (Jordan, 2001b). The racist attitudes in schools typified by bullying and name calling are described to be one of the main reasons for Gypsy Travellers' lack of success in educational achievement (Liegeois, 1998). Often Traveller groups are branded by practitioners within the education system as victims, and this coupled with the racism they experience serves to reinforce and enhance their failure in schools. It is possible that Gypsy Travellers will continue to remain marginalised in educational settings that are not designed for their nomadic needs.

The coincidence of an excluding school system and self-excluding Gypsy Traveller pupils perpetuates cycles of underachievement and marginalisation and contributes to their wider social exclusion in society (Jordan, 2001a). Research has found that Gypsy Travellers remain socially excluded and are formally being excluded from state schools once enrolled (Lloyd et al, 1999). The school education system presents many barriers to learning and achievement for Gypsy Traveller pupils, from overt racism, name calling and other forms of bullying to institutional racism (Jordan, 2001a).

Common themes to emerge from research in this field over many years are the continuing existence of serious obstacles to securing for Gypsy Traveller children ready access, regular attendance, continuity of educational experience and satisfactory levels of achievement. Many of these observations and conclusions have been contained within official reports, often marginal to the main objective of the research or other formal investigation. Over the years, the extent of detail surrounding good practice has markedly increased and this is a sign of positive progress. Identifying good practice has simultaneously highlighted many of the factors responsible for hindered access and poor or irregular attendance. There is less confident evidence regarding the range of reasons for the seeming persistence of underachievement, despite the measured increase in school attendance. Recent research (Bhopal et al, 2000) into successful schools and issues of good practice concludes that the low attendance, access to the curriculum and achievement levels of many such children can be successfully addressed by schools, LEAs and TES.

Working towards inclusive education

In 1999 the then Department for Education and Employment (DfEE) commissioned a research project to examine examples of successful initiatives in mainstream education by schools that aimed to promote more effective teaching and learning by improving attendance and raising attainment. The main aim was to identify the key elements of successful schemes and to disseminate them in order to promote more effective teaching and learning. The conclusions of this research were published by the DfEE as *Working towards inclusive education: Aspects of good practice for Gypsy Travellers* (Bhopal et al, 2000). Although outside the direct terms of the DfEE brief, it became apparent that issues of rurality had an influence on the work of schools when tackling racism towards Gypsy Traveller children.

Since the project was to focus on examples of successful initiatives, the most appropriate methodology was that of case studies (Yin, 1984). In the project, participants included parents and pupils, head teachers, class teachers, peripatetic specialist teachers, learning support assistants and representatives of the LEA TES. The project was conducted in six schools, four primary and two secondary. Six was considered enough to get a spread of experience; more primary schools than secondary were chosen for two reasons: first, because primary schools are generally smaller, so each secondary school accounts for more pupils. In addition, it was believed that the primary school is key in that it can lay the basis for later attendance and attainment for Gypsy Traveller pupils. Schools were selected equally from a range of rural, semi-rural and urban geographical areas. All the schools had a relatively large Gypsy Traveller intake.

One secondary school in the research, South Hall Village School,[2] was set in a rural setting just outside a local village. Although the school's location has the appearance of a rural idyll, the area in common with much of the countryside has been subject to enormous change in the last 20 years. What was predominantly a farming community is now reliant on a more mixed economy. There are still, however, a large number of people living in small isolated communities.

South Hall Village School has a population of mainly white children and staff. There are 780 pupils on its roll (380 boys and 400 girls). About 3% of pupils come from Gypsy Traveller homes or have a Gypsy Traveller background.[3] In addition, less than 0.4% of the school population come from other ethnic minority groups. The vast majority of pupils are classified as white. The children who attend the school are mainly from the local area. Children from the neighbouring villages also attend the school. Many of the children live in the local village or travel to the school by bus from outlying villages. Their parents work in trade, commerce and agriculture.

The school's 1997 OFSTED report emphasises that very good relationships have been fostered and developed over a long period with the settled Gypsy Traveller community. A spirit of mutual trust exists between them and the school. The TES supports the parents of the Gypsy Traveller children. The Gypsy Traveller community live in close proximity to South Hall Village School. There are two established Gypsy Traveller sites, which have been used by Gypsy Travellers for 12 and 18 years respectively. Many of the Gypsy Travellers no longer travel due to lack of work.

Results in the national Standard Assessment Tests (SATs) at the end of Key Stage 3 show that the percentages of pupils achieving level 5 or above are not significantly differently from national averages. At Key Stage 4, results in GCSE examinations across subjects indicate that in 1996 the performance of pupils at the school is not significantly different from national averages.

The school has 30 pupils with statements of Special Educational Needs (SEN). Provision for SEN pupils and for the education of pupils from the local Gypsy Traveller community are noted as major strengths of the school according to the OFSTED report. The assessment of the individual needs of the pupils on the SEN register and the action taken to support their academic and social development is noted as excellent. Progress of SEN pupils is better among girls and for those pupils who have a statement of SEN.

Pupils who come from a semi-settled Gypsy Traveller background generally make good progress. The progress and attainment that these pupils make in literacy skills is noted as being particularly good. The curriculum provision and pastoral support between the school and the LEA TES are very effective and of a high quality. Gypsy Traveller children are very well integrated into the school. Their attendance is significantly higher in comparison with national figures, and their attainment across a range of subjects is often good and sometimes very good. The school has a national reputation for good practice regarding Gypsy Traveller Education. The Travellers are mainly English Gypsy Travellers. The TES has excellent links with Gypsy Traveller families (school's 1997 OFSTED report).

The culturally affirmative curriculum: anti-racist strategies and integration

The cohort of pupils included in the case-study data in this research mainly belong to the semi-nomadic communities who live on official public or private caravan/mobile home sites. While many of these families travel only for limited periods during a year, some are more routinely nomadic and a proportion periodically become victims of the national lack of official sites. As a result, some of the children have more limited educational opportunities and varied attendance at schools, which can have a negative impact on their levels of achievement.

School policies

In common with other schools and institutions, South Hall Village School publishes a number of policies that outline anticipated norms of behaviour by pupils, members of staff, parents, contractors and other visitors to the school. The school has an exclusion policy, a health and safety policy, discipline and behaviour policies and an Equal Opportunities policy.

> At South Hall Village School we see equal opportunities as a cross-cultural dimension and as such it should permeate every aspect of the curriculum. We believe equal opportunities should mean freedom from discrimination for all and equal access to both education and employment, irrespective of gender, class, race and disability. (South Hall Village School Equal Opportunities Policy)

The policies were in existence for all children and no children were singled out when it came to enforcing the policies. At the same time, on more than one occasion and by more than one interviewee the issue of racism was mentioned as something that was very worrying and happened a lot: 'Sometimes you get children calling the Gypsy Travellers horrible names and they think they can get away with it. But we have to tackle it and we tell them that ("dirty gypo") is a derogatory remark and will not be accepted' (Andy,[4] TES teacher). The TES teacher said this was also echoed in the wider community, outside the school gates and beyond the remit of the school policy:

> 'We don't even begin to touch on the wider community; the attitudes and prejudices towards Gypsy Travellers are extreme. And for some of the children, their attitudes are brought into the school. Perhaps this is one of the reasons why the Traveller children like to stick together because they know they won't experience racism from each other.'

Although there was recognition by the teaching staff of a great deal of racism and prejudice against Gypsy Travellers, there is still an indication that this is something that the school is unable to tackle in its entirety. Recognition within the confines of the school alone is not enough to combat racism. More worryingly, the head indicated that racist incidents were *not* recorded in the school and there was no system in place to deal effectively with the issue of racism. The head felt that if the incidents were recorded this would in fact benefit the school; staff and students would think before they made racist remarks towards or about Gypsy Travellers: 'If the school recorded racist incidents and was given the impetus to have that system, that would mean that racism and racist incidents were taken seriously.'

There is an indication that, because the school is an all-white school, the issue of racism is not considered a problem. Whereas many schools in urban contexts have easily identifiable communities of black or Asian children in predominantly white populations who by their visibility prompt schools to be proactive in responding not just to isolated incidents of racism but also to trends and general low-level racist moods within these schools. In the rural setting of South Hall Village school there are no black or Asian children, as a result racism is *not seen* to be an issue. The *visibility* of race is replaced with the *invisibility* of being a white 'other' in an all-white school. It is clear that racism exists for Gypsy Traveller children, but because they are white the issue is not taken seriously by the school/LEA.

School ethos

A key factor of the success to date of the school in terms of good practice was the strong leadership quality of the head and the insistence that the school should epitomise an 'inclusive' ethos. Although the school did achieve this aim, the lack of recording of racist incidents brought into question whether or not they were being as successful as they could be. The leadership role of the head did contribute significantly to the success with Gypsy Travellers in terms of confident relationships, secure access, regular attendance and academic achievement. The influence of the head is crucial in setting the tone or culture of the institutional response and in providing a gateway for the wider community to embrace the school's ethos.

The recognition and acceptance of the ethnic and cultural status of pupils contributes to the development of confidence and trust and in consequence, the breaking down of mistrust and the fear of 'official' type institutions that some Gypsy Travellers face. The head's acceptance at South Hall Village School of Gypsy Traveller pupils had an influence on the success of the educational provision made for them. The school as a whole had an informed appreciation of the importance of Gypsy Traveller communities and the head was proactive in ensuring that their culture was recognised and celebrated within the curriculum for *all* pupils. However, the institution's vision of seeing its worth and richness did not necessarily contribute to how Gypsy Travellers were seen by others, even though a positive group image was portrayed by the school. At the same time, some staff were reluctant to try and build relationships with the Gypsy Travellers:

> 'I try and encourage staff to build relationships with the families, because I think this makes a difference. Most of the staff are not forthcoming, this may be due to the boundaries they have against them and they may feel they have to visit every family and perhaps just don't have the time. But I think getting to know more about the family will help staff understand the children and where they're coming from.' (Andy, TES teacher)

The motivation of Gypsy Traveller pupils to attend school and fully participate is strongly influenced by the quality of intercultural relations in the school and the anti-racist policies and practices. South Hall Village School tries to reflect the culture of Gypsy Travellers by including it in some English and history lessons. The school is also flexible in timetabling issues for those children who have difficulty in attending and these children are also taught 'friendly' subjects to encourage them to attend.

> 'If children have some difficulty attending, then we can create an individual timetable for them. We can give them part-time subjects and plan it for the individual child. We find out from the head of year which subjects the child enjoys and then pick these out so that the children can attend these first. This has worked positively, because then they have a positive experience at school.' (Julie, TES teacher)

This flexibility of approach is based on a clear understanding of the distinctive nature of a nomadic culture and the negative impact of social exclusion. So continuity of education is recognised and dealt with. At the same time a positive reflection of Gypsy Traveller culture is included within the curriculum. However, as noted earlier, despite these efforts on the part of the school there is still a worrying degree of racism among the pupils.

Role of TES

The role of the TES in the school was seen as being crucial to the success of the Gypsy Travellers. The high regard within the LEA for the TES was a positive element for the school in its development of policy and provision for Gypsy Traveller pupils. The TES had a high profile at South Hall Village School and was seen to be taken seriously by the school and other support services. The level of respect by senior management within the LEA for the work of the TES appears to be a further important factor in influencing the changing attitudes and practices both within the school and across the education service as a whole.

> 'We have a high profile, but this has only happened recently. It was different before. Here it is taken seriously due to the work that we do. For example lots of people within the LEA are sympathetic and approachable to what we do and we need that because sometimes people don't really take us seriously.' (Janet, TES teacher)

One of the main aims of the TES is to encourage mainstream providers of education to understand and to take on board issues that are relevant to Gypsy Traveller children; sometimes this can be difficult, because it is seen as the role of the TES and not the role of teachers. Their role is seen to teach. The problem here lies in the issue that the Gypsy Traveller children often become seen to be a 'problem' (even when they may not be) as they become attached to the TES teacher, as he/she is the one who understands them and gives them time. For example, there is the designation of sanctuary territory for Gypsy Travellers. In South Hall Village School, there is a special room or place where the Gypsy Traveller children can go to if they have a problem, or if they just want to feel they are in a safe place. The Gypsy Traveller pupils have a named person and a 'place of safety' to encourage their confidence and overcome fears they may have of the school setting. This may also encourage them to seek advice and support for any difficulties they may be experiencing. Having a named person in an institution is an important point of call for Gypsy Traveller children. Such sensitive provision can enhance the confidence that some pupils have in the school and the staff. There was an indication, however, from the TES team at South Hall Village School that mainstream staff at the school had not taken on board that they also had to accept responsibility for the Gypsy Traveller children. Often the Gypsy Traveller children were labelled as 'your children' to the TES:

> 'Often, when there is a problem with one of the Gypsy Traveller children, we are told it's "your children" again and so we have to deal with it. The staff have to also accept

> and take responsibility for the children, because only then
> can they understand that Gypsy Traveller children are truly
> a part of the school and must be integrated rather than
> segregated as they are.' (Janet, TES teacher)

This particular TES teacher found that her role was somewhat
marginalised in the school and as a result she was often excluded from
circulars and memos and felt she missed out information that was
useful and relevant to her. She also felt there was no real physical base
for her and lack of immediate support when a problem arose. She did
not feel that there were staff she could approach and would probably
have to seek support from other members of the TES who may not be
in the immediate vicinity. She also felt that those children who missed
out on their education because of their nomadic lifestyle were classed
as having Special Educational Needs. So, although the TES role
benefited from the support and sanctioning of the LEA and the head
and in terms of the school's ethos there was a sense of its effectiveness
being compromised to some degree at the level of delivery.

The school does aim to integrate the children by, for example, the
inclusion of Gypsy Traveller culture within the curriculum and by an
even-handed application of school policies. One aim of this approach
is that Gypsy Traveller children should not be seen as being 'different'.
One class teacher, Marie, said: 'We try to integrate Traveller children,
try to treat them like everyone else, with the proviso that we have to
treat them differently.' Even though Gypsy Traveller children may be
integrated to an extent (such as in the playground and in some of the
classrooms), they tended to be an exclusive group. Marie went on to
say: 'We want the children to mix with the other children and they are
given this opportunity for example in the playground and in the dinner
hall. But they make themselves into an exclusive group, so this becomes
a problem.'

Such efforts at trying to integrate the children generally did not
succeed, one result being that Gypsy Traveller children are more likely
to be picked on and experience some form of racism and bullying.
However, the self-exclusion of Gypsy Traveller children may also be a
reason for them having experienced racism and bullying in the first
place. One of the teachers indicated that the main problem the Gypsy
Traveller children face is that their lifestyle is so different from their
peers that it is very difficult to integrate with them. This lack of
integration makes it more likely that they may experience some form
of bullying. The perception on the part of some teaching staff that at
some level responsibility for lack of integration lies within the ambit

of Gypsy Traveller culture suggests that responses towards incidents of bullying or racist name-calling may not be dealt with adequately.

The culturally affirmative curriculum

There is a need for Gypsy Traveller children to be included in the mainstream experiences of schooling for all children. This includes the development of more flexible curricula and the removal of all derogatory references to Gypsy Travellers from school texts and other materials, as well as the inclusion of references to Gypsy Travellers and other ethnic minority groups in a positive and balanced way. It also includes a long-term commitment on the part of LEAs to resource reforms aimed at ending discrimination adequately and to ensure that systems are in place to monitor and evaluate outcomes effectively. In rural settings this means a recognition that bullying and racist name-calling of Gypsy Travellers by white pupils are treated as racist incidents and dealt with similarly to incidents between white, black or Asian children.

Generally most schools are aware of the need for books and learning materials to reflect Gypsy Traveller culture in as many ways as possible. Although South Hall Village School was one of the schools that had established positive links with the local Gypsy Traveller community, when the school was visited there were no visible displays of Traveller education materials or resources. Compared to other schools that had a visible presence of Gypsy Travellers in the form of a board that displayed pictures of Gypsy Traveller culture, including photographs of a wedding and visits to local sites, no such material was evident in South Hall Village School. Surprisingly this was true not just in the main corridors but also the area designated for the TES. Furthermore, there was no awareness regarding the bilingual status[5] of many Gypsy Traveller pupils. This indicated that the pupils' knowledge of a second language is rarely recognised, commended or promoted. When asked about the visible presence of Gypsy Travellers, Andy, a TES teacher, replied:

> 'I just don't think they have the space. The school is small as it is and things that go on the walls in the corridors are the most important things. These are not seen to be those related to Gypsy Travellers. The issue of language is something the school has to think about and has to recognise that Gypsy Traveller children as well as being the

same as other children, they are also different. They have different backgrounds and they have different needs.'

The inclusion of the Gypsy Traveller background in the curriculum is first and foremost to provide an environment in which Gypsy Traveller pupils feel welcome and thus want to come to the school: 'The school has to be welcoming and has to celebrate their culture to do this' (Andy, TES teacher).

Apart from the importance of learning materials having relevance to pupils' real-life experiences and their understanding of the world in which they live, it is also fundamentally important in the context of the affirmation of self and group identity.

As part of the attempt to affirm Gypsy Traveller pupils' values and identities, another school visited in the project in an urban setting had a number of very large and visible display boards near the entrance of the school celebrating Gypsy Traveller culture. The Gypsy Traveller pupils are the ones who frequently develop the display boards themselves. The children take photographs of their trips, for example to Appleby Horse Fair (an annual event in the calendar of most Gypsy Travellers) and other positive depictions of their way of life. This is an implicit and at the same time an unequivocal confirmation that Gypsy Traveller culture, history and language are legitimate, relevant and worth celebrating. Such practice would seem to be vital for many Gypsy Traveller pupils who may feel they are not valued in a strange institutional school setting, when the majority of their peers are likely to subscribe to the commonly perceived negative public stereotypes of Gypsy Travellers.

Interestingly, the use of photography projects within urban schools to record Gypsy Traveller pupils' cultural experiences is increasingly becoming commonplace (Myers and Bhopal, 2005). The results either appear on large display boards or prominently placed photography albums in the schools. One distinctive appeal of these records is their apparent exoticism in the urban context; they tend to highlight the Gypsy Traveller link to the countryside, with pictures of trips to horse fairs being a particular favourite. As discussed earlier Sibley (1981, 1986) has shown how positive accounts of Gypsy Travellers tend to focus on a romanticised image. In the rural context it appears the lack of exoticism contributes to a devaluing of these cultural markers, essentially this aspect of Gypsy Traveller culture is a familiar part of rural society. The distinctiveness of Gypsy Traveller culture is clearly *felt* within the rural context but perhaps harder to delineate or define, it therefore becomes harder to establish within the contexts of a school's curriculum and ethos.

In addition to affirming identities, the inclusion of Gypsy Traveller culture in the curriculum is to the educational benefit of all pupils in the school. Including Gypsy Traveller culture into the main body of 'knowledge' is not just in the interests of Gypsy Traveller pupils, but *all* pupils. Gypsy Travellers have a long-standing presence in the locality of the school; they are and will remain part of the local community. It is justified on the grounds that it improves the quality and the accuracy of 'knowledge' learned by *all* pupils in the school.

The TES teachers at South Hall Village School felt that the culture of Gypsy Traveller children should be celebrated more than it was. They felt the presence of Gypsy Traveller children in school made all children aware of ethnic and cultural diversity and its value in an otherwise 'mono-ethnic' (all-white) institution. It would also emphasise the gaps and perhaps the degree of accuracy in the body of 'knowledge' that is currently presented to all children. The children can add richness to the school population (which is neither culturally nor ethnically diverse), which extends important opportunities for curriculum development: 'By Gypsy Traveller children taking a part in the school, they see their culture is worth defending and it empowers them. By their presence they make a tremendous contribution to the learning experience of other children and adults' (Janet, TES teacher).

Conclusion

This chapter has argued that the rural setting can affect aspects of good practice for Gypsy Traveller pupils in schools. The contextual definition and spatial location in which racism occurs is a fundamental part of how racism is viewed. In South Hall Village School there was a sense that racism was not being defined as such because it defied standard expectation around the visibility of skin colour. The rural environment plainly contributed to a lack of contact with ethnic minorities other than Gypsy Travellers and the position of Gypsy Travellers in relation to the wider community was not generally equated to their being seen as a group who would be accorded the same status as a visible ethnic minority (that is, Asian or Black). Lack of contact with ethnic minority groups does not mean lack of conceptions about them. Those who seldom have contact with ethnic minorities often perceive them through stereotypes and as 'other'. Ironically, the perception of Gypsy Travellers in the rural context is one that is both familiar and alien; despite a long-standing involvement in rural life, Gypsy Travellers remain seen as 'other' by the dominant white culture.

Schools need equal opportunities and race equality policies and practices that are explicitly inclusive of Gypsy Traveller pupils. Furthermore, all schools should record racist incidents and deal with them effectively. Name-calling associated with ethnic background must be seen as racist bullying. There is a need for racist incidents to be recorded and formally investigated. There must also be effective and explicit sanctions to deal with and/or prevent racist behaviour. School pastoral systems need to assist sensitively in the combating of racist attitudes and behaviour. Incidents of racist bullying should be recorded and investigated in accordance with the 2000 Race Relations (Amendment) Act and dealt with in terms of managing diversity.

The DfEE research identified a worrying approach towards the management of racist problems within rural schools. Reflecting the wider community, the majority population of the schools (teachers, children, support, administrative and other staff) was overwhelmingly white. The presence of a 'white other' group did not trigger the same responses that would be commonplace in a typical urban school where black or Asian minority groups are easily recognisable. As a result, racist behaviour was not necessarily tackled as vigorously as it would be in an urban setting. Simple systems to monitor racist incidents, for example, and the schools' responses to these incidents were not in place.

It was clear these systems had been overlooked by the schools rather than deliberately omitted, but this in itself raised questions about what else would be overlooked for the similar reasons. At the level of an individual racist attack or incident there was a clear possibility that neither the victim nor the perpetrator would be recognised by the school institution. In other words, in addition to the known incidents of racist behaviour, there is a likelihood that there is large degree of unknown incidents: unknown to the institution, though accepted as the norm by the wider Gypsy Traveller and non-Gypsy Traveller communities.

These identifiable problems contribute not only to the devaluing of education for Gypsy Travellers but also for the wider community. An inclusive education system is critical to the delivery of education to Gypsy Traveller children but it also contributes greatly to the education of the white majority rural population who have little or no direct exposure to other cultures. Involving the whole school community, including pupils and parents, to identify problems and generate solutions is one aspect of inclusionary practice. This involves careful planning, monitoring and documenting outcomes for children and educators and an awareness that diversity is not merely tolerated, but accepted and celebrated by all groups. Such thinking has become standard practice throughout many urban schools with a diverse intake of pupils; it is still a novelty in the rural setting, despite the long-established presence of Gypsy Travellers in rural culture.

The creative work and practice of the TES can certainly contribute to the quality of learning for all pupils. TES work is, however, seen as being isolated to the Gypsy Traveller community. There is little linkage between the work of TES teachers and their non-TES colleagues. Problems surrounding the education of Gypsy Traveller children are seen as being solely the responsibility of the 'specialists', the TES teachers. Responsibility is not seen as being owned by the wider teaching profession. On the flip side, where Gypsy Traveller children could contribute to a wider, diversity-driven education for the whole school there is little enthusiasm or support for this. Again this situation appears to be driven by the peculiarities of having a 'white other' group historically resented by the white majority. In comparable urban locations schools enthusiastically embrace celebrations of Diwali and Eid just as they do Christmas, children hear stories of Anancy and Good King Wenceslas and Little Miss Trouble. The culture of Gypsy Traveller children – Appleby horse fair, the extraordinary story of the Romani diaspora and dialect – all goes unnoticed by other children. This is a missed opportunity.

Tony Boxall's photographs seem dated and at times overly quaint in the harsh glare of the 21st century. What remains, though, leafing through his photographs, is a recognisable sense of the otherness of the Gypsy Traveller community compared to the settled population. That otherness remains a significant factor in the education of many children from many different communities; currently it is a cause of discrimination and inequality. There is, however, a huge and pressing need to turn the tables on this state of affairs by including Gypsy Traveller culture within mainstream education.

Acknowledgements

I would like to thank the DfEE for providing funding to carry out the research. The views expressed in this chapter are the views of the author and not the department. I would like to express my thanks to the school and TES who participated in the research and gave generously of their time. I would also like to thank Martin Myers who read earlier drafts of this chapter.

Notes

[1] Recently, the terms used to describe those from nomadic or semi-nomadic communities have become problematic and controversial. The generic term 'Travellers' has become acceptable and the preferred terminology to describe a number of distinct communities who either are, or have been, traditionally associated with a nomadic way of life. These communities can include Gypsies/Romanies of English, Scottish or Welsh heritage; Gypsies and Travellers of Irish heritage; Roma/Gypsies mainly from Eastern and Central Europe; Fairground families or Showpeople; Circus families/groups; New Travellers and Bargees. The use of some of the specific and traditional definitions of the different communities is being insisted upon by members of the communities themselves. For this reason, the use of the generic term 'Travellers' is unhelpful as it uses families to distinguish the main target group. The aim of the research project was to specifically investigate the education of Gypsy Travellers. While in the main, the majority of pupils were from Gypsy/Romany backgrounds of English, Scottish or Welsh heritage, a number were of Irish Gypsy or Traveller heritage. Most of the schools also made provision for children from Fairground and/or Circus backgrounds. For this chapter the term 'Gypsy Traveller' has been used to represent the main groups who participated in the research. However, I accept the continuing evolution of terms used to describe these groups. Given this context, it was noted that the use of this term should not contribute to any stereotypical or inaccurate definitions.

[2] This is a pseudonym.

[3] These figures are from the 1997 school OFSTED report. The school was due to be re-inspected in the 2003-04 academic session.

[4] All the names cited from the research project are pseudonyms.

[5] Some groups within the Romany diaspora speak a version of Romanes, the Romany language that has travelled and developed with the Romany people, since they left India. The Roma communities from Eastern European countries speak inflected, complete versions of Romanes, while the English Romanies (Romanichals) speak a dialect where the nouns are Romany and the grammar is English. This dialect is called 'Pogadijib', meaning 'broken tongue'.

References

Acton, T. and Kenrick, D. (1991) 'From summer voluntary to European Community bureaucracy: the development of special provision for Traveller education in the United Kingdom since 1967', *European Journal of Intercultural Studies*, vol 1, no 3, pp 47-62.

Agyeman, J. and Spooner, R. (1997) 'Ethnicity and the rural environment', in P. Cloke and J. Little (eds) *Contested countryside cultures: Otherness, marginalization and rurality*, London: Routledge, pp 197-217.

Bhopal, K., Gundara, J., Jones, C. and Owen, C. (2000) *Working towards inclusive education: Aspects of good practice for Gypsy Travellers*, Research Report RR238, London: Department for Education and Employment.

Boxall, T. (1992) *Gypsy camera*, Surrey: Creative Monochrome Publishers.

Broadhurst, K. and Wright, A. (2004) 'Challenging rural racism through education', in J. Garland and N. Chakraborti (eds) *Rural racism*, Cullompton: Willan Publishing, pp 161-74.

Cambridgeshire Travellers Review (2003) *Gypsy council for education, welfare and civil rights*, Cambridge: Cambridgeshire Research Group.

Casciani, D. (2004) 'Rural England, Gypsies and land reform', BBC, available at www.bbc.co.uk.

Chakraborti, N. and Garland, J. (2004) (eds) *Rural racism*, Cullompton: Willan Publishing.

Cloke, P. and Little, J. (1997) (eds) *Contested countryside cultures: Otherness, marginalization and rurality*, London: Routledge.

Commission for Racial Equality (2001) *Gypsy Travellers enquiry*, London: Commission for Racial Equality.

Dorset County Council Gypsy Traveller Policy (2002) *Gypsy and Traveller liaison policy*, Dorset: Dorset County Council.

Jordan, E. (2001a) 'Exclusion of Travellers in state schools', *Educational Research*, vol 43, no 2, pp 117-32.

Jordan, E. (2001b) 'From interdependence, to dependence and independence: home and school learning for Traveller children', *Childhood*, vol 8, no 1, pp 57-74.

Kiddle, C. (1999) *Traveller children: A voice for Themselves*, London: Jessica Kingsley.

Liegeois, J.P. (1987) *School provision for Gypsy and Traveller children: A synthesis report*, Luxembourg: Office for Official Publications of the European Communities.

Liegeois, J.P. (1998) *School provision for ethnic minorities: The Gypsy paradigm*, Hatfield: University of Hertfordshire Press.

Lloyd, G., Stead, J. and Jordan, E. (1999) *Travellers at school: The experience of parents, pupils and teachers*, Edinburgh: University of Edinburgh.

Local Government Association (2003) *Gypsies and Travellers: Moving forward on policy and service development*, London: Local Government Association.

Minority Cohesion Team (2003) *Gypsy Traveller funding*, London: Department for Education and Skills.

Myers, M. and Bhopal, K. (2005) '"Because they're black they're better off than us" – Gypsy Travellers, social exclusion and marginalisation', paper presented at the BSA 2005 conference, University of York, 21–23 March 2005.

NATT (1999) *National Association of Teachers of Travellers, annual report*, Wolverhampton: NATT.

Neal, S. (2002) 'Rural landscapes, representations and racism: examining multicultural citizenship and policy-making in the English countryside', *Ethnic and Racial Studies*, vol 25, no 3, pp 442-61.

NFU (2004) 'Human Rights Usurp Planning Laws', at www.nfucountryside.org.uk.

OFSTED (1996) *The education of travelling children*, London: OFSTED.

OFSTED (1999) *Raising the attainment of minority ethnic pupils: school and LEA responses*, London: OFSTED.

Okely, J. (1983) *The Traveller-Gypsies*, Cambridge: Cambridge University Press.

Plowden Report (1967) *Children and their primary schools*, London: Her Majesty's Stationery Office.

Save The Children (2001) *Denied a future*, London: Save The Children.

Scottish Equal Opportunities Committee (2001) *Inquiry into Gypsy Travellers and public bodies*, Edinburgh: Equal Opportunities Commission.

Scottish Parliament (2001) *Gypsy Travellers and public sector policies*, London: Her Majesty's Stationery Office.

Sibley, D. (1981) *Outsiders in urban society*, Oxford: Blackwell.

Sibley, D. (1986) 'Persistence or change? Conflicting interpretations of peripheral minorities', *Environment and Planning: Society and Space*, vol 4, no 2, pp 57-70.

Swann Report (1985) *Education for all: The report of the committee of enquiry into the education of children from ethnic minority groups*, London: Her Majesty's Stationery Office.

Thomas, R. (2003) 'Pride & Prejudice', *Country Living*, October, pp 78-85, at www.countryliving.co.uk.

Turner, R. (1999) 'Fellow Travellers', *Guardian*, 24 August, pp 5-6.

Yin, R. (1984) *Case study research: Design and methods*, London: Sage Publications.

NINE

Rethinking rural race equality

Early interventions, continuities and changes

Perminder Dhillon

Introduction

This chapter highlights the key successes and challenges of the National Council of Voluntary Organisations' Rural Anti-Racism Project in promoting race equality within the rural voluntary sector. It addresses the gaps left by the project and in light of more recent legislative changes and political priorities, examines a series of issues that need to be addressed in order that the current and emerging rural race equality initiatives are inclusive and relevant today.

Agyeman (1989) highlighted the problems experienced by Black and minority ethnic communities in accessing the countryside. However, it was not until 1992, that the concept of 'rural racism' gained prominence in describing the experiences of visitors as well as dwellers from Black and minority ethnic communities in rural areas. Racial prejudice and discrimination had existed in rural areas for decades but had remained largely uncharted and unacknowledged in academia, rural policy and practice.

Eric Jay's (1992) report, *Keep them in Birmingham*, set out to examine the extent of racial prejudice and discrimination in the rural counties of Cornwall, Devon, Dorset and Somerset in the South-West of England. Contrary to the usual 'no problem here' assertion, this report, which took its title from an interview quote with a white college student, highlighted countless examples of racial harassment and discrimination across key rural agencies and service providers. There was also evidence of organised activity by right-wing organisations such as the British National Party (BNP) in the South-West.

In response to the recommendations contained in the Jay Report aimed at the voluntary sector, the National Council for Voluntary Organisations (NCVO) set up a consultative group that was comprised of the Commission for Racial Equality (CRE), the Rural Development Commission (RDC) and 15 national voluntary organisations.[1] This group debated the issues raised by the report and contributed to the development of a proposal that led to the setting up of the Rural Anti-Racism Project (RARP). The RARP was the first funded national initiative aimed at addressing rural racism by building the capacity of the voluntary sector in England and Wales to tackle the issue.

The Rural Anti-Racism Project

The RARP was originally conceived as a full-time project for a period of three to five years. However, only part funding was secured from the CRE and the Baring Foundation (with the RDC undertaking to support some specific initiatives) for a three-year period. NCVO decided to proceed with the project on a part-time basis. The project had two initial aims: to work collaboratively with at least six national voluntary organisations in developing race equality policies and practices in rural areas and to provide education and information on rural race equality issues. A number of related objectives were identified:

- to support isolated workers in rural areas;
- to set up a national forum on rural race equality issues;
- to develop race equality training materials suitable for use in rural areas.

The RARP was based in the NCVO's rural team and started in October 1994, when I was appointed part-time as the national project coordinator. My skill base in training, community development, race equality and women's equality issues was essential in giving shape to the priorities of the project. Having been a print and television journalist, I was also able to use my networks in ensuring that the project reached a wider audience through coverage on radio, television and in the print media.

The project was formally launched in February 1995 by the BBC's *The Archers*[2] team (to coincide with *The Archers* storyline on rural racism) and by Baroness Shreela Flather who herself had been subject to racial attacks in her rural home in Berkshire. The launch attracted national coverage on radio and in print media. The launch and the RARP's first conference – Challenging Rural Racism (see Dhillon, 1994) – which was supported by the RDC, immediately gave the project a high profile. From this basis the project was able to begin to interest a broad range of organisations in the issue of rural racism. The Challenging

Rural Racism conference considered the findings of a new report by the National Alliance of Women's Organisations (NAWO) (Goldsmith and Makris, 1994), outlined the practical rural race equality strategies devised by the CRE, explained the remit of the RARP and detailed the discrimination faced by Travellers and Black women in rural areas.

Building on Jay's evidence base

The Jay and the NAWO reports paved the way for similar investigations in other parts of the UK (Derbyshire, 1994; Nizhar, 1995; Suzin, 1996; Kenny, 1997). As well as these reports, a number of conferences and seminars were organised in different geographical areas (for example Action for Racial Equality across Leicestershire (AREAL), 1996). Conclusions from the research and meetings were similar. They revealed a widespread pattern in which racial prejudice, discrimination and harassment were everyday realities for many people from Black and minority ethnic communities visiting, living, working and studying in rural areas. Many people were subjected to numerous incidents of racial harassment and violence; and the rural idyll was marred by ugly views perpetuated by organisations such as the National Front, Combat 18 and the BNP. Further, there was little effective action to challenge any of these issues.

At the same time, the CRE followed up the Jay Report by holding regional conferences in all of the four rural counties investigated in the report. The aim of these events was to foster some cohesive plan of action and resulted in race equality networks being initiated in the South-West, some of which went on to develop as Racial Equality Councils. The RARP was involved in two of these events and again received much exposure. The plethora of national research and regional events, combined with the fact that the RARP was based in the NCVO's rural team, ensured that from the onset the project was in touch with a broad range of rural voluntary organisations from which to enlist partnership and collaboration.

Working in partnership

The RARP devised a partnership framework to work with national and local partners. This clearly stated what the project could offer and the commitment required from partners. The aim of working with at least six national organisations was exceeded as the project managed to engage over 27 national voluntary bodies. These included major national rural organisations such as the National Federation of Women's

Institutes, Action for Communities in Rural England (ACRE) and the National Federation of Young Farmers' Youth Clubs. Some of these organisations were targeted specifically as they represented major rural constituencies. Others, like ACRE and the National Association of Citizens' Advice Bureaux (NACAB), had been members of the NCVO's steering group that developed the concept for the RARP. The project also worked with many regional and local voluntary organisations and a further ten largely urban-based organisations.[3]

Most partner organisations saw the RARP as a vital resource in tackling this uncharted issue and made a firm commitment to the partnership agreement. One or two organisations were involved because they had to be seen to be 'politically correct'. Whatever the motivation, all partners attested to the benefit of this collaboration in the evaluation of the project (Walker, 1999). Again, major rural organisations were represented on the advisory group of the project set up to support, monitor and evaluate its work. Right from the onset, the RARP included Gypsy and Traveller issues and representative organisations were involved in the advisory group.[4]

Key successes: raising awareness and building capacity

The project was successful in two areas: in raising awareness of rural racism and in building the capacity of the rural voluntary sector in tackling this issue. Partners benefited from a range of support activities organised by the RARP. Summaries and case studies were produced regularly to broadcast findings of new research, to highlight experiences of rural racism and to provide guidance for partners (NCVO, 1994, 1997, 2000).

The RARP also produced an information briefing on a quarterly basis for partners, the RARP News Roundup. This included information about joint activities, news from partners that required wider circulation, media coverage of rural racism, national and regional events, training resources and emerging reports on racism and exclusion in rural areas. The RARP News Roundup was also circulated via the NCVO rural team's quarterly mailing reaching over 500 individuals and organisations and was sent in response to queries from students, researchers and individuals living or working in rural areas. The project annually dealt with over 300 enquiries on rural race-equality related issues. The RARP partners also received the NCVO's Rural Information Service mailings, which included comprehensive briefing on rural issues.

Regular events, either informal meetings or focused workshops, were held at the NCVO where partners could receive information and training, share their expertise, network and support each other. Topics included devising race equality policies, the Rural White Paper (HM Government, 2000) and assessing rural race equality training needs.

Specific seminars and conferences were organised in collaboration with a number of partners and were held in different geographical regions. The topics ranged from addressing children's issues to looking at more generic issues of community care and voting patterns; for example 'Valuing Children: Nurturing Racial Identity in the Early Years', which was held in Norwich in partnership with the Working Group Against Racism in Children's Resources; 'Community Care Needs of People from Black and Minority Ethnic Groups' (Marsh, 1996), which was held in Atherstone and was organised with North Warwickshire Community Volunteer Services and 'Supporting Operation Black Vote in Rural Areas', which was organised with Charter 88 and held in Exeter. Partners therefore received information on specific rural as well as more generic race equality issues.

This partnership arrangement meant that the project was able to issue guidance to organisations at short notice. For example, verbal and written guidance was given by the project when one of the RARP's partners alerted the coordinator to right-wing neo-Nazi groups targeting village halls for their social gigs and speaking events. This guidance resulted in many village committees blocking these bookings for community halls and rooms in local pubs.

Partners were also supported on issues through a 'case work' approach. This sometimes involved getting more support secured from their head office – largely urban based – for the rural constituency. Examples include getting the national policy officer to work with a local rural constituency in drawing up a detailed work programme on race equality. Another approach was to secure additional training resources from the central training team to enable a specific training event around rural racism to take place, enabling the good practice to be cascaded to other parts of the organisation. Partners were also able to call on my expertise to deliver specific tailored training events for a number of organisations. Among these were the National Federation of Young Farmers' Youth Clubs, the National Council for Voluntary Childcare Organisations and Victim Support.

The RARP was also instrumental in supporting organisations in addressing support issues for isolated workers. Initiatives such as working with the Devon Probation Service saw the emergence of a Black Workers Support Group that became a key partner in the South-West

Race Equality Network. I was invited to speak on rural racism at a number of national and regional conferences in England, Wales and Scotland. This included ACRE's annual conferences that brought together all rural community councils, the Scottish Council for Voluntary Organisations, Victim Support and MIND. This again contributed to the project reaching a much wider audience.

The success in gaining a high profile on rural racism in the media was partly due to my background and my written and broadcast work. The RARP had also prepared media packs to answer general queries. Another contributing factor was the wide coverage received by the BBC Radio 4's *The Archers* serial following the introduction of racial attacks in Ambridge. The project was featured in numerous articles in national and regional newspapers as well as in rural magazines. Regional television newsrooms covered the issue as new research emerged or when certain personal experiences were highlighted. BBC Radio 4's *Farming Today* dedicated a whole programme to rural racism, featuring the RARP as a key project. *Farming Today* went on to regularly feature news from the project. I also managed to include rural experiences of racial harassment in a BBC 2 documentary called *Skin* (1995). This exposure in the media enabled a much wider publicity of the work of the project.

As part of capacity building, the RARP started a debate about 'rurally relevant race equality' practice and challenged generic rural policy through its work with its partners and major rural organisations. This debate sought to use the 'Think Global, Act Local' notion, and advanced that it was necessary to encompass the governing principles of key race equality frameworks developed in an urban context but that it was essential for the local communities and organisations to determine the right solutions for their needs and profiles. Urban models could not be transported lock, stock and barrel to rural settings.

Some funders sought to impose funding criteria from an urban context to a rural one, encompassing issues such as including a certain percentage of users from Black and minority ethnic communities. Others wanted issue-based projects to be funded, for example on immigration advice, Black women-only groups or the setting up of 24-hour crisis lines based on models developed largely in London. The RARP supported local solutions that enabled organisations to think through key issues relating to the small numbers of Black and minority ethnic communities, the constraints of rural funding and lack of sustainable local infrastructure. The project advanced that it was necessary for generic projects to deal with a number of local issues and it worked to build the capacity of mainstream rural organisations like Citizens'Advice Bureaux and the National Federation of Women's Institutes to adopt a more inclusive approach to their activities.

The separation of rural and race equality issues were challenged on many occasions with the partner organisations. Indeed, similar parallels were drawn between the problems faced by the rural voluntary sector and many Black organisations. It was emphasised that equality should be integral to rural policy and practice and not be seen to be an addendum to be discarded when it appeared not to be relevant. The project was also able to influence the promotion of equality in all of NCVO's rural work. A submission to the consultation on the Rural White Paper (HM Government, 2000) ensured that issues related to minority ethnic communities in rural areas were officially acknowledged.

Key successes: expanding the agenda and disseminating good practice

The project organised three national conferences to expand the debate on rural racism and to spread good practice. The first anniversary of the project brought together the RARP partners and key organisations in the Germinating the Seeds of Equality conference. This conference assessed the impact of the work initiated by the project. The conclusion of the day is summed up by one quote from a RARP partner, the Rural Group of Churches/Arthur Rank Centre: 'This must be treated as phase one of the work in view of the deep rooted racist attitudes in the countryside. The project has tried to tackle the impossible with slender resources – you cannot move the mountain with a firework.'

The second conference sought to include issues concerning Traveller (Irish and New Travellers) and Romany Gypsies in the rural race-equality agenda. With the collaboration of Cambridgeshire County Council Gypsy section, the project brought together key players in a landmark conference, the only one of its kind ever held, titled Land, People and Freedom, in June 1997 (Acton et al, 1998). The title summed up issues concerning Traveller and Romany communities in rural areas.[5]

Prominent members from all the major Romany, including the International Romani Union Presidium, Traveller and New Traveller organisations delivered keynote speeches. Workshops were facilitated by professionals from or working with Gypsies and Travellers. Nearly 200 Travellers, liaison workers, practitioners and policy makers from a wide variety of voluntary and statutory sectors from England, Wales and Ireland attended the conference. The primary purpose of this event was to address and overcome two false dichotomies. The first was the separation that existed between most mainstream race equality initiatives and Traveller liaison work. The second was the way that Traveller liaison work was seen as distinct from the work of the rural voluntary sector.

The RARP's third conference, titled Black, White and Green (1998), organised in collaboration with Worcester Racial Equality Council and held at the completion of the project, brought together key RARP partners and major rural race equality projects. The aim of the conference was to disseminate good practice and to make recommendations for ongoing work, including the proposed rural anti-racism forum. The conference emphasised that the work of the RARP must be taken forward through the development of a national initiative. This led to the setting up of a steering group that developed the Rural Race Equality Action Programme (RREAP). Two years later, RREAP was launched at the NCVO's annual conference, supported by all political parties, to take forward the work developed by the RARP. RREAP was set up to be a national forum on rural race equality issues. The organisation still remains an embryonic body. This is largely due to divided views about the political focus of the organisation.

Key difficulties: constraints and limitations

Developing Black organisations in rural areas

Although the RARP achieved much success in raising awareness and engaging the voluntary sector, a number of initiatives did not come to fruition. In part this was due to the project being delivered on a part-time basis for three years, resulting in lack of development time. There were also other reasons. For example, the work that was initiated with Sia, the national Black Development Agency, to develop Black voluntary organisations in rural areas was an ambitious national project and required substantial committed time, resources and funding from both organisations, which neither could commit at that time.

Developing a national forum on rural race equality issues

The South-West of England had received focused support from the CRE (regional conferences; funding specific pilot projects and the

South-West Race Equality Network) and the RDC, whereas the infrastructure for promoting rural race equality was less developed in other parts of England and Wales. Advancing rural race equality strategies in other geographical areas was largely left to the local CREs and race equality networks (for example, Charnwood, Norwich, Sussex and Worcester RECs and York REN). Regional infrastructure was less well developed or non-existent. The RARP had hoped that similar regional forums would emerge in different areas to feed into a national forum on rural race equality as all regions of England and Wales required the same level of development and funding as was afforded to the South-West of England. It was outside the scope of the project to begin the development of regional structures. As a result, the national forum could not be initiated at that stage.

The RARP also had a remit to develop rurally relevant race equality training that could be used at local and regional levels. Funding was secured to initiate the first stage of this development in 1997 with a grant from the Gulbenkian Trust. The project carried out an audit of existing resources via a questionnaire survey and by organising two consultative seminars to determine the gaps in knowledge, skills and resources. A consultant was hired to write a report on the outcome of the audit and to develop a checklist of needs and issues, together with a three-stage development plan. The plan could not proceed due to the absence of further RARP resources.

Race equality initiatives after Jay

Many rural race equality initiatives initiated after the Jay Report were funded on a short-term and ad hoc basis. Many networks were encouraged by the CRE to progress towards becoming local race equality councils, bound by the same relationship to the CRE as the long-established local CREs. The underpinning principle was that rural areas were lagging behind urban areas in their capacity to tackle race equality issues. It was therefore inevitable that some newly set-up CREs sought to follow the practice established in urban areas. There was also a reliance on individual efforts and commitment and an expectation that rural Black and minority communities would champion the cause of race equality.

Further, whereas the RARP had acknowledged the need to build the capacity of the generic voluntary organisations to deliver race equality initiatives, there was a call for specialist support services. Most of these services could not be justified on the numbers of dwellers in the local areas (see de Lima, this volume) except on one issue – that of supporting victims of racist harassment and violence. Another perceived issue was the homogeneous nature of rural dwellers. In the same way that Black and minority ethnic communities are regarded as a homogeneous group, dwellers in rural areas were talked about in the same way. These perceptions were also present among some of the RARP's urban and rural partners. Often they manifested at meetings and seminars where use of certain terminology by members of a rurally based organisation would be used to exemplify 'deeply entrenched racist views of rural dwellers' (a quote from one participant representing a very urban organisation).

The promotion of activities to develop mutual understanding of different cultures was seen by some as shifting the focus from anti-racist work to multiculturalism. Yet this was one of the greatest needs presented by the RARP partners. This, and many more issues, impressed on the RARP that there was a need to educate urban-based organisations about rural issues (Walker, 1999).

One of the partnership aims of the project was to link organisations in rural areas with those in urban areas. Although the National Federation of Young Farmers' Youth Clubs had been doing exchange visits with young farmers in Africa, it proved impossible to find suitable hosts in places like Brixton or Southall. A number of factors contributed to this. Most urban-based organisations did not see educating the rural constituency as part of their role. There was also a profound lack of knowledge about rural communities and related issues. The RARP did not have the resources to engage meaningfully with urban-based organisations to build their capacity to engage with rural issues. No systematic evaluation exists that assesses the effectiveness of the approaches and processes of the race equality initiatives that emerged after the Jay Report. The CRE did commission an overview but this has remained unpublished.

New urgencies: the increase in racial harassment and violence in rural areas

Thirteen years after the publication of the Jay Report, racial incidents continue to rise (Chakraborti and Garland, 2004). In 2001, based on Home Office figures on racial incidents for England and Wales, Rayner (2001) indicated that people from minority ethnic communities in low-density 'ethnic' areas were ten times more likely to be attacked on racial grounds. The likelihood of experiencing racial harassment and violence was estimated at being one in 16 in Devon and Cornwall, one in 15 in South Wales and one in 12 in Northumbria. Other areas included were Somerset, Norfolk, Avon, Durham and Cumbria. These areas represented the ten worst constabularies for racial incidents in England and Wales and yet between them they only accounted for 5% of the total minority ethnic population. Figures from the North Wales Police over a three-year period from April 2001 to March 2004 logged 205 racially motivated hate crimes in the county. Research by Chakraborti and Garland (2004) provides the data that show the correlation between the BNP setting up an operation in an area and the corresponding increase in racist attacks. The Institute of Race Relations (IRR) and the National Civil Rights Movement (NCRM) continue to catalogue the attacks on asylum seekers and refugees. Further, national figures show that deaths where a racial motive is involved have also increased. In 2004 the IRR set the figure at 11 since 1991. The NCRM have put this figure at 157 and included deaths in police and psychiatric custody, from racial harassment and where asylum seekers have died seeking entrance to the UK. Despite these figures, research shows that racist incidents are grossly under-reported and by extrapolation this must be even more of a case in rural areas. The most recent study of rural racism shows that the 'invisibility' of racist crimes continues to go unnoticed by rural agencies (Grewal, 2004).

New guidance for the police on the logging and monitoring of racial incidents, community safety initiatives, multi-agency forums and networks have produced an increase in the availability of statistics on racial incidents. However, there is a dearth of information about incidents involving asylum seekers, refugees and the long-established rural communities of Roma Gypsies and Travellers. There is also no national overview of incidents in rural areas according to DEFRA's definition of rurality. This key gap must be addressed.

Defining perpetrators of racial harassment and violence

Sibbit's work on racist perpetrators was based on two London boroughs (Sibbit, 1997, 2004) but it is worth considering the model in relation to rural areas. Sibbit's model describes three layers within a community – *the actual perpetrators* (those who actually commit the act), *the potential perpetrators* (those who are 'around' and may get involved if the opportunity arises) and *the perpetrator community* (the community that allows this to take place). Contrary to the conclusions by some reports that minority ethnic households living in rural areas suffer from racist language and violence 'as a result of white communities' fear of the unknown and unfamiliar' (Grewal, 2004), research shows that most racial harassment and violence is motivated by hate and aggression (Searchlight Educational Trust, 1995).

According to the experiences reported to victim support organisations, there are three types of harassment experience: those offences that are committed by lone individuals (either as a one-off or sustained offending); harassment carried out by groups 'looking for trouble' and harassment committed by groups where the offences are premeditated and organised. National analysis is required to understand the extent, the pattern and the motivation behind racial harassment in rural areas for lone, group and premeditated offenders – the 'actual perpetrators' defined by Sibbit. Sibbit also states that perpetrators can be any age and the popular image of 'skinhead thugs' doesn't hold true. Research by Searchlight shows that many 'respectable' members of the community can be perpetrators. For example, the local British National Party (BNP) organiser in a village near Burnley was an ex-police officer. In certain parts of England, significant sections of the 'ordinary' population had voted for the BNP's councillors in 2003.

Again, research by Searchlight has shown that attacks in rural areas on Black individuals and families are often premeditated and organised. Some have been incited by organisations like the BNP and Combat 18 who are known to target rural areas for recruitment, especially of young men. Gordon (1994) has also noted the role played by extremist organisations in relation to the bulk of racial harassment and racist violence in Britain.

Research commissioned by the Joseph Rowntree Charitable Trust, (Joseph Rowntree Foundation, 2004) and conducted by the Searchlight Educational Trust and Vision 21, looked at the 2003 elections voting patterns for the BNP. The report, which was based on exit polls of 539 voters and focus groups, was carried out in Burnley, Oldham and Calderdale: three areas where the BNP had potential or actual electoral success. The three wards studied were around 95% white areas. A BNP councillor was elected in Mixenden in January 2003 and another in Lanehead in May 2003.

The most startling finding was that younger people were more likely to vote for the BNP. Around one in three of 18–25 year olds said that they voted for the BNP, suggesting that those who voted for the BNP did so tactically and really did support the party's views. The analysis of voting patterns for the BNP is useful for two reasons – in understanding how the BNP *is* targeting rural areas for recruitment and in determining the most appropriate interventions in tackling actual perpetrators.

Many racist views and attitudes are perpetrated by people who themselves are incomers to rural areas (fleeing the cities because 'too many Blacks there'). This was described as 'white flight' during the time of the RARP. The BNP has taken the phrase, subverted it and called it 'ethnic cleansing' to describe white people who are forced to flee cities because 'they feel they are no longer welcome there' (also see Jay, 1992).

Although, the RARP did not get directly involved in supporting victims of racial harassment, the project supported and guided its partners like Victim Support and Crime Concern to tackle the issue. The RARP dealt more with educating what Sibbit has categorised as *the potential perpetrators* and the *perpetrator community*. The potential perpetrator community can include the local politicians and the local media. These play a crucial role in defining local opinion. For example, in Dover when the local paper ran a campaign against asylum seekers, attacks on the local refugee communities went up by 40%. On the other hand, a local Welsh paper ran a campaign of editorials denouncing racial harassment experienced by Asian hospital staff travelling to and from the hospital. To stem this, members of the local community offered to walk the Asian staff! On a positive note, despite initial scepticism by parish councils, the RARP was successful in writing well-received guidance for parish councils on using their powers to tackle local racist actions (Crime Concern, 1995).

The police are the primary agency dealing with racial violence and crime, particularly in the rural context. The Metropolitan Police's intelligence-led policing went a long way in building up patterns of racist crime and profiles of perpetrators. This approach has to be commended to rural police services in order to tackle race hate crime. Following the BBC documentary, *The Secret Policeman* (2003), which exposed racially biased attitudes among recruits at a police training college in Cheshire, the CRE launched an investigation into police services in England and Wales. In an interim report published in June 2004, the CRE stated that 14 out of 43 police services were found to be in breach of the 2000 Race Relations Amendment Act, which required them to compile action plans on how to eliminate discrimination and promote equality. Yet, according to this report, only two services were issued with compliance notices.

It is vital that local communities have full confidence and trust in the police to tackle race hate crime. A national analysis of racial incidents, perpetrators and effective action must include the responses of the local police, media, support agencies, local authorities, employers, the local churches, religious bodies and local politicians.

Victims of racial harassment and violence

The proposed national overview of racial incidents must include the support or lack of it as afforded to victims. Many people feel a profound sense of shame in admitting that they are being targeted and, combined with the fear of becoming repeat victims, they would rather not report such incidents to the police. This is especially the case in rural areas where the isolation is intense and often there is no family or community support.

In 1996, the RARP put a BBC Radio 4 reporter in touch with a number of people in rural areas that had experienced or were experiencing racist violence and harassment. He was shocked to note that people did not even want to acknowledge the everyday harassment they were subjected to. This included name-calling, things through their letter box and racist graffiti outside their homes or businesses. It was only when things escalated to violence that victims thought of reporting the events (see *Farming Today*, 1996; also Chahal and Julienne, 1999). Further, both Sibbit and Chahal have recorded that people will only seek help from statutory agencies as a last not first resort (Sibbit, 1997, 2004; Chahal, 2003).

In recent years, a number of independent organisations have emerged to work with victims of racial harassment in rural areas. They believe that a 'victim-centred' approach is vital in developing the confidence of those who are affected. This includes the successful Rural Racism Project in the South-West of England set up by the monitoring group (based in Southall, West London). Chahal (2003) evaluated a small number of such initiatives. He found that independent, community-based support groups offered victims of racism a sense of empowerment and a validation of their experience, which they did not find from other agencies, such as the police, housing departments or racial equality councils.

A comprehensive evaluation of organisations that support victims of racial harassment in rural areas will provide vital information about effective action and good practice. The recommended detailed analysis of racial incidents, perpetrators and responses must also include the experiences of the Gypsy, Traveller, refugee and asylum seeking communities.

Gypsy and Traveller issues

According to the Gypsy Council, Romany Gypsies are thought to be the largest ethnic minority in Europe (an estimated 10 million Gypsies and Travellers across Europe). The Gypsy and Traveller population in Britain is estimated at 300,000, mainly composed of English and Welsh Romanichal or 'Romany' Gypsies and Irish and Scottish Travellers. Gypsies are recognised as a distinct ethnic group and together with Travellers have always been part of rural communities providing essential labour for farming and crafts (see Bhopal, this volume).

Like Black and minority ethnic communities, Gypsy/Roma and Travellers continue to be subjected to prejudice and discrimination. Yet there is still the tendency to see problems relating to the Gypsy/ Roma and Traveller communities as associated with sites and land use, neglecting the communities' needs on racial harassment, health, education and access to information, which have to be addressed appropriately (Dhillon, 1992; Bhopal, this volume). The RARP had sought to include Traveller (Irish) and Romany Gypsy issues in the rural race equality agenda. This the project did by including key organisations in the advisory group, raising the profile of these issues through a major conference and seeking to establish an ongoing network that would debate and clarify key policy and practice issues.

The CRE investigation launched in 2004, into issues affecting Gypsies and Travellers, is to be welcomed. The research focuses on potential direct or indirect discrimination against Gypsies and Irish Travellers in planning, site provision and eviction, and will lead to detailed practical guidance for local authorities. The inquiry will also examine how local authorities integrate Gypsy and Traveller issues within their Race Equality Schemes. It is not clear whether there will be a focus on rural areas. These areas, as defined by the new definition of 'rurality' by DEFRA, should be included and the issues unique to these areas placed at the centre of this investigation.

Asylum seekers and refuges

The 2002 Nationality, Immigration and Asylum Act, the fourth major piece of asylum legislation in a decade, introduced further measures to deter asylum seekers from applying to the UK. The 'dispersal policy' was introduced to alleviate the housing burden on the South-East and London authorities by proposing to build 'holding centres' or 'accommodation centres', mainly in rural areas.

Sections of the media whipped up hysteria and launched 'crusades' against asylum seekers in relation to the government's dispersal policy (see also Neal and Agyeman, this volume). Many 'ad hoc' committees and coalitions of villages emerged to stop the housing of asylum seekers or the building of accommodation centres in places, such as near Bicester, Oxfordshire. Many local authorities collaborated to highlight why planning consent should be withheld. Again, organisations like the BNP rallied around this issue and introduced a racial dimension to the issue. These protests existed at the same time as active recruitment from abroad continued to fill crucial vacancies in services such as transport, building, health, food processing and education in the rural areas. Often these predominantly new male recruits, particularly from Europe, experienced racial harassment and discrimination.

In 2005, the Home Office dropped plans to build the multimillion-pound network of centres after spending more than £1 million searching for sites throughout the UK and after contesting a series of bitterly fought planning applications. 'Victory for rural revolt as asylum centre plan is scrapped' was how one national newspaper summed up the issue (*The Times*, 2005). Yet, despite the fact that asylum/refugee issues inform the debate on race equality, particularly in the media and the New Labour government agenda, there is still separation between asylum/refugee issues and mainstream race equality policy.

Defining rurality

The definition of the term 'rural' has to be clearly understood so that race equality initiatives can be pitched appropriately. The term 'rural' has often been used to describe communities that are seen to be homogenous and static. Further, settlements of populations under 10,000 had remained the basis of the definition until recently. The reality couldn't be further from the truth. Rural areas vary according to population, transport links and social issues. It was only a decade ago that rural deprivation, poverty and mental stress became acknowledged as crucial issues (ACRE, 2003).

According to figures from DEFRA, rural populations are growing considerably faster than urban populations. Between the years 1991 and 2002, the rural population grew a net migration of 60,000 people per year into wholly or predominantly rural districts. No systematic figures are available that provide migrant figures according to ethnicity or capture patterns of recruitment from overseas.

The new definition for rural now consists of two parts:

- the *settlement morphology*, comprised of all places with a population of under 10,000, made up of small ('rural') towns, villages and scattered dwellings; and
- the wider geographic *context* in which individual settlements are located, that is, whether the wider area is defined as being 'sparsely' populated or not. Settlements and context are identified on a grid consisting of one-hectare cells. This grid is the foundation of the definition.

Using the new rural definition, 19% of the population (9.5 million) live in rural areas. Of these, 6% live in rural areas where the surrounding region is particularly sparsely populated. Among those in less sparse rural areas, 47% (4.2 million) live in small towns, 37% (3.3 million) in villages and 16% (1.4 million) in hamlets or isolated dwellings. According to the 2001 census, minority ethnic communities made up 9% of the total population in England, 2% in both Scotland and Wales, and less than 1% in Northern Ireland. The census figures put the presence of 'non-white' people in rural areas at 0.2% to 2.4%. No statistical breakdown exists according to DEFRA's definition of 'rural'.

The Rural Strategy

The Rural Strategy (DEFRA, 2004) sets out the government's policy and practice for rural areas for the next three to five years and boosts a new devolved approach to rural policy and delivery. Many changes have been announced, for example, to rural funding. And, despite the work on rural race equality, the Rural Strategy makes no reference to racism in rural areas. There is one reference to Black and minority ethnic communities:

> The Countryside Agency is investigating what can be done to provide more opportunities for disabled people, Black and minority ethnic people, people who live in inner city areas, and young people to enjoy countryside recreation. This is taking place under the Countryside Agency's Diversity Review. (DEFRA, 2004, p 44)

The publication does make an attempt to include images of Black and minority ethnic communities. There are two photographs in the publication: one on the cover with a party presumably visiting the countryside with their backs to the reader and a picture of a group of predominantly Black children learning about the countryside in the body text of the report.

Under the theme of 'Social Justice for All' there is no reference to people from Black and minority ethnic communities as socially excluded groups or as marginalised communities. Further, there is no mention of minority ethnic communities in Shucksmith's (2004) review of recent research on social exclusion in rural areas. This is a serious omission in the New Labour government's current strategy and policy on rural areas and its neglect will continue to produce the racialised equivalences of urban=Black, and rural=white. Moreover, it relegates Black people and people from minority ethnic groups as 'visitors' to the countryside and invisible as dwellers (see Askins, Tyler, and Neal and Agyeman, this volume). The continuation of this binary will inevitably impact on the way organisations in rural areas are (or are not) funded or supported to carry out race equality work. Further it renders ineffective the numerous initiatives announced in the Rural Strategy that are designed to empower, educate and advance local rural communities.

Conclusion

Contrary to the notion that 'it doesn't happen here', racial discrimination and harassment is very much part of rural life in England and Wales. There is a consistent pattern of racial harassment and violence in many rural areas against Black people and people from minority ethnic, asylum-seeker, Gypsy and Traveller communities, and evidence of involvement of right-wing organisations. Yet, this still remains relatively uncharted at a national level. Too little is known about the actual perpetrators or the activities of the local communities in condemning or supporting these. Given this, a national overview that determines the nature, the extent and the pattern of racial harassment and violence in rural areas and information about actual and potential perpetrators, including right-wing activity, is urgently needed.

Separately, specific organisations working with and supporting victims of racial harassment and violence need to be assessed for their success and experiences especially in relation to supporting victims of all hate crimes. There is also a continuing need to evaluate, post-Macpherson Report, those generic and specific race equality programmes and initiatives that emerged after the Jay Report in order to determine good practice and to highlight gaps that exist in different geographical regions.

Recent local and world events have produced a complex web of issues for the race equality agenda to address. As Sivanandan (2004) argues, 'The two trajectories then – the war on asylum and the war on terror – have converged to produce a racism which cannot tell a settler from an immigrant, an immigrant from an asylum seeker, an asylum seeker from a Muslim, a Muslim from a terrorist'. In this context, it is crucial that there is a reflexive selection of the language and terminology used in promoting equality policy and practice. Although the concept of 'race' is problematic and has its origins in colonialism and imperialism, it is widely used to describe prejudice and discrimination based on someone's colour (Fredrickson, 2002). Part of the success of the RARP was to allow debate on the concept of 'race' and 'racial equality' in order that all equality issues could be discussed and advanced through a rights-based approach. Increasingly, language of race equality is being replaced by terminology such as 'community cohesion', 'valuing diversity' and 'active citizenship'. This seems to be an attempt to shift the focus away from a rights-based equality framework to an approach that is governed by a law and order approach. It is important that education and awareness in rural areas adopt appropriate terminology and concepts to reflect the discrimination faced by all communities, not just those who are visibly different.

The rural race equality agenda must continue to build capacity in all sectors and address issues of terminology in education and training issues. Similarly, urban-based organisations must also be supported in attempts to develop and address rural issues. DEFRA should commission an 'equality impact' study of the Rural Strategy (DEFRA, 2004) so that at every stage an equality component is built into its programmes. Equality impact study should go further than race equality and should include sex, gender, disability, ethnic, nationality, cultural, sexuality, religious and age issues. This would lead to a national rural equality strategy that will inform *all* rural policy and practice. It will also determine toolkits for the Rural Development Agencies and the funding programmes established under the Rural Strategy (DEFRA, 2004). It is essential that there is appropriate monitoring of ethnicity and nationality of migration patterns to rural areas. Again, it is vital to include the Gypsy, Traveller, asylum and refugee communities and those who are contracted from abroad to work in rural areas.

Notes

[1] The Consultative Group membership involved Action with Communities in Rural England, National Association of Citizens' Advice Bureaux, Rural Development Commission.

[2] *The Archers* is the BBC's long-running radio agricultural soap opera.

[3] The RARP partners included the Churches Commission for Racial Justice, Crime Concern, National Federation of Women's Institutes, National Federation of Young Farmers'Youth Clubs.

[4] The RARP Advisory Group included Action with Communities in Rural England, Arthur Rank Centre, Friends, Families and Travellers Support Group, Gypsy Council for Education, Culture, and Welfare.

[5] Both the Countryside Alliance and the BNP have used a similar title for their own campaigns. Both organisations pose as representative of 'oppressed minorities' who experience prejudice while other groups – Black communities – get preferential treatment. The Countryside Alliance, in their campaign for fox hunting have used 'Land and Freedom' as a slogan (see Neal and Agyeman, this volume). The BNP has used 'Land and People' for its website on country issues.

References

Action for Communities in Rural England (ACRE) (2003) *Updating the English indices of deprivation, stage 2 consultation*, Cirencester: ACRE.

Action for Racial Equality across Leicestershire (AREAL) (1996) *Suffering in silence: A conference on racial harassment in rural Leicestershire*, Loughborough: AREAL.

Acton T., Samblas, C. and Coke P. (1997) *Land, people and freedom: Conference report*, London: National Council for Voluntary Organisations.

Agyeman, J. (1989) 'Black people, white landscape', *Town and Country Planning*, vol 58, no 12, pp 336-8.

Agyeman, J. and Spooner, R. (1997) 'Ethnicity and the rural environment', in P. Cloke and J. Little (eds) *Contested countryside cultures: Otherness, marginalization and rurality*, London: Routledge, pp 197–217.

BBC 1 (2003) 'The Secret Policeman' documentary (broadcast 21 October)

BBC 2 (1995) 'Skin' documentary about racist attacks.

BBC Radio 4 (1996) *Farming Today*.

Chahal, K. (2003) *Racist harassment support projects: Their role, impact and potential*, London: Joseph Rowntree Foundation

Chahal, K. and Julienne, L. (1999) *We can't all be white! Racist victimisation in the UK*, London: Joseph Rowntree Foundation.

Chakraborti, N. and Garland, J. (eds) (2004) *Rural racism*, Cullompton: Willan Publishing.

Crime Concern (1995) *Cutting crime in rural areas: A practical guide for parish councils*, Swindon: Crime Concern.

DEFRA (Department for Environment, Food and Rural Affairs) (2004) *Rural strategy 2004*, London: DEFRA, at www.defra.gov.uk.

de Lima, P. (2001) *Needs not numbers – An exploration of minority ethnic groups in Scotland*, London: Commission for Racial Equality and Community Development Foundation.

Derbyshire, H. (1994) *Not in Norfolk: Tackling the invisibility of racism*, Norwich: Norfolk and Norwich Racial Equality Council.

Dhillon, P. (1992) *At your service: A video for accessing services for Travellers*, Cambridge: Cambridgeshire County Council.

Dhillon, P. (1994) *Challenging rural racism: Conference report*, London: National Council for Voluntary Organisations.

Fredrickson, G. (2002) *Racism: A short history*, Princeton, NJ: Princeton University Press.

Goldsmith, J. and Makris, M.-L. (eds) (1994) 'Staring at invisible women, Black and minority ethnic women in rural areas', London: National Alliance of Women's Organisations.

Gordon, P. (1993) 'The police and racist violence in Britain', in T. Bjorgo and R. Witte (eds) *Racist violence and harassment in Europe*, London: Macmillan.

Gordon, P. (1994) 'Racist harassment and violence', in E. Stanko (ed) *Perspectives on violence*, London: Howard League.

Grewal, H. (2004) *Green and pleasant lands 'no place to be Black'*, Leicester: University of Leicester.

HM Government (2000) *Our countryside: The future, a fair deal for rural England*, Rural White Paper, London: HMSO.

Institute of Race Relations (IRR) www.irr.org.uk

Jay, E. (1992) *'Keep them in Birmingham': Challenging racism in South-West England*, (The Jay Report), London: Commission for Racial Equality.

Joseph Rowntree Charitable Trust and the Joseph Rowntree Charitable Reform Trust Ltd in association with Searchlight Educational Trust (2004) and undertaken by Vision 21, *539 voters' views: A voting behaviour study in three northern towns*, London: Joseph Rowntree Foundation.

Kenny, N. (1997) *It doesn't happen here?*, Somerset: Somerset Equality Forum.

Marsh, B. (1996) *Community care needs of people from minority ethnic groups in North Warwickshire*, Warwickshire: North Warwickshire Council for Voluntary Service.

Monitoring Group (nd) Rural racism project in the Southwest, at www.monitoring-group.co.uk

National Civil Rights Movement (South West) (2001) *South West Attacks Bulletin* (website: www.ncrm.org.uk; email: ncrmsouthwest@aol.com).

NCVO (National Council for Voluntary Organisations) (1994) *Testimony of a schoolgirl*, London: NCVO.

NCVO (1997) *Germinating the seeds of equality*, London: NCVO.

NCVO (2000) *Rural anti-racism project report*, London: NCVO.

Nizhar, P. (1995) *No problem?*, Telford: Race Equality Forum for Telford and Shropshire.

Rayner, J. (2001) 'The hidden truth behind race crimes in Britain', *Observer*, 18 February.

Searchlight Educational Trust (1995) *When hate comes to town: Community responses to racism and Fascism*, London: Searchlight Educational Trust.

Searchlight Information services (2005) *Searchlight Media Pack, a journalist's guide to race hate in Britain* (at www.s-light.demon.co.uk/presspack/mediaPackFrame1.htm).

Shucksmith, M. (2004) *Social exclusion in rural areas: A review of recent research*, Aberdeen: Arkleton Centre for Rural Development Research, University of Aberdeen.

Sibbit, R. (1997, 2004) *The perpetrators of racial harassment and racial violence*, A Research and Statistics Directorate Report, London: HMSO.

Sivanandan, A. (2004) *Racism in the age of globalisation*, London: Institute of Race Relations.

Suzin, K. (1996) *Voices from the margins: A qualitative study of the experiences of Black people in Devon*, Exeter: University of Exeter.

Times, The (2005) 'Victory for rural revolt as asylum centre plan is scrapped', 11 June.

Walker, J. (1999) *Rural anti-racism project: An evaluation report*, London: NCVO.

Afterword

Sarah Neal and Julian Agyeman

Beyond the familiar absence, unfamiliar presence paradigm

Kye Askins' chapter mentions an article in the *Guardian* newspaper. As Askins critically notes, the article, 'Countryside retreat' by Raekha Prasad (28 January 2004), examined ethnicity and the countryside through the premise of the familiar absence of black and minority ethnic visitors. Prasad's article includes short 'interviews' with six high-profile British black and minority ethnic figures about their autobiographic thoughts on the countryside. While Cloke (2004, pp 17-18) has detailed their accounts of racism, exclusion and uncomfortableness in rural areas, what some of these accounts also reveal is a significant rural relation; there is a positive rural presence in a number of these stories. For example Benjamin Zephaniah (poet and children's author) describes how he 'loves the countryside'; he highlights the rural legacy of black and minority settlers 'most black people I know, certainly Jamaicans, are rural' and in a direct echo of Dabydeen (Neal and Agyeman, this volume) Zephaniah concludes 'we should be confident enough to see the countryside ... as ours to enjoy'(Prasad, 2004, p 3). Shaks Ghosh (chief executive of the charity organisation Crisis) explains how she 'lives and works in the inner city and finds that her need to get out into the countryside is huge' and Kwame Kwe-Armah (playwright) described how he now enjoys the countryside and of 'overcoming my own prejudices [of the rural]' to such an extent that he would now at least consider living in a rural area. Kwame Kwe-Armah and Andrea Levy (novelist) show how other factors seep into the ethnicity–rural relation. Kwe-Armah explained how 'I didn't associate the countryside with me or anyone with an ethnic background. Most people from the black community felt they were not in the same social class as the stereotype of the affluent country squire' (Prasad, 2004, p 3) and Levy remembered how being brought up in North London, poor and without a car 'we couldn't get into the countryside' (Prasad, 2004, p 3). There is more than one narrative at work even in Prasad's small collection of short autobiographic stories: racism and exclusion is one, but class can also be seen to be at work in how the rural is conceived and accessed. Also, and significantly, what is in these accounts are expressions of attachment, pleasure, entitlement and belonging. That there was a plurality in these narratives that went beyond the familiar absence, unfamiliar presence understanding of black and minority people's relation with the countryside was confirmed the following week in the letters that readers had written in response to Prasad's article. One of these letters challenged the dominant theme of the article 'I disagree strongly with you that black and Asian people rarely visit rural Britain. There are thousands of us who live in rural Britain and get on with the countryside people. For once please try to show the positive side rather than the negative side' (*Guardian*, 2 February 2004). Another letter pointed out, in response to Levy's argument about the difficulties of getting into the countryside, that in the 1930s, 1940s and 1950s working-class Londoners would take the underground to the final station where 'there is countryside at the end of every underground line' (*Guardian*, 2 February 2004). A third letter detailed a (white?) reader's feelings of 'out of placeness' as a socialist (*Guardian*, 2 February 2004). We have spent some time detailing this media story and reader correspondence because it does reflect, albeit in a limited way, some of the arguments that have been part of the chapters presented in this collection. The *Guardian* article's autobiographic accounts, the readers' responses and, of course, the research and arguments in the chapters collected here all reveal a more *broken narrative* of the ethnicity–rural–excluded relation than the now-established familiar absence, unfamiliar presence paradigm allows. In the final section of this collection it is the contributors' telling of a more complex rural narrative that we briefly scrutinise.

Broken narratives

In the Introduction we argued that the work of social theorists Henri Lefebvre and Ed Soja could be usefully applied to rural spaces and the alchemic processes by which these can become *country/side*. The trialectics of space have been evident to differing extents, in all of the chapters. We have seen how *perceived space* – the countryside itself, national contexts (Connolly, de Lima, Robinson and Gardner, Neal and Agyeman); *conceived space* – the tenacious dominant rural imaginary, planners, policy makers, service providers, media representations (Tyler, Askins, Hetherington, Bhopal, Dhillon) and *lived space* – the real-and-imaginary, the experiences and navigation of rural spaces by those that live in them (all chapters but see especially, Connolly, Robinson and Gardner, Neal and Agyeman, Tyler, Askins and Hetherington) constantly bleed between each other. It is the blurring of the edges of these domains that has featured, to different extents, in the work of each of the contributors. However, it has been Lefebvre's lived space or Soja's thirdspace that has been particularly documented in this collection. Soja reminds us that, although Lefebvre did not privilege any of the three spatial domains there is an:

> implied preference in all of Lefebvre's (and my) spatial trialectics and thirdings that derives not from ontological privilege or priority but from that political choice that is so central to Lefebvre's spatial imagination. It is political choice, the impetus of an explicit political project, that gives special attention and particular contemporary relevance to... *lived space as a strategic location* from which to encompass, understand and potentially transform all spaces simultaneously. (Soja, 1996, p 68, original emphasis)

The nationalist discourses examined in Connolly, Robinson and Gardner, and de Lima, Neal's and Agyeman's concept of rural citizenship, Askins' concept of resistance, Hetherington's rural as a landscape of freedom and Tyler's investigation of troubled village whiteness are all accounts that directly challenge the dominant rural imaginary and break into and disrupt conceived space notions of the rurality–ethnicity relation. We would suggest that previous, existing media and academic commentary on this relation has tended to work very much within the secondspace or conceived space domain (Jay, 1992; Derbyshire, 1994; Agyeman and Spooner, 1997; Dhalech, 1999; Henderson and Kaur, 1999; Neal, 2002). In other words, this work has been preoccupied with two issues. On the one hand the focus has been on the symbolism of the countryside, the linkages between the idea of, in particular, the English countryside and the idea of nation. On the other hand it has been preoccupied with the spatial practices of service deliverers and countryside agencies and those figures responsible for the well-being of rural communities that have served to reinforce this connection either negatively – the 'no race problem here' position evidenced in Jay's research – or positively, as in the Council for National Parks and the Countryside Agency approach of trying to encourage more ethnic minority visitors to the countryside.

While this secondspace dual focus has been, and continues to be of critical importance, this collection develops the rurality–ethnicity debate by illuminating the countryside as 'a space of social struggle' (Soja, 1996, p 68) and as 'alive ... the loci of passion, of action, of lived situations' and as 'qualitative, fluid and dynamic' (Lefebvre, 1991, p 24, cited in Soja, 1996, p 69). It is through a combination of a theoretical and empirical emphasis on human agency and spatiality that the authors' work presented here forms what we identify as a newer narrative of the countryside and its 'legitimate' constituent inhabitants and users. This more complex and broken narrative has been particularly viewed through the collection's systematic presentation of qualitative and quantative research data. With the exception of Dhillon each contributor introduces us to different data-sets that allow us glimpses into the lived space of the contemporary countrysides.

Un/settled rural spaces

We have argued earlier that the contributors to this volume have, in their provision of glimpses into the lived space of the rural, presented newer narratives of countrysides. They do this through an intellectually interdisciplinary approach that, combines the cultural turn of geography and the spatial turn of sociology and pulls into the subsequently broad analytical frame a range of social theorists from Lefebvre, Soja, Bakhtin and Marshall to Hall, Ahmed and Probyn. There is a need for this theoretical plurality or bricolage because, as the data-sets drawn on in this collection also indicate, the categories of rurality and ethnicity are incredibly complex and protean, seemingly concrete and obvious but also shifting, elusive and intangible. It is the diverse relational configurations that occur at the intersections between these categories that are repeatedly demonstrated in the data and its analysis in the collection. Connolly, de Lima, and Robinson and Gardner have each shown how the historical legacy of English intervention in national spaces bends and re-coordinates the rural in national stories. From the ruralism of Nationalist Celtic imagery through to concepts of *gwerin* and Scottish leftism through to the contemporary partial devolvement of Northern Ireland, Wales and Scotland, an anti-English legacy adds another dimension to the un/settling of rural spaces in these countries. What these chapters show is the Englishness at the heart of the debates about racialised exclusion in and from the countryside. This is not to argue, of course, that racism and racialised exclusions do not occur or are not present in Northern Ireland, Wales and Scotland. Connolly, Robinson and Gardner, and de Lima clearly show, through their qualitative and quantative data, how very present these processes and experiences are. It is to argue, though, that there has been a neglect of the rural–ethnicity relation outside of the parameters of England and Englishness. At a time of partial devolution, the processes of post-devolution nation building that Scotland and Wales are currently undergoing open up the possibilities for the reconstitution of these countries' countrysides. For example, the demographic situation in Scotland is such that Scotland will need to rethink and re-present itself as a country *desiring* migration. For Wales the making of a contemporary Welsh identity through a devolutionary political and policy framework presents the possibilities for a new inclusiveness in a country which had (as Robinson and Gardner note) the first 'race riot' in Britain *and* famously embraced into its national story the African-American communist, lawyer, singer and actor, Paul Robeson.

Certainly, as we argued in the Introduction, the effect of looking at rural spaces in national contexts, especially those with a historical relation in which England had a political, economic and cultural dominance, presents a set of differing conditions in which racialised exclusion, processes of racism and processes of inclusion, claiming and entitlement have to be understood. These differing conditions and specificities need to be incorporated into analyses of exclusion and belonging within different rural areas. However, specificity does not mean that the issues, problems and possibilities are confined within those particular contexts. This is exactly what Connolly urges us to remember when he argues that, even in the distinctive context of Northern Ireland, the findings detailed in his chapter have a wider applicability to other rural settings. This argument is echoed by Robinson and Gardner in their concluding caveat that a process by which there is an ever more finely distilled analysis of racism in rural areas is one that runs the risk of losing sight of the similarities and continuities of racism and racist practices and thus the coherency of potential and actual political and policy responses and interventions. The accounts voiced by those respondents in Connolly's, Robinson's and Gardner's, and de Lima's research are marked by their commonality of the experiences of exclusion, violence and invisiblisation as well as more uneven experiences of belonging, identification and attachment. However, these continuities across national spaces have to be viewed alongside the historical, political, socio-economic and cultural distinctiveness of those same spaces. As each of these authors show, it is this distinctiveness that continues to shape specific racist practices *as well as* anti-racist and multiculturalist strategies and rhetorics of belonging and post-(partial) devolution nation building.

The argument that the rural as repository of nation is a particularly English metanarrative is at the centre of Neal and Agyeman's chapter.

There has been a massive re-population of rural England – the *State of the countryside report* (Countryside Agency, 2004) figures reveal that between 1981 and 2002 the rural population grew by 14%, compared to 3% growth in urban areas. The report also notes that migration from urban to rural areas is four times the rate of migration from the North of England to the South (Countryside Agency, 2004). This process has un/settled the English countryside and has been a key driver in its reconstitution alongside the decline in agricultural production and the increase in geographic mobility. This un/settlement has, as Neal and Agyeman's chapter argued, fed into the securing of the countryside on public agendas and a framing of this place through a narrative of rural crisis. This narrative of crisis is imbued with senses of nation and endangerment – in his recent speech on English identity the former Home Secretary David Blunkett noted that the outlawing of hunting 'has been seen by some to mark the end of Englishness'[1] – but this un/settling has also opened up the English countryside. It may have been opened up to those drawn by a rural idyll discourse and 'white flight' urban migrants (Robinson and Gardner, Tyler this volume) but the opening up has played a part in creating space for other groups to insert themselves in, and make claims on, the countryside. The rural idyll, rural crisis narrative is one that reflects uncertainty and change in relation to space and identity. We argued in the Introduction that anxieties flowing from the perception of increasingly permeable and fraying dominant nation borders – brought about by globalisation, and devolution – can lead to a social imaginary that seeks to shore up particular spaces as 'reassurance sites', that is, those in which national identity can be 'seen'. In this way a rurally based English white ethnicity relates very much to an imagined pastoral world in which the social actors ascribing to this version of English ethnicity observe social and cultural change and this amplifies anxiety and uncertainty and strengthens the boundary of ethnic identity. It is a process that urban anthropologist Sandra Wallman has describes as 'the ethnic double bind ... tightly bounded networks preserve the integrity of the local system and they also limit its ability to adapt to change' (1986, p 231).

The chapters in the second part of this collection can be seen as explorations of the challenges and pressures on the 'ethnic double bind' and each serves to remind us of the relational core of ethnicity as well as its social constructedness. This is evident in Tyler's village residents' anxious attempts to create an exclusively (white) middle-class, English village utopia in the green hinterlands of a multicultural city and is there in the belonging claims made by members of Askins' focus groups. It is present in the deliberate design and assembling of an ethnic identity based on another way of seeing rural belonging that is detailed by Hetherington. It is there in Dhillon's descriptions the educational experiences of Gypsy Traveller children. It is also there in the early political and policy efforts to secure the gaze on racism and exclusion and the need to address their related processes to the lives of those who visit, work and live in rural areas. All these accounts act as markers of the perils posed by narrow rurally based English ethnicities *but also* indicate the possibilities for a broader, reconfigured rural multi-ethnicity, in effect, a new countryside.

In closing, the story that has been differently told across these chapters and through the research evidence can be delineated into a number of interconnected concluding thoughts. First, the chapters demonstrate, along with previous literatures, that mainly white areas do have problems of racism and exhibit patterns of racialised exclusion and racial violence. These processes and practices excavate ideas of biological difference and fetishise the visible as markers of undesirability and non-belonging. These processes and practices also excavate and work with cultural difference as a marker of undesirability and non-belonging. Gypsy Travellers and New Age Travellers and, albeit more historically, urban-based working classes have shown how whiteness is of itself not sufficient to be rurally included and that undesirable white presences continue to trouble dominant rural imaginaries. It is the dominant rural imaginary's excavation of ideas of biological difference and cultural difference that highlight Hall's (2000) two logics of racism. Each chapter presents research evidence of the material outcome of these two logics.

Second, the countryside needs to be understood as a non-homogeneous space and as locally, regionally and nationally configured. This comes back to the argument for the importance of the specificity of particular areas as well as a recognition of the wider applicability of patterns and findings within these. Third, related to the non-homogeneity of the countryside itself is the importance of recognising contemporary rural communities as being plurally constituted and not simply representing static sites of socio-economic affluence and rightist political consent. This is a representation that conceals the extent of social exclusion and the presence of political dissent and transgressive others in rural areas. Fourth, again bearing a connection to the previous points, there is an urgent need for a much more mainstream recognition of the existence of a black and minority ethnic rural population. Multicultural Britain cannot be defined as multicultural only in its urban areas. Black and minority ethnic people do live in, work in, study in and visit rural Britain and this is likely to continue and increase. As Prime Minister Tony Blair observed in a keynote speech on immigration in April 2004, 'in an integrated, culturally diverse and dispersed Britain successful migrant populations have moved onwards and outwards over generations. *From...Southall to leafy Hertfordshire*'[2] (emphasis added). Fifth, what each of these concluding thoughts demonstrate is an urgency for (secondspace) planners, policy makers, service deliverers, countryside agencies and those figures responsible for the well-being of rural communities to all work from a 'four r premise' of recognition, relevance, resources and review. By this we mean the need to *recognise* the existence and importance of rural multiculture; design and deliver policies on the basis that multiculturalism, heterogeneity, racialised exclusion and racism are all highly *relevant* considerations and issues in rural areas; have a political commitment to a project of rural inclusion that is adequately *resourced* and the need to not only monitor but constantly *review* policy approaches to rural policy-making and ethnicity in terms of their effectiveness and implementation.

Our final and critical argument, and one that threads through this collection, is the importance of spatialising the concept of social citizenship and extending this concept into the thicker category of spatialised belonging. The recognition of spatialised social citizenship and belonging needs to sit alongside a commitment to the countryside itself and the possibilities it offers for a re-imagined inclusive country/ side and rural narrative in which the familiar multicultural absence and unfamiliar multicultural presence is irrevocably erased from discourses of nation and rurality. In this way, thirdspace possibilities of the countrysides of contemporary Britain become much more limitless.

Notes
[1] D. Blunkett, 'A new England, an English identity within Britain', speech given to the Institute of Public Policy Research, 14 March 2005.
[2] T. Blair, speech given to the CBI, 27 April 2004 (www.number-10.gov.uk/output/page5708).

References
Agyeman, J. and Spooner, R. (1997) 'Ethnicity and the rural environment', in P. Cloke and J. Little (eds) *Contested countryside cultures: Otherness, marginalization and rurality*, London: Routledge, pp 197–217.

Cloke, P. (2004) 'Rurality and racialised others: out of place in the countryside?', in N. Chakraborti and J. Garland (eds) *Rural racism*, Cullompton: Willan Publishing, pp 17–35.

Countryside Agency (2004) *State of the countryside report*, Yorkshire: Countryside Agency Publications.

Derbyshire, H. (1994) *Not in Norfolk: Tackling the invisibility of racism*, Norwich: Norwich and Norfolk Racial Equality Council.

Dhalech, M. (1999) *Challenging racism in the rural idyll: Final report*, Exeter: National Association of Citizens' Advice Bureaux.

Hall, S. (2000) 'The multicultural question', in B. Hesse (ed) *Un/settled multiculturalisms: Diasporas, entanglements, transruptions*, London: Zed Books, pp 209–41.

Henderson, P. and Kaur, R. (eds) (1999) *Rural racism in the UK: Examples of community based responses*, London: Community Development Foundation.

Jay, E. (1992) *'Keep them in Birmingham': Challenging racism in South-West England*, London: Commission for Racial Equality.

Lefebvre, H. (1991) *The production of space*, Oxford: Blackwell.

Neal, S. (2002) 'Rural landscapes, representations and racism: examining multicultural citizenship and policy-making in the English countryside', *Ethnic and Racial Studies*, vol 25, no 3, pp 442–61.

Soja, E. (1996) *Thirdspace, journeys to Los Angeles and other real-and-imagined places*, Oxford: Blackwell.

Wallman, S. (1986) 'Ethnicity and the boundary process in context', in J. Rex and D. Mason (eds) *Theories of race and ethnicity*, Cambridge: Cambridge University Press, pp 226–45.

Index

Note: Page numbers in *italics* indicate an illustration, page numbers in **bold** indicate a chapter by an author, and page numbers followed by *n* indicate information is in a note.